Other Books and Series by Jeff Bowen

Applications for Enrollment of Chickasaw Newborn Act of 1905
Volumes I thru VII

Cherokee Intermarried White 1906 Volume I thru X

Applications for Enrollment of Creek Newborn Act of 1905
Volumes I thru XIV

Applications for Enrollment of Choctaw Newborn Act of 1905
Volume I, II, III, IV, V & VI

Visit our website at **www.nativestudy.com** to learn more about these and other books and series by Jeff Bowen

APPLICATIONS FOR ENROLLMENT OF CHOCTAW NEWBORN ACT OF 1905

VOLUME VII

TRANSCRIBED BY
JEFF BOWEN

NATIVE STUDY
Gallipolis, Ohio
USA

Other Books and Series by Jeff Bowen

1901-1907 Native American Census Seneca, Eastern Shawnee, Miami, Modoc, Ottawa, Peoria, Quapaw, and Wyandotte Indians (Under Seneca School, Indian Territory)

1932 Census of The Standing Rock Sioux Reservation with Births And Deaths 1924-1932

Census of The Blackfeet, Montana, 1897- 1901 Expanded Edition

Eastern Cherokee by Blood, 1906-1910, Volumes I thru XIII

Choctaw of Mississippi Indian Census 1929-1932 with Births and Deaths 1924-1931 Volume I
Choctaw of Mississippi Indian Census 1933, 1934 & 1937, Supplemental Rolls to 1934 & 1935 with Births and Deaths 1932-1938, and Marriages 1936-1938 Volume II

Eastern Cherokee Census Cherokee, North Carolina 1930-1939 Census 1930-1931 with Births And Deaths 1924-1931 Taken By Agent L. W. Page Volume I
Eastern Cherokee Census Cherokee, North Carolina 1930-1939 Census 1932-1933 with Births And Deaths 1930-1932 Taken By Agent R. L. Spalsbury Volume II
Eastern Cherokee Census Cherokee, North Carolina 1930-1939 Census 1934-1937 with Births and Deaths 1925-1938 and Marriages 1936 & 1938 Taken by Agents R. L. Spalsbury And Harold W. Foght Volume III

Seminole of Florida Indian Census, 1930-1940 with Birth and Death Records, 1930-1938

Texas Cherokees 1820-1839 A Document For Litigation 1921

Choctaw By Blood Enrollment Cards 1898-1914 Volumes I thru XVII

Starr Roll 1894 (Cherokee Payment Rolls) Districts: Canadian, Cooweescoowee, and Delaware Volume One
Starr Roll 1894 (Cherokee Payment Rolls) Districts: Flint, Going Snake, and Illinois Volume Two
Starr Roll 1894 (Cherokee Payment Rolls) Districts: Saline, Sequoyah, and Tahlequah; Including Orphan Roll Volume Three

Cherokee Intruder Cases Dockets of Hearings 1901-1909 Volumes I & II

Indian Wills, 1911-1921 Records of the Bureau of Indian Affairs Books One thru Seven;
Native American Wills & Probate Records 1911-1921

Other Books and Series by Jeff Bowen

Turtle Mountain Reservation Chippewa Indians 1932 Census with Births & Deaths, 1924-1932

Chickasaw By Blood Enrollment Cards 1898-1914 Volume I thru V

Cherokee Descendants East An Index to the Guion Miller Applications Volume I
Cherokee Descendants West An Index to the Guion Miller Applications Volume II (A-M)
Cherokee Descendants West An Index to the Guion Miller Applications Volume III (N-Z)

Applications for Enrollment of Seminole Newborn Freedmen, Act of 1905

Eastern Cherokee Census, Cherokee, North Carolina, 1915-1922, Taken by Agent James E. Henderson   Volume I (1915-1916)
Volume II (1917-1918)
Volume III (1919-1920)
Volume IV (1921-1922)

Complete Delaware Roll of 1898

Eastern Cherokee Census, Cherokee, North Carolina, 1923-1929, Taken by Agent James E. Henderson   Volume I (1923-1924)
Volume II (1925-1926)
Volume III (1927-1929)

Applications for Enrollment of Seminole Newborn Act of 1905 Volumes I & II

North Carolina Eastern Cherokee Indian Census 1898-1899, 1904, 1906, 1909-1912, 1914 Revised and Expanded Edition

1932 Hopi and Navajo Native American Census with Birth & Death Rolls (1925-1931) Volume 1 - Hopi
1932 Hopi and Navajo Native American Census with Birth & Death Rolls (1930-1932) Volume 2 - Navajo

Western Navajo Reservation Navajo, Hopi and Paiute 1933 Census with Birth & Death Rolls 1925-1933

Cherokee Citizenship Commission Dockets 1880-1884 and 1887-1889 Volumes I thru V

Copyright © 2013
by Jeff Bowen

ALL RIGHTS RESERVED
No part of this publication may be reproduced
or used in any form or manner whatsoever
without previous written permission from the
copyright holder or publisher.

Originally published:
Baltimore, Maryland
2013

Reprinted by:

Native Study LLC
Gallipolis, OH
www.nativestudy.com
2020

Library of Congress Control Number: 2020918113

ISBN: 978-1-64968-100-3

Made in the United States of America.

This series is dedicated to the descendants of the
Choctaw newborn listed in these applications.

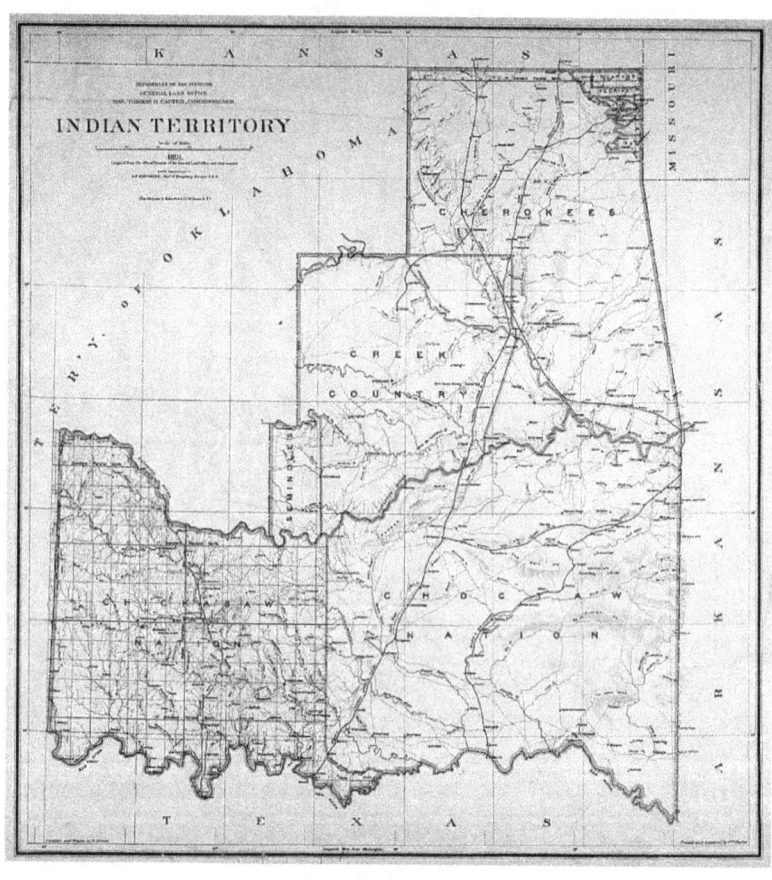

This map of Indian Territory shows how large the Choctaw and Chickasaw Nations' land base was that contained huge deposits of asphalt and coal. Just the size and territory involved was flooded with the "Grafters".

DEPARTMENT OF THE INTERIOR.
Commissioner to the Five Civilized Tribes.

NOTICE.

Opening of Land Office at Wewoka,
IN THE SEMINOLE NATION, INDIAN TERRITORY.

Notice is hereby given that on Monday, September 4, 1905, the Commissioner to the Five Civilized Tribes will establish a land office at Wewoka, in the Seminole Nation, Indian Territory, for the purpose of allowing citizens and freedmen of the Seminole Nation to select allotments of land for their minor children enrolled under the Act of Congress approved March 3, 1905 (33 Stat. L. 1060), and for the further purpose of allowing citizens and freedmen of the Seminole Nation, whose allotments are incomplete, to select additional land in order to bring the value of their allotments up to the standard of $309.09, as nearly as may be practicable.

Each child whose enrollment in accordance with the Act of March 3, 1905, has been duly approved by the Secretary of the Interior, is entitled to receive an alllotment of forty acres without regard to the character or value of the land selected.

Selection of allotments for minor children must be made by their citizen or freedmen parents or by a duly appointed guardian, or curator, or by a duly appointed administrator.

TAMS BIXBY,
Commissioner.

Muskogee, Indian Territory,
July 29, 1905.

This particular notice for the Seminole and Creek Newborn makes mention of the Act of 1905. It is likely that a similar notice was posted in the Choctaw and Chickasaw Nations for the registration of newborn children.

DEPARTMENT OF THE INTERIOR,
Commission to the Five Civilized Tribes.

Rules and Regulations Governing the Selection of Allotments and the Designation of Homesteads in the Choctaw and Chickasaw Nations.

1. Selections of allotments and designations of homesteads for adult citizens and selections of allotments for adult freedmen must be made in person except as herein otherwise provided.

2. Applications to have land set apart and homesteads designated for duly identified Mississippi Choctaws must be made personally before the Commission to the Five Civilized Tribes. Fathers may apply for their minor children and if the father be dead the mother may apply. Husbands may apply for wives. Applications for orphans, insane persons and persons of unsound mind may be made by duly appointed guardian or curator, and for aged and infirm persons and prisoners by agents duly authorized thereunto by power of attorney, in the discretion of said Commission.

3. At the time of the selection of allotment each citizen and duly identified Mississippi Choctaw shall designate as a homestead out of said selection land equal in value to one hundred and sixty acres of the average allottable land of the Choctaw and Chickasaw Nations, as nearly as may be.

4. Each Choctaw and Chickasaw freedman, at the time of selection shall designate as his or her allotment of the lands of the Choctaw and Chickasaw Nations, land equal in value to forty acres of the average allottable land of the Choctaw and Chickasaw Nations.

5. Citizens, freedmen and identified Mississippi Choctaws who are married, whether they have attained their majority or not, will be regarded as of age for the purpose of making selections.

6. Selections may be made by citizen and freedman parents for unmarried male children under twenty-one years of age and for unmarried female children under eighteen years of age, and a male citizen or freedman may make selection for his wife, if she is entitled to make selection, unless she shall, at the time or previously thereto, protest in writing.

7. Where the father of an unmarried minor citizen, freedman or identified Mississippi Choctaw is a non-citizen, the citizen, freedman or identified Mississippi Choctaw mother of such children must make selection in person in behalf of said children.

8. Selections of allotments and designations of homesteads for minor citizens and selections of allotments for minor freedmen may be made by the citizen father or mother or freedman father or mother, as the case may be, or by a guardian, curator, or an administrator having charge of their estate, in the order named.

9. Selections of allotments and designations of homesteads for citizen, and selections of allotment for freedmen, prisoners, convicts, aged and infirm persons and soldiers and sailors of the United States on duty outside of Indian Territory, may be made by duly appointed agents under power of attorney, and for incompetents by guardians, curators, or other suitable person akin to them.

10. Selections may be made and homesteads designated by duly identified Mississippi Choctaws, who have, within one year after the date of their identification as such, made satisfactory proof of bona fide settlement within the Choctaw-Chickasaw country, at any time within six months after the date of their said identification.

11. Persons authorized to make selections by power of attorney, as provided in rules 2 and 9 hereof, must be the husband or wife, or a relative not further removed than a cousin of the first degree of the person for whom such selection is made.

12. It shall be the duty of the Commission to the Five Civilized Tribes to see that selections of allotments and designations of homesteads for the classes of persons mentioned in rules 2, 6, 7, 8 and 9 hereof, are made for the best interests of such persons.

13. Selections of allotments for citizens, freedmen and identified Mississippi Choctaws who have died subsequent to September 25, 1902, and before making a selection of allotment, shall be made by a duly appointed administrator or executor. If, however, such administrator or executor be not duly and expeditiously appointed, or fails to act promptly when appointed, or for any other cause such selections be not so made within a reasonable and practicable time, the Commission to the Five Civilized Tribes shall designate the lands thus to be allotted.

14. In determining the value of a selection the appraised value of the land selected shall be increased by the appraised value of such pine timber on such land as has heretofore been estimated by the Commission to the Five Civilized Tribes.

15. Selections of allotments may be made only by citizens and freedmen whose enrollment has been approved by the Secretary of the Interior, and by persons duly identified by the Commission to the Five Civilized Tribes as Mississippi Choctaws, and by none others.

16. When a selection of land has been made by a citizen, freedman or identified Mississippi Choctaw, and the land so selected is claimed by a person whose rights as a citizen or freedman have not been finally determined, contest for the land so selected may be instituted by the person claiming the land, formal application for the land being first made as is required by the Rules of Practice in Choctaw and Chickasaw allotment contest cases.

THE COMMISSION TO THE FIVE CIVILIZED TRIBES.
TAMS BIXBY, Chairman.

Muskogee, Indian Territory, March 24, 1903.

The above statement published prior to 1905, was established for what was supposed to be a set of guidelines when it came to allotments. But with supplemental agreements and Congressional legislation, time frames as well as rules and regulations often changed and were not the same for every tribe.

INTRODUCTION

The *Applications for Enrollment of Choctaw Newborn Act of 1905*, National Archive film M-1301, Rolls 50-57, are found under the heading of Applications for Enrollment of the Commission to the Five Civilized Tribes. For this series, I have transcribed the application forms filled out by individuals applying for enrollment in the Five Civilized Tribes under the Dawes Commission. These applications contain considerably more information than stated on the census cards found in series M-1186. M-1301 possesses its own numerical sequence, separate from M-1186. To find each party's roll number you would have to reference M-1186.

The Choctaw as well as the Chickasaw allotments were likely some of the most sought after properties in Indian Territory. There was supposed to be a 25-year restriction on the sale or lease of any Indian lands so as to insure that the owners wouldn't be swindled, but that isn't what happened. This fact is borne out in the Dawes Commission General Allotment Act, of February 8, 1887, Section 5, which "Provides that after an Indian person is allotted land, the United States will hold the land 'in trust [1] for the sole use and benefit of the Indian' (or his heirs if the Indian landowner dies) for a period of 25 years. (Land held in trust by the United States government cannot be sold or in anyway alienated by the Indian landowner, since the United States government considers the underlying ownership of the land held by itself and not the tribe. After the period of trust ends, the Indian landowner is free to sell the land and is free from any encumbrance from the United States.)"[1] Instead, Native Americans were exploited by the devious. The Choctaw and Chickasaw Districts both had huge asphalt and coal deposits, so there was pressure from outsiders to acquire them from the minute they were discovered. After repeated attacks throughout the years and many legislative changes, President "Roosevelt finally signed the Five Tribes Bill at noon on April 26, 1906, the forces seeking to end all restrictions were disappointed. Section 19 removed restrictions from the sale of all inherited land but directed that no full-bloods could sell their land for twenty-five years. The Act also prohibited leases for more than one year without the approval of the Secretary of the Interior."[2]

Angie Debo described the opportunists that wanted these Native American allotments as, "Grafters". The parents of the newborns enumerated within this series would no sooner receive the approval for their child's allotment than there would be someone there with cash in hand holding a new deed or lease for the parents to sign their child's birthright away. Angie Debo said it best, "As the business incapacity of the allottees became apparent, a horde of despoilers fastened themselves upon their property." According to Debo, "The term 'grafter' was applied as a matter of course to dealers in Indian land, and was frankly accepted by them. The speculative fever also affected Government employees so that it was almost impossible to prevent them from making personal investments."[3]

---

[1] General Allotment Act, Act of Feb. 8, 1887 (24 Stat. 388, ch. 119, 25 USCA 331)
[2] The Dawes Commission and the Allotment of the Five Civilized Tribes, 1893-1914 by Kent Carter, pg. 173
[3] And Still the Waters Run, Angie Debo, p. 92.

INTRODUCTION

According to the Department of Interior in 1905, "It is estimated that there will be added to the final rolls of the citizens and freedmen of the Choctaw and Chickasaw nations the names of 2,000 persons, including 1,500 new-born children to be enrolled under the provisions of the act of Congress approved March 3, 1905."[4]

The quote below explains, in detail, the requirements for qualifying as a newborn Choctaw, "By the act of Congress approved March 3, 1905 (H.R. 17474), entitled 'An act making appropriations for the current and contingent expenses of the Indian Department and for fulfilling treaty stipulations with various Indian tribes for the fiscal year ending June 30, 1906, and for other purposes,' it was provided as follows:

'That the Commission to the Five Civilized Tribes is hereby authorized for sixty days after the date of the approval of this act to receive and consider applications for enrollment of infant children born prior to September twenty-fifth, nineteen hundred and two, and who were living on said date, to citizens by blood of the Choctaw and Chickasaw tribes of Indians whose enrollment has been approved by the Secretary of the Interior prior to the date of the approval of this act; and to enroll and make allotments to such children.'

'That the Commission to the Five Civilized Tribes is authorized for sixty days after the date of the approval of this act to receive and consider applications for enrollment of children born subsequent to September twenty-fifth, nineteen hundred and two, and prior to March fourth, nineteen hundred and five, and who were living on said latter date, to citizens by blood of the Choctaw and Chickasaw tribes of Indians whose enrollment has been approved by the Secretary of the Interior prior to the date of the approval of this act; and to enroll and make allotments to such children.'

"Notice is hereby given that the Commission to the Five Civilized Tribes will, up to and inclusive of midnight, May 2, 1905, receive applications for the enrollment of infant children born prior to September 25, 1902, and who were living on said date, to citizens by blood of the Choctaw and Chickasaw tribes of Indians whose enrollment has been approved by the Secretary of the Interior prior to March 3, 1905."[5]

Following is the scope of these transcriptions: Besides the applications themselves, researchers will find the identities of other individuals within these applications -- doctors, lawyers, mid-wives, and other relatives -- that may help with you genealogical research.

Jeff Bowen
Gallipolis, Ohio
NativeStudy.com

---

[4] Annual Reports of the Department of the Interior For the Fiscal Year Ended June 30, 1905, p. 609.
[5] Annual Reports of the Department of the Interior For the Fiscal Year Ended June 30, 1905, p. 593.

Applications for Enrollment of Choctaw Newborn
Act of 1905 Volume VII

Choc New Born 374
　　Richard B. Sexton b. 12-7-03

BIRTH AFFIDAVIT.

DEPARTMENT OF THE INTERIOR.
COMMISSION TO THE FIVE CIVILIZED TRIBES.

　　IN RE APPLICATION FOR ENROLLMENT, as a citizen of the　　Choctaw　　Nation, of Richard B Sexton　　, born on the　7th　day of　Dec　, 1903

Name of Father: Jonas Sexton　　　　　　a citizen of the　Choctaw　　Nation.
Name of Mother: Jessie L Sexton　　　　a citizen of the　Choctaw　　Nation.

　　　　　　　　　　　Postoffice　　McAlester, I.T.

AFFIDAVIT OF MOTHER.

UNITED STATES OF AMERICA, Indian Territory, }
　Central　　　　　　DISTRICT.

　　I,　Jessie L Sexton　　, on oath state that I am　22　years of age and a citizen by　marriage　, of the　Choctaw　Nation; that I am the lawful wife of　Jonas Sexton　, who is a citizen, by blood　of the　Choctaw　Nation; that a male　child was born to me on　7th　day of　December　, 1903; that said child has been named　Richard B Sexton　, and was living March 4, 1905.

　　　　　　　　　　　　　　　　Jessie L Sexton
Witnesses To Mark:
　{

　　Subscribed and sworn to before me this　17th　day of　March　, 1905

　　　　　　　　　　　　　　Wirt Franklin
　　　　　　　　　　　　　　　Notary Public.

AFFIDAVIT OF ATTENDING PHYSICIAN OR MID-WIFE.

UNITED STATES OF AMERICA, Indian Territory, }
　Central　　　　　　DISTRICT.

　　I,　W E Abbott　　, a　Physician　, on oath state that I attended on Mrs.　Jessie L Sexton　, wife of　Jonas Sexton　on the　7th　day of　December　, 1903; that there was born to her on said date a　male　child; that said child was living March 4, 1905, and is said to have been named Richard B Sexton

Applications for Enrollment of Choctaw Newborn
Act of 1905 Volume VII

W.E. Abbott M.D.

Witnesses To Mark:
{

Subscribed and sworn to before me this 17th day of March , 1905

R.B. Coleman
Notary Public.

<u>Choc New Born 376</u>
    Elbert Hubbard Gotcher   b. 4-15-04

BIRTH AFFIDAVIT.

DEPARTMENT OF THE INTERIOR.
COMMISSION TO THE FIVE CIVILIZED TRIBES.

IN RE APPLICATION FOR ENROLLMENT, as a citizen of the Choctaw Nation, of Elbert Hubbard Gotcher , born on the 15th day of April , 1904

Name of Father: Walter E. Gotcher   a citizen of the United States Nation.
Name of Mother: Susan E. Gotcher   a citizen of the Choctaw Nation.

Postoffice   Savanna, I.T.

AFFIDAVIT OF MOTHER.

UNITED STATES OF AMERICA, Indian Territory, }
    Central   DISTRICT.

    I, Susan E. Gotcher , on oath state that I am 28 years of age and a citizen by blood , of the Choctaw Nation; that I am the lawful wife of Walter E. Gotcher , who is a citizen, ~~by~~ .... of the Choctaw Nation; that a male child was born to me on the 15th day of April , 1904; that said child has been named Elbert Hubbard Gotcher , and was living March 4, 1905.

                              Susan E. Gotcher

Witnesses To Mark:
{

Applications for Enrollment of Choctaw Newborn
Act of 1905   Volume VII

Subscribed and sworn to before me this   17th day of   March   , 1905

                         Wirt Franklin
                         Notary Public.

AFFIDAVIT OF ATTENDING PHYSICIAN OR MID-WIFE.

UNITED STATES OF AMERICA, Indian Territory,
   Central   DISTRICT.

    I,   S.P. Ross   , a   physician   , on oath state that I attended on Mrs. Susan E. Gotcher   , wife of   Walter E. Gotcher   on the 15th day of April   , 1904; that there was born to her on said date a   male   child; that said child was living March 4, 1905, and is said to have been named Elbert Hubbard Gotcher

                     S.P. Ross MD

Witnesses To Mark:

Subscribed and sworn to before me this   17th day of   March   , 1905

                     Wirt Franklin
                     Notary Public.

<u>Choc New Born 377</u>
      Pearlie M. Freeman   b. 9-20-04

BIRTH AFFIDAVIT.
DEPARTMENT OF THE INTERIOR.
COMMISSION TO THE FIVE CIVILIZED TRIBES.

   IN RE APPLICATION FOR ENROLLMENT, as a citizen of the   Choctaw   Nation, of Pearlie M. Freeman   , born on the 20th   day of Sept   , 1904

Name of Father: Jasper N. Freeman   a citizen of the   Choctaw   Nation.
Name of Mother: Maria J.   "   a citizen of the   Choctaw   Nation.

              Postoffice   Howe, I.T.

Applications for Enrollment of Choctaw Newborn
Act of 1905   Volume VII

AFFIDAVIT OF MOTHER.

UNITED STATES OF AMERICA, Indian Territory,
Central   DISTRICT.

I, Maria J. Freeman, on oath state that I am 34 years of age and a citizen by blood, of the Choctaw Nation; that I am the lawful wife of Jasper N. Freeman, who is a citizen, by Intermarriage of the Choctaw Nation; that a female child was born to me on 20th day of September, 1904; that said child has been named Pearlie M. Freeman, and was living March 4, 1905.

Maria J. Freeman

Witnesses To Mark:

Subscribed and sworn to before me this 15th day of March, 1905

W.H. Angell
Notary Public.

AFFIDAVIT OF ATTENDING PHYSICIAN OR MID-WIFE.

UNITED STATES OF AMERICA, Indian Territory,
Central   DISTRICT.

I, Jane Ward, a midwife, on oath state that I attended on Mrs. Maria J. Freeman, wife of Jasper N. Freeman on the 20th day of September, 1904; that there was born to her on said date a female child; that said child was living March 4, 1905, and is said to have been named Pearlie M. Freeman

her
Jane x Ward
mark

Witnesses To Mark:
WH Martin
(Name Illegible)

Subscribed and sworn to before me this 15th day of March, 1905

W.H. Angell
Notary Public.

Applications for Enrollment of Choctaw Newborn
Act of 1905 Volume VII

BIRTH AFFIDAVIT.

DEPARTMENT OF THE INTERIOR.
COMMISSION TO THE FIVE CIVILIZED TRIBES.

IN RE APPLICATION FOR ENROLLMENT, as a citizen of the Choctaw Nation, of Pearlie M. Freeman, born on the 20th day of Sept, 1904

Name of Father: Jasper N. Freeman   a citizen of the Choctaw Nation.
Name of Mother: Maria J. Freeman   a citizen of the Choctaw Nation.

Postoffice   Howe, Ind. Ter.

AFFIDAVIT OF MOTHER.

UNITED STATES OF AMERICA, Indian Territory,
Central DISTRICT.

I, Maria J. Freeman, on oath state that I am 34 years of age and a citizen by Blood, of the Choctaw Nation; that I am the lawful wife of Jasper N. Freeman, who is a citizen, by Intermarriage of the Choctaw Nation; that a Female child was born to me on 20th day of Sept, 1904; that said child has been named Pearlie M. Freeman, and was living March 4, 1905.

                         Maria J. Freeman

Witnesses To Mark:

Subscribed and sworn to before me this 5th day of June, 1905

                         W.N. Ester
                         Notary Public.

AFFIDAVIT OF ATTENDING PHYSICIAN OR MID-WIFE.

UNITED STATES OF AMERICA, Indian Territory,
Central DISTRICT.

I, Jane Ward, a mid-wife, on oath state that I attended on Mrs. Maria J. Freeman, wife of Jasper N. Freeman on the 20 day of Sept, 1904; that there was born to her on said date a Female child; that said child was living March 4, 1905, and is said to have been named Pearlie M. Freeman

                         her
                         Jane x Ward
                         mark

Applications for Enrollment of Choctaw Newborn
Act of 1905   Volume VII

Witnesses To Mark:
{ Rebecca Anderson
  Lenola Anderson

Subscribed and sworn to before me this 9th day of June , 1905

Thos. B. Losene
Notary Public.

My Commission expires Jan 17th 1909

Affidavit of Attending Physician or Midwife

UNITED STATES OF AMERICA,
INDIAN TERRITORY,
Central   DISTRICT

I, Jane Ward a Mid Wife on oath state that I attended on Mrs. Maria J Freeman wife of Jasper N. Freeman on the 20th day of September , 190 4, that there was born to her on said date a Female child, that said child is now living, and is said to have been named Perley[sic] M Freeman

her   Mid Wife
Jane x Ward   ~~M. D.~~
mark

Subscribed and sworn to before me this the 23 day of February 1905

A.E. Folsom
Notary Public.

WITNESSETH:

Must be two witnesses
who are citizens and
know the child.
{ Ben Moses
  F.C. Jackson

We hereby certify that we are well acquainted with Mrs Jane Ward a Mid Wife and know her to be reputable and of good standing in the community.

Must be two citizen
witnesses.
{ Ben Moses
  F.C. Jackson

6

Applications for Enrollment of Choctaw Newborn
Act of 1905 Volume VII

NEW-BORN AFFIDAVIT.

Number..................

...Choctaw Enrolling Commission...

IN THE MATTER OF THE APPLICATION FOR ENROLLMENT, as a citizen of the Choctaw Nation, of Perley[sic] M Freeman

born on the 20th day of September 1904

Name of father   Jasper N Freeman   a citizen of   Choctaw
Nation final enrollment No.   1139
Name of mother   Mariah[sic] J Freeman   a citizen of   Choctaw
Nation final enrollment No.   12855

Postoffice   Atoka I.T.

AFFIDAVIT OF MOTHER.

UNITED STATES OF AMERICA
INDIAN TERRITORY
Central   DISTRICT

I   Mariah J. Freeman   , on oath state that I am 34 years of age and a citizen by blood of the Choctaw Nation, and as such have been placed upon the final roll of the Choctaw Nation, by the Honorable Secretary of the Interior my final enrollment number being 12855 ; that I am the lawful wife of Jasper N. Freeman , who is a citizen of the Choctaw Nation, and as such has been placed upon the final roll of said Nation by the Honorable Secretary of the Interior, his final enrollment number being 1139 and that a Female child was born to me on the 20th day of September 1903[sic] ; that said child has been named Perley M Freeman , and is now living.

Witnesseth.   Mariah J Freeman

Must be two ⎫   Ben Moses
Witnesses who ⎬
are Citizens. ⎭   F.C. Jackson

Subscribed and sworn to before me this   23   day of   February   1905

A.E. Folsom
Notary Public.

My commission expires:
Jan 9 - 1909

Applications for Enrollment of Choctaw Newborn
Act of 1905   Volume VII

7-4651

Muskogee, Indian Territory, March 20, 1905.

Maia J. Freeman,
    Howe, Indian Territory.

Dear Madam:

    Receipt is hereby acknowledged of the affidavits of Maria J. Freeman and Jane Ward to the birth of Pearlie M. Freeman, infant daughter of Jasper N. and Maria J Freeman, September 20, 1904, and the same have been filed with our records as an application for the enrollment of said child.

    Respectfully,

    Chairman.

Sub.

7-NB-377.

Muskogee, Indian Territory, May 26, 1905.

Jasper M[sic]. Freeman,
    Howe, Indian Territory.

Dear Sir:

    Referring to your letter of the 8th instant, in which you ask whether the application for the enrollment of your infant child, Pearlie M. Freeman, has been approved; it is noted that in the application filed in this office on March 17, 1905, the date of the applicant's birth is given as September 20, 1904, while in the one filed on the 25th ultimo, it is given as September 20, 1903.

    There is enclosed you herewith for execution application for the enrollment of this child in which the date of Birth has been left blank. Before this matter an be finally determined it will be necessary that you return this application to this office properly executed, giving the correct date of birth.

    In having these affidavits executed care should be exercised to see that all names are written in full, as they appear in the body of the affidavit, and in the event that either of the persons signing the affidavit are unable to write, signatures by mark must be attested by two witnesses. Each affidavit must be executed before a Notary Public and the notarial seal and signature of the officer must be attached to each separate affidavit.

Applications for Enrollment of Choctaw Newborn
Act of 1905 Volume VII

Respectfully,

Chairman.

---

7 NB 377

Muskogee, Indian Territory, June 15, 1905.

Jasper N. Freeman,
    Howe, Indian Territory.

Dear Sir:

    Receipt is hereby acknowledged of the affidavits of Maria J. Freeman and Jane Ward to the birth of Pearlie M. Freeman, daughter of Jasper N. and Maria J. Freeman, September 20, 1904, and the same have been filed in the matter of the enrollment of said child.

Respectfully,

Chairman.

<u>Choc New Born 378</u>
    Ellen Campelube b. 1-5-05

(The letter below does not belong with the current applicant.)

Muskogee, Indian Territory, November 17, 1906.

S. J. Belvin,
    Jackson, Indian Territory.

Dear Sir:

    Receipt is hereby acknowledged of your letter of November 1, 1906, in the matter of the right to enrollment as minor citizens of the Choctaw Nation of children of Impson Sharkey, Lamus Belvin, Robert Belvin and Thomas Belvin.

    In reply to your letter you are advised that it appears from your testimony of May 18, 1906, that Robert and Sallie A. Belvin had on child Williamson Belvin born about the year 1903. Subsequently affidavits of Sallie Jackson and Jane Ward were forwarded to

Applications for Enrollment of Choctaw Newborn
Act of 1905   Volume VII

the birth of Raymus Belvin referred to in the affidavits was the Williamson Belvin concerning when you testified, but no definiate[sic] information has yet been obtained.

You also testified on the same date to the birth of Eva Belvin, child of Thomas and Lena Belvin, born sometime in the year 1906. Affidavits of Lane Wilson and Galloway Williams were subsequently received to the birth of Jonas Belvin, child of Thomas and Lena Belvin, February 20, 1906, and it has so far been impracticable to secure information as to whether your testimony of May 18, 1906, and the affidavits of Lane Wilson and Calloway Williams referre[sic] to the same child or if Thomas and Lena Belvin have two children, a girl born sometime during the year 1905 and Jonas a boy born February 20, 1906.

Your testimony was also taken on the same date at Bennington, Indian Territory, to the birth of Annie Belvin, child of Lamos and Sis Belvin sometime in the year 1903. The affidavits of Sallie Jackson and Sebbie[sic] R. Scott to the birth of this child December 24, 1904, have subsequently been received and it will be necessary that affidavits be secured showing the correct date of the birth of this child, the names of her parents and that she was living March 4, 1906. If possible the affidavit of the mother Sis Belvin should be secured to the birth of this child.

You also testified at Bennington, Indian Territory, May 18, 1905, to the birth of Fleny and Lanca Sharkey, children of Lupson and Susan Sharkey born in February 1903 and _____ 1905 respectively. Subsequently affidavits of Sallie Jackson and Lane Wilson to the birth of Selener and Lemus Sharkey January 14, 1903 and February 10, 1906 were filed.

It will be necessary that this office be advised if Selener and Fleny Sharkey are the same child and if so her correct name.

Affidavits of the mother should be secured to the birth of all the children above referred to if it is possible to secure the same, and there are inclosed herewith blanks for the purpose of securing additional evidence to the birth of these children.

Respectfully,

Commissioner.

Applications for Enrollment of Choctaw Newborn
Act of 1905   Volume VII

NEW BORN AFFIDAVIT

No ....

CHOCTAW ENROLLING COMMISSION

IN THE MATTER OF THE APPLICATION FOR ENROLLMENT as a citizen of the Choctaw Nation, of Helen[sic] Campelube   born on the   5   day of   January   190 5

Name of father   Columbus Campelube   a citizen of   Choctaw   Nation, final enrollment No.   12861
Name of mother   Sallie Pusley   a citizen of   Choctaw   Nation, final enrollment No.   12866

McAlester I.T.   Postoffice.

AFFIDAVIT OF MOTHER

UNITED STATES OF AMERICA
INDIAN TERRITORY
DISTRICT   Central

I   Sallie Pusley   , on oath state that I am   23   years of age and a citizen by   blood   of the   Choctaw   Nation, and as such have been placed upon the final roll of the   Choctaw   Nation, by the Honorable Secretary of the Interior my final enrollment number being   12866   ; that I am the lawful wife of   not married Columbus Campelube   , who is a citizen of the   Choctaw   Nation, and as such has been placed upon the final roll of said Nation by the Honorable Secretary of the Interior, his final enrollment number being   12861   and that a   female   child was born to me on the   5   day of   January   190 5; that said child has been named   Helen[sic] Campelube   , and is now living.

                 her
WITNESSETH: Sallie x Pusley
Must be two witnesses { Silas Nail   mark
who are citizens   *(Name Illegible)*

Subscribed and sworn to before me this, the   15   day of   March   , 190 5

           James Bower
             Notary Public.

My Commission Expires:
Sept 23 1907

Applications for Enrollment of Choctaw Newborn
Act of 1905 Volume VII

Affidavit of Attending Physician or Midwife

UNITED STATES OF AMERICA, }
    INDIAN TERRITORY,
  Central   DISTRICT

I, Nancy Pusley   a   midwife
on oath state that I attended on Mrs. Sallie Pusley   ~~wife of~~ Columbus Campelube
on the 5 day of January, 190 5, that there was born to her on said date a female child, that said child is now living, and is said to have been named Helen[sic] Campelube

                          her
                     Nancy x Pusley   M. D.
                         mark

Subscribed and sworn to before me this the 16 day of March 1905

                       (Name Illegible)
                            Notary Public.

WITNESSETH:
Must be two witnesses { *(Name Illegible)*
who are citizens and
know the child.   Frank Pope

We hereby certify that we are well acquainted with Nancy Pusley
a mid wife and know her to be reputable and of good standing in the community.

                Must be two citizen { *(Name Illegible)*
                witnesses.   Frank Pope

BIRTH AFFIDAVIT.

DEPARTMENT OF THE INTERIOR.
COMMISSION TO THE FIVE CIVILIZED TRIBES.

IN RE APPLICATION FOR ENROLLMENT, as a citizen of the Choctaw Nation, of Ellen Compelube[sic], born on the 5th day of January, 1905

Name of Father: Columbus Compelube   a citizen of the Choctaw Nation.
Name of Mother: Sallie Pusley   a citizen of the Choctaw Nation.

                Postoffice   McAlester, I.T.

Applications for Enrollment of Choctaw Newborn
Act of 1905 Volume VII

AFFIDAVIT OF MOTHER.

UNITED STATES OF AMERICA, Indian Territory, }
Central   DISTRICT.

I, Sallie Pusley, on oath state that I am 24 years of age and a citizen by blood, of the Choctaw Nation; that I am not the lawful wife of Columbus Compelube[sic], who is a citizen, by blood of the Choctaw Nation; that a female child was born to me on 5th day of January, 1905; that said child has been named Ellen Compelube, and was living March 4, 1905.

                                             her
                                   Sallie x Pusley
Witnesses To Mark: mark
{ Silas Nail
{ D. J. Byington

Subscribed and sworn to before me this 17th day of March, 1905

                                   Wirt Franklin
                                   Notary Public.

AFFIDAVIT OF ATTENDING PHYSICIAN OR MID-WIFE.

UNITED STATES OF AMERICA, Indian Territory, }
Central   DISTRICT.

I, Nancy Pusley, a mid-wife, on oath state that I attended on Mrs. Sallie Pusley not, wife of Columbus Compelube on the 5th day of January, 1905; that there was born to her on said date a female child; that said child was living March 4, 1905, and is said to have been named Ellen Compelube

                                             her
                                   Nancy x Pusley
Witnesses To Mark: mark
{ Silas Nail
{ D.J. Byington

Subscribed and sworn to before me this 17th day of March, 1905

                                   Wirt Franklin
                                   Notary Public.

Applications for Enrollment of Choctaw Newborn
Act of 1905   Volume VII

Choc New Born 379
Ellen Amos b. 10-10-02

BIRTH AFFIDAVIT.

DEPARTMENT OF THE INTERIOR.
COMMISSION TO THE FIVE CIVILIZED TRIBES.

IN RE APPLICATION FOR ENROLLMENT, as a citizen of the   Choctaw   Nation, of Ellen Amos   , born on the   15[sic]   day of   October   , 1902

Name of Father: Sanders Amos   a citizen of the   Choctaw   Nation.
Name of Mother: Ann Amos   a citizen of the   Choctaw   Nation.

Postoffice   Krebs, Ind Ter.

AFFIDAVIT OF MOTHER.

UNITED STATES OF AMERICA, Indian Territory, }
Central   DISTRICT.

I,   Ann Amos   , on oath state that I am   33   years of age and a citizen by Blood   , of the   Choctaw   Nation; that I am the lawful wife of   Sanders Amos   , who is a citizen, by Blood   of the   Choctaw   Nation; that a   Female   child was born to me on   the 15[sic]   day of   October   , 1902; that said child has been named   Ellen Amos   , and was living March 4, 1905.

                                 her
                          Ann x Amos
Witnesses To Mark: mark
  { B.M. Gregg
  { Johnie Watson

Subscribed and sworn to before me this   10 day of   August   , 1905

                          Allen C Gregg
                             Notary Public.

AFFIDAVIT OF ATTENDING PHYSICIAN OR MID-WIFE.

UNITED STATES OF AMERICA, Indian Territory, }
Central   DISTRICT.

I,   Sallie Ridley   , a   woman   , on oath state that I attended on Mrs.   Ann Amos   , wife of   Sanders Amos   on the   15[sic]   day of   October   ,

Applications for Enrollment of Choctaw Newborn
Act of 1905   Volume VII

1905; that there was born to her on said date a   Female   child; that said child was living March 4, 1905, and is said to have been named Ellen Amos

Witnesses To Mark:
{ B.M. Gregg
  Johnie Watson

Sallie x Ridley
her   mark

Subscribed and sworn to before me this   10   day of   August   , 1905

Allen C Gregg
Notary Public.

- D E P A R T M E N T OF THE I N T E R I O R -
Commision[sic] to the Five Civilized Tribes.

APPLICATION FOR ENROLLMENT, as a citizen of the   Choctaw   Nation, of   Ellen Amos   born on the   10   Day of   Oct   1902. Name of Father, Sanders Amos   a citizen of the   Choctaw   Nation. Name of Mother   Ann Amos   a citizen of the   Choctaw   Nation.

POST OFFICE   Carbon I.T.

AFFIDAVIT OF MOTHER

UNITED STATES OF AMERICA |
   Indian Territory. |
Central   District.

I   Ann Amos   on oath state that I am   35   years of age and a Citizen by   Blood   of the   Choctaw   Nation, that I was the lawful wife of   Sanders Amos *deceased* who was a citizen by   Blood   of the   Choctaw   Nation, that a   Female   child was born to me on the   10   day of   Oct   1902, that said child has been Named   Ellen Amos   and is now liveing[sic] .....

Ann x Amos
her   mark

Must be 2   Lee Silmon
witnesses   Gilbert Pope

Subscribed and sworn to before me this   9   day of   Jan   1905

W.J. Oglesby
Notary Public.

Applications for Enrollment of Choctaw Newborn
Act of 1905   Volume VII

Affidavid[sic] of attending Physican[sic] or Midwife.

Central District.
Indian Territory.

I Sallie Ripley a midwife on oath state that I attended on Mrs. Ann Amos wife of Sanders Amos on the 10 day of Oct 1902 ; that there was born to her on said date a Female child; that said child was living March 4, 1905, and is said to have been named Ellen Amos

her
Sallie x Ripley
mark

Lee Silmon
Gilbert Pope

Subscribed and sworn to before me this 9 day of Jan 1905

W.J. Oglesby
Notary Public.

BIRTH AFFIDAVIT.   7-NB-379

DEPARTMENT OF THE INTERIOR.
COMMISSION TO THE FIVE CIVILIZED TRIBES.

IN RE APPLICATION FOR ENROLLMENT, as a citizen of the Choctaw Nation, of Ellen Amos , born on the 15[sic] day of October , 1902

Name of Father: Sanders Amos   a citizen of the Choctaw Nation.
Name of Mother: Ann Amos   a citizen of the Choctaw Nation.

Postoffice   Krebs Ind Ter

AFFIDAVIT OF MOTHER.

UNITED STATES OF AMERICA, Indian Territory, }
Central   DISTRICT. }

I, Ann Amos , on oath state that I am 35 years of age and a citizen by blood , of the Choctaw Nation; that I am the lawful wife of Sanders Amos , who is a citizen, by blood of the Choctaw Nation; that a female child was born to me on 15[sic] day of October , 1902; that said child has been named Ellen Amos , and was living March 4, 1905.

her
Ann x Amos
mark

16

Applications for Enrollment of Choctaw Newborn
Act of 1905   Volume VII

Witnesses To Mark:
{ B.M. Gregg
{ Nellie Winnett

    Subscribed and sworn to before me this   30 day of   August   , 1905

                          Allen C Gregg
                          Notary Public.

AFFIDAVIT OF ATTENDING PHYSICIAN OR MID-WIFE.

UNITED STATES OF AMERICA, Indian Territory, }
   Central   DISTRICT. }

    I,   Sallie Ripley   , a   midwife   , on oath state that I attended on Mrs. Ann Amos , wife of Sanders Amos dec'd   on the 15[sic] day of October , 1902; that there was born to her on said date a   female   child; that said child was living March 4, 1905, and is said to have been named Ellen Amos

                            her
                      Sallie x Ripley
Witnesses To Mark: mark
{ B.M. Gregg
{ Nellie Winnett

    Subscribed and sworn to before me this   30 day of   August   , 1905

                          Allen C Gregg
                          Notary Public.

BIRTH AFFIDAVIT.

DEPARTMENT OF THE INTERIOR,
COMMISSION TO THE FIVE CIVILIZED TRIBES.

    IN RE Application for Enrollment, as a citizen of the   Choctaw   Nation, of   Ellen Anos , born on the   15[sic]   day of   October   , 1902

Name of Father: Sanders Amos   a citizen of the   Choctaw Nation.
Name of Mother: Ann Amos   a citizen of the   Choctaw Nation.

                      Post-Office: Krebbs Ind. Ter.

Applications for Enrollment of Choctaw Newborn
Act of 1905   Volume VII

AFFIDAVIT OF MOTHER.

UNITED STATES OF AMERICA,
   INDIAN TERRITORY.
Central   District.

I, Ann Amos , on oath state that I am 30 years of age and a citizen by blood , of the Choctaw Nation; that I am the lawful wife of Sanders Ams , who is a citizen, by blood of the Choctaw Nation; that a female child was born to me on 15th[sic] day of October , 1902 , that said child has been named Ellen Amos , and is now living.

                        her
                    Ann x Amos
WITNESSES TO MARK: mark
  { Wm C Brown
    Freddie Kinkade

Subscribed and sworn to before me this 22nd *day of* December , 1902

                    J C Humphrey
                      NOTARY PUBLIC.

AFFIDAVIT OF ATTENDING PHYSICIAN OR MID-WIFE.

UNITED STATES OF AMERICA,
   INDIAN TERRITORY.
Central   District.

I, Sallie Riddle[sic] , a midwife , on oath state that I attended on Mrs. Ann Amos , wife of Sanders Amos on the 15th[sic] day of October , 1902 ; that there was born to her on said date a female child; that said child is now living and is said to have been named Ellen Amos

                      her
                Sallie x Riddle
WITNESSES TO MARK: mark
  { Wm C Brown
    Freddie Kinkade

Subscribed and sworn to before me this 22nd *day of* December , 1902

                    J C Humphrey
                      NOTARY PUBLIC.

Applications for Enrollment of Choctaw Newborn
Act of 1905   Volume VII

BIRTH AFFIDAVIT.

DEPARTMENT OF THE INTERIOR.
COMMISSION TO THE FIVE CIVILIZED TRIBES.

    IN RE APPLICATION FOR ENROLLMENT, as a citizen of the   Choctaw   Nation, of Ellen Amos   , born on the   10   day of   Oct , 1902

Name of Father: Sanders Amos   a citizen of the   Choctaw   Nation.
Name of Mother: Ann Amos   a citizen of the   Choctaw   Nation.

    Postoffice   Carbon I.T.

AFFIDAVIT OF MOTHER.

UNITED STATES OF AMERICA, Indian Territory, }
    Central   DISTRICT. }

    I,   Ann Amos   , on oath state that I am   35   years of age and a citizen by Blood , of the   Choctaw   Nation; that I am the lawful wife of   Sanders Amos , who is a citizen, by Blood   of the   Choctaw   Nation; that a   Female   child was born to me on the 10   day of   Oct   , 1902; that said child has been named   Ellen Amos   , and was living March 4, 1905.

    Ann x Amos

Witnesses To Mark:
  { Jno Perteet
    Minnie Oglesby

    Subscribed and sworn to before me this   22 day of   March   , 1905

    W.J. Oglesby
    Notary Public.

AFFIDAVIT OF ATTENDING PHYSICIAN OR MID-WIFE.

UNITED STATES OF AMERICA, Indian Territory, }
    Central   DISTRICT. }

    I,   Sallie Riply   , a   Mid Wife   , on oath state that I attended on Mrs. Ann Amos   , wife of Sanders Amos   on the 10 day of Oct   , 1902; that there was born to her on said date a   Female   child; that said child was living March 4, 1905, and is said to have been named Ellen Amos

    Sallie x Riply

Applications for Enrollment of Choctaw Newborn
Act of 1905 Volume VII

Witnesses To Mark:
{ Jno Perteet
{ Minnie Oglesby

Subscribed and sworn to before me this 22 day of March , 1905

W.J. Oglesby
Notary Public.

7-4749.

Muskogee, Indian Territory, October 28, 1902.

Sanders Amos,
    Care R.B. Coleman,
        McAlester, Indian Territory.

Dear Sir:

    Receipt is hereby acknowledged of your letter of the 23d inst., enclosing the application for enrollment as a citizen of the Choctaw Nation of Ellen Amos, infant daughter of Sanders and Annie[sic] Amos, born October 10, 1902; and the same is returned to you herewith.

    You are informed that the Commission cannot now receive or consider the application for the enrollment of this child as a citizen of the Choctaw Nation, it appearing that said child was born October 10, 1902, subsequent to the ratification by the citizens of the Choctaw an Chickasaw Nations on September 25, 1902, of an agreement recently entered into between the United States and the citizens of these two Nations.

    Section twenty-eight of the agreement above referred to provides as follows:

    "The names of all persons living on the date of the final ratification of this agreement entitled to be enrolled as provided in section 27 hereof shall be placed upon the rolls made by said Commission; and no child born thereafter to a citizen or freedman and no person intermarried thereafter to a citizen shall be entitled to enrollment or to participate in the distribution of the tribal property of the Choctaws and Chickasaws."

                Respectfully,

                Acting Chairman.

Enc B I 196.

Applications for Enrollment of Choctaw Newborn
Act of 1905   Volume VII

7-4749

Muskogee, Indian Territory, January 19, 1905.

Ann Amos,
    Carbon, Indian Territory.

Dear Madam:

    Receipt is hereby acknowledged of your affidavit and the affidavit of Sallie Ritley[sic] to the birth of Ellen Amos, infant daughter of Sanders Amos, deceased, and Ann Amos December 10, 1902, which it is presumed have been forwarded as an application for the enrollment of said child.

    You are advised that under the provisions of the act of Congress approved July 1, 1902, no children born to citizens of the Choctaw and Chickasaw Nations subsequent to September 25, 1902, the date of the ratification of said act, are entitled to enrollment and allotment in the Choctaw and Chickasaw Nations.

Respectfully,

Chairman.

7-4749

Muskogee, Indian Territory, March 25, 1905.

Sanders Amos,
    Carbon, Indian Territory.

Dear Sir:

    Receipt is hereby acknowledged of the affidavits of Ann Amos and Sallie Ripley to the birth of Ellen Amos daughter of Sanders and Ann Amos, October 10, 1902, and the same have been filed with our records as an application for the enrollment of said child.

Respectfully,

Chairman.

Applications for Enrollment of Choctaw Newborn
Act of 1905   Volume VII

7-NB-379.

Muskogee, Indian Territory, May 25, 1905.

Sanders Amos,
   Krebs, Indian Territory.

Dear Sir:

There is enclosed you herewith for execution application for the enrollment of your infant child, Ellen Amos.

In the affidavits of December 22, 1903, heretofore filed in this office, the date of the applicants[sic] birth is given as October 15, 1902, while in the affidavits of January 9, 1905, and March 22, 1905, it is given as October 10, 1902. In the enclosed application the date of birth is left blank, in which you will please insert the correct date, and, when properly executed, return the application to this office.

In having these affidavits executed care should be exercised to see that all names are written in full, as they appear in the body of the affidavit, and in the event that either of the persons signing the affidavit are unable to write, signatures by mark must be attested by two witnesses. Each affidavit must be executed before a Notary Public and the notarial seal and signature of the officer must be attached to each separate affidavit.

Respectfully,

VR 25-3.   Chairman.

7-NB-379

Muskogee, Indian Territory, July 29, 1905.

Ann Amos,
   Krebs, Indian Territory.

Dear Madam:

There is inclosed you herewith for execution application for the enrollment of your infant child, Ellen Amos.

In the affidavits of December 23, 1903, heretofore filed in this office, the date of applicant's birth is given as October 15, 1902, while in the affidavits of January 9, 1905, and March 22, 1905, the date of birth is given as October 10, 1902.

In the inclosed application the date of birth is left lank. You will please insert the correct date and when properly executed return to this office immediately.

Applications for Enrollment of Choctaw Newborn
Act of 1905 Volume VII

In having these affidavits executed care should be exercised to see that all names are written in full, as they appear in the body of the affidavit, and in the event that either of the persons signing the affidavit are unable to write, signatures by mark must be attested by two witnesses. Each affidavit must be executed before a Notary Public and the notarial seal and signature of the officer must be attached to each separate affidavit.

This matter should receive your immediate attention as no further action can be taken relative to the enrollment of your said child, until the evidence requested is supplied.

Respectfully,

LM 4/29

Commissioner.

---

7 N B 379

Muskogee, Indian Territory, August 14, 1905.

Ann Amos,
    Krebbs, Indian Territory.

Dear Madam:

Receipt is hereby acknowledged of your affidavit and the affidavit of Sallie Ridley[sic] to the birth of Ellen Amos, daughter of Sanders and Ann Amos, October 15, 1902, and the same have been filed with the record in the matter of the enrollment of said child.

Respectfully,

Acting Commissioner.

Choc New Born 380
    Wynema Hill b. 4-8-04

Applications for Enrollment of Choctaw Newborn
Act of 1905   Volume VII

7-4756

Muskogee, Indian Territory, March 10, 1905.

Bone[sic] & Melton,
    Attorneys at Law,
        Chickasha, Indian Territory.

Gentlemen:

    Receipt is hereby acknowledged of your letter of March 7, 1905, enclosing the affidavits of Nellie B. Hill and E. L. Dawson to the birth of Wyonia[sic] Hill, infant daughter of Dave and Nellie B. Hill, April 7, 1904, and the same have been filed with our records as an application for the enrollment of said child.

        Respectfully,

                Chairman.

N. B. 380

Muskogee, Indian Territory, April 7, 1905.

David Hill,
    Chickasha, Indian Territory.

Dear Sir:

    There is inclosed you herewith for execution application for the enrollment of your infant child, Wynema Hill, born April 4, 1904.

    The affidavits heretofore filed with the Commission show the child was living on February 16, 1905. It is necessary, for the child to be enrolled, that she was living on March 4, 1905.

    In having these affidavits executed care should be exercised to see that all names are written in full, as they appear in the body of the affidavit, and in the event that either of the persons signing the affidavit are unable to write, signatures by mark must be attested by two witnesses. Each affidavit must be executed before a Notary Public and the notarial seal and signature of the officer must be attached to each separate affidavit.

        Respectfully,

LM 7-27   Commissioner in Charge.

Applications for Enrollment of Choctaw Newborn
Act of 1905 Volume VII

7-7456

Muskogee, Indian Territory, April 20, 1904.

Bond & Melton,
    Attorneys at Law,
        Chickasha, Indian Territory.

Gentlemen:

    Receipt is hereby acknowledged of your letter of the 16th inst., enclosing the affidavits of Nellie B. Hill and E. L. Dawson, relative to the birth of Wynema Hill, infant daughter of David D. and Nellie B. Hill, April 8, 1904, which you have forwarded to this Commission as an application for the enrollment of said child as a citizen of the Choctaw Nation.

    You are advised that under the provisions of the Act of Congress approved July 1, 1902, the Commission is now without authority to receive or consider the original application for enrollment of any person whomsoever as a citizen of the Choctaw or Chickasaw Nation.

    Respectfully,

    Chairman.

7-NB-380.

Muskogee, Indian Territory, April 25, 1905.

David Hill,
    Chickasha, Indian Territory.

Dear Sir:

    Receipt is hereby acknowledged of the affidavits of Nellie B. Hill and E. L. Dawson, to the birth of Wynema Hill, child of David and Nellie B. Hill, April 7, 1904, and the same have been filed with our records in the matter of the enrollment of said child.

    Respectfully,

    Chairman.

Applications for Enrollment of Choctaw Newborn
Act of 1905   Volume VII

7-NB-380.

Muskogee, Indian Territory, May 25, 1905.

Dave Hill,
    Chickasha, Indian Territory.

Dear Sir:

There is enclosed you herewith for execution application for the enrollment of your infant child, Wynema Hill.

In the application field in this office on March 4, 1904, the date of the applicants[sic] birth is given as April 8, 1904, while in the one filed April 14, 1905, the date of birth is given as April 8, 1905. In the application filed April 25, 1905, the mother gives the date of birth as April 8, 1904, and the physician gives it as April 7, 1904. In the enclosed application the date of birth is left blank in which you will please insert the correct date of birth, and, when the affidavits are properly executed, return the application to this office.

In having these affidavits executed care should be exercised to see that all names are written in full, as they appear in the body of the affidavit, and in the event that either of the persons signing the affidavit are unable to write, signatures by mark must be attested by two witnesses. Each affidavit must be executed before a Notary Public and the notarial seal and signature of the officer must be attached to each separate affidavit.

Respectfully,

Vr 25-4.   Chairman.

7-N.B. 380.

Muskogee, Indian Territory, June 5, 1905.

Dave Hill,
    Chickasha, Indian Territory.

Dear Sir:

Receipt is hereby acknowledged of the affidavits of Nellie B. Hill and E. L. Dawson to the birth of Wynema Hill, daughter of Dave and Nellie B. Hill, April 8, 1904, and the same have been filed with our records in the matter of the enrollment of said child.

Respectfully,

Commissioner in Charge.

Applications for Enrollment of Choctaw Newborn
Act of 1905 Volume VII

BIRTH AFFIDAVIT.

DEPARTMENT OF THE INTERIOR.
COMMISSION TO THE FIVE CIVILIZED TRIBES.

IN RE APPLICATION FOR ENROLLMENT, as a citizen of the Choctaw Nation, of Wynema Hill, born on the 7 day of April, 1904.

Name of Father: Dave Hill   a citizen of the Chocktaw[sic] Nation.
Name of Mother: Nellie B. Hill   a citizen of the Chocktaw[sic] Nation.

Postoffice   Chickasha, I.T.

AFFIDAVIT OF MOTHER.

UNITED STATES OF AMERICA, Indian Territory,
Southern DISTRICT.

I, Nellie B. Hill, on oath state that I am 27 years of age and a citizen by blood, of the Chocktaw Nation; that I am the lawful wife of Dave Hill, who is a citizen, by intermarriage of the Chocktaw Nation; that a female child was born to me on 7th day of April, 1904, that said child has been named Wynema Hill, and is now living.

                 Nellie B. Hill

Witnesses To Mark:

Subscribed and sworn to before me this 18th day of Feby, 1905.

           (Name Illegible)
           Notary Public.

AFFIDAVIT OF ATTENDING PHYSICIAN OR MID-WIFE.

UNITED STATES OF AMERICA, Indian Territory,
Southern DISTRICT.

I, E.L. Dawson, a physician, on oath state that I attended on Mrs. Nellie B. Hill, wife of Dave Hill on the 7th day of April, 1904; that there was born to her on said date a female child; that said child is now living and is said to have been named Wynema Hill

           E. L. Dawson, M.D.

Witnesses To Mark:

Applications for Enrollment of Choctaw Newborn
Act of 1905 Volume VII

Subscribed and sworn to before me this   16 day of Feb , 1905.

(Name Illegible)
Notary Public.

Birth AFFidavit[sic].

---DEPARTMENT OF THE INTERIOR---

Commission to the five[sic] Civilized Tribes,

IN RE APPLICATION FOR ENROLLMENT, as a citizen of the Chocktaw[sic] Nation, of Wynema Hill, born on the 8th day of April 1904, Daughter of Dave D. Hill, a citizen of the Chocktaw[sic] Nation, by Intermarriage and Nellie B. Hill a citizen of the Chocktaw[sic] Nation by blood, of Chickasha, Indian Territory.

AFFIDAVIT OF MOTHER.

United States of America,)
   Indian Territory,   )
   Southern District,   )

I, Nellie B. Hill, on oath state that I am   26   years old, a Citizen of the Chocktaw[sic] Nation, that I am the lawful wife of Dave D. Hill, who is a citizen by intermarriage of the Chocktaw[sic] nation; that a female child was born to me on the 8th day of April, 1904, that said child has been named Wynema, and is now living.

Nellie B. Hill

Witnesses to mark, Mrs. Millie Morgan
must be two wit-
nesses.   Dave Hill

Subscribed and sworn to before me this the   15   day of April, 1904.

Alger Melton
Notary Public.

Applications for Enrollment of Choctaw Newborn
Act of 1905 Volume VII

AFFIDAVIT OF ATTENDING PHYSICIAN, OR MID-WIFE.

United States of America,)
    Indian Territory,   )
    Southern District,)

    I, E. L. Dawson, a practicing physician, on oath state that I attended Mrs. Nellie B. Hill, wife of Dave D. Hill, on the 8th day of April, 1904; that there was born to her on said date a female child; that said child is now living and is said to have been named Wynema.

                                                E. L. Dawson, M.D.
Witnesses to mark.

    Subscribed and sworn to before me this the ~~xxx~~ *15* day of ~~April~~ *April*, 1904.

                                             Alger Melton
                                             Notary Public.

My commission expires on the 24th day of February, 1907.

BIRTH AFFIDAVIT.

DEPARTMENT OF THE INTERIOR.
COMMISSION TO THE FIVE CIVILIZED TRIBES.

    IN RE APPLICATION FOR ENROLLMENT, as a citizen of the   Choctaw   Nation, of Wynema Hill   , born on the   7"[sic] day of   April   , 1904

Name of Father: David Hill   a citizen of the   Choctaw   Nation.
Name of Mother: Nellie B Hill   a citizen of the   Choctaw   Nation.

                          Postoffice   Chickasha Ind. Ter.

AFFIDAVIT OF MOTHER.

UNITED STATES OF AMERICA, Indian Territory, }
.... DISTRICT. }

    I, Nellie B. Hill   , on oath state that I am   27   years of age and a citizen by Blood   , of the   Choctaw   Nation; that I am the lawful wife of   David Hill   , who is a citizen, by Intermarriage   of the   Choctaw   Nation; that a   Female

Applications for Enrollment of Choctaw Newborn
Act of 1905   Volume VII

child was born to me on 7 8 day of   April , 1904; that said child has been named Wynema Hill , and was living March 4, 1905.

Nellie B Hill

Witnesses To Mark:
{

Subscribed and sworn to before me this 20th day of   April   , 1905

(Illegible) Melton
Notary Public.

AFFIDAVIT OF ATTENDING PHYSICIAN OR MID-WIFE.

UNITED STATES OF AMERICA, Indian Territory, }
....DISTRICT.}

I,   E L Dawson   , a   Physician   , on oath state that I attended on Mrs. Nellie B Hill , wife of   David Hill   on the 7"[sic] day of April   , 1904; that there was born to her on said date a   Female   child; that said child was living March 4, 1905, and is said to have been named   Wynema Hill

E L Dawson M.D.

Witnesses To Mark:
{

Subscribed and sworn to before me this 20th day of   April   , 1905

(Illegible) Melton
Notary Public.

BIRTH AFFIDAVIT.

DEPARTMENT OF THE INTERIOR.

COMMISSION TO THE FIVE CIVILIZED TRIBES.

IN RE APPLICATION FOR ENROLLMENT, as a citizen of the   Choctaw   Nation, of Wynema Hill   , born on the 8 day of April , 1904

Name of Father: Dave Hill	a citizen of the Choctaw Nation.
Name of Mother: Nellie B Hill	a citizen of the Choctaw Nation.

Postoffice   Chickasha I.T.

Applications for Enrollment of Choctaw Newborn
Act of 1905   Volume VII

AFFIDAVIT OF MOTHER.

UNITED STATES OF AMERICA, Indian Territory,   }
    Southern   DISTRICT.

    I, Nellie B. Hill, on oath state that I am 27 years of age and a citizen by Blood, of the Choctaw Nation; that I am the lawful wife of Dave Hill, who is a citizen, by Intermarriage of the Choctaw Nation; that a Female child was born to me on 8 day of April, 1904; that said child has been named Wynema Hill, and was living March 4, 1905.

                                        Nellie B Hill

Witnesses To Mark:
{

    Subscribed and sworn to before me this 31 day of May, 1905

                                        (Illegible) Melton
                                                        Notary Public.

AFFIDAVIT OF ATTENDING PHYSICIAN OR MID-WIFE.

UNITED STATES OF AMERICA, Indian Territory,   }
    Southern   DISTRICT.

    I, E. L. Dawson, a Physician, on oath state that I attended on Mrs. Nellie B Hill, wife of Dave Hill on the 8 day of April, 1904; that there was born to her on said date a Female child; that said child was living March 4, 1905, and is said to have been named Wynema Hill

                                        E L Dawson M.D.

Witnesses To Mark:
{

    Subscribed and sworn to before me this 31 day of May, 1905

                                        (Illegible) Melton
                                                    Notary Public.

Applications for Enrollment of Choctaw Newborn
Act of 1905 Volume VII

Choc New Born 381
Ruth Smart b. 3-6-03

BIRTH AFFIDAVIT.

DEPARTMENT OF THE INTERIOR.
COMMISSION TO THE FIVE CIVILIZED TRIBES.

IN RE APPLICATION FOR ENROLLMENT, as a citizen of the Choctaw Nation, of Ruth Smart , born on the 6th day of March , 1903

Name of Father: James H. Smart a citizen of the United States Nation.
Name of Mother: Annie Smart a citizen of the Choctaw Nation.

Postoffice Crowder, I.T.

AFFIDAVIT OF MOTHER.

UNITED STATES OF AMERICA, Indian Territory,
Central DISTRICT.

I, Annie Smart , on oath state that I am 32 years of age and a citizen by blood , of the Choctaw Nation; that I am the lawful wife of James H Smart , who is a citizen, by .... of the United States Nation; that a female child was born to me on 6th day of March , 1903; that said child has been named Ruth Smart , and was living March 4, 1905.

Annie Smart

Witnesses To Mark:

Subscribed and sworn to before me this 17th day of March , 1905

Wirt Franklin
Notary Public.

AFFIDAVIT OF ATTENDING PHYSICIAN OR MID-WIFE.

UNITED STATES OF AMERICA, Indian Territory,
Western DISTRICT.

I, Thomas T Morris M.D. , a Physician , on oath state that I attended on Mrs. Annie Smart , wife of James H Smart on the 6th day of March , 1903; that there was born to her on said date a female child; that said child was living March 4, 1905, and is said to have been named Ruth

Applications for Enrollment of Choctaw Newborn
Act of 1905   Volume VII

Thomas T. Morris M.D.

Witnesses To Mark:

Subscribed and sworn to before me this 17 day of   March   , 1905

T. D. Tignor
Notary Public.

7-4771

Muskogee, Indian Territory, March 21, 1905.

Annie Smart,
    Crowder, Indian Territory.

Dear Madam:

Receipt is hereby acknowledged of the affidavits of Annie Smart and Thomas T. Morris to the birth of Ruth S. daughter of James H. and Annie Smart, March 6, 1903, and the same have been filed with our records as an application for the enrollment of said child.

Respectfully,

Chairman.

NEW BORN AFFIDAVIT

No ....

CHOCTAW ENROLLING COMMISSION

IN THE MATTER OF THE APPLICATION FOR ENROLLMENT as a citizen of the Choctaw Nation, of   Ruth Smart   born on the 6 day of   March   190 3

Name of father   James Smart   a citizen of   White   Nation, final enrollment No. ———
Name of mother   Annie Smart   a citizen of   Choctaw   Nation, final enrollment No. 13177

Crowder I.T.   Postoffice.

33

Applications for Enrollment of Choctaw Newborn
Act of 1905 Volume VII

AFFIDAVIT OF MOTHER

UNITED STATES OF AMERICA
INDIAN TERRITORY
DISTRICT   Central

I   Annie Smart   , on oath state that I am   32   years of age and a citizen by   blood   of the   Choctaw   Nation, and as such have been placed upon the final roll of the   Choctaw   Nation, by the Honorable Secretary of the Interior my final enrollment number being   13177   ; that I am the lawful wife of   James Smart   , who is a citizen of the   non   Nation, and as such has been placed upon the final roll of said Nation by the Honorable Secretary of the Interior, his final enrollment number being   ——   and that a   Female   child was born to me on the   6   day of   March   190 3; that said child has been named   Ruth Smart   , and is now living.

WITNESSETH: Annie Smart

Must be two witnesses   { Sarah A Harlow
who are citizens   Joseph C Jones

Subscribed and sworn to before me this, the   16   day of   March   , 190 5

James Bower
Notary Public.

My Commission Expires:
Sept 23 - 1907

Affidavit of Attending Physician or Midwife

UNITED STATES OF AMERICA,
INDIAN TERRITORY,
Central   DISTRICT

I,   T.T. Norris[sic]   a   Practicing Physician on oath state that I attended on Mrs.   Annie Smart   wife of   James Smart   on the   6   day of   March   , 190 3, that there was born to her on said date a   female   child, that said child is now living, and is said to have been named   Ruth Smart

Thos.T. Morris   M. D.

Subscribed and sworn to before me this the   16   day of   March   1905

James Bower
Notary Public.

WITNESSETH:
Must be two witnesses   { Sarah A Harlow
who are citizens and
know the child.   Joseph C Jones

Applications for Enrollment of Choctaw Newborn
Act of 1905   Volume VII

We hereby certify that we are well acquainted with   T. T. Norris[sic] a   Practicing Physician   and know   him   to be reputable and of good standing in the community.

Must be two citizen ⎰ Sarah A Harlow
witnesses.   ⎱ Joseph C Jones

Choc New Born 382
Benjamin Paul Choote[sic]   b. 8-23-03

BIRTH AFFIDAVIT.

DEPARTMENT OF THE INTERIOR.
COMMISSION TO THE FIVE CIVILIZED TRIBES.

IN RE APPLICATION FOR ENROLLMENT, as a citizen of the   Choctaw   Nation, of Benjamin Paul Choate   , born on the   23   day of August   , 1903

Name of Father: William F Choate   a citizen of the   Choctaw   Nation.
Name of Mother: Mary Elizabeth Choate   a citizen of the   Choctaw   Nation.

Postoffice   Indianola I.T.

AFFIDAVIT OF MOTHER.

UNITED STATES OF AMERICA, Indian Territory, ⎫
   Western   DISTRICT. ⎭

I,   Mary Elizabeth Choate   , on oath state that I am   37   years of age and a citizen by   intermarriage   , of the   Choctaw   Nation; that I am the lawful wife of   William F Choate   , who is a citizen, by Blood   of the   Choctaw Nation; that a   male   child was born to me on   23   day of August   , 1903; that said child has been named   Benjamin Paul Choate   , and was living March 4, 1905.

Mary Elizabeth Choate

Witnesses To Mark:
⎰ G. W. Choate
⎱ Tobe Taylor

Applications for Enrollment of Choctaw Newborn
Act of 1905   Volume VII

Subscribed and sworn to before me this   24   day of   March   , 1905

My Commission Expires   T. J. Rice
Aug. 1st. 1906
Notary Public.

AFFIDAVIT OF ATTENDING PHYSICIAN OR MID-WIFE.

UNITED STATES OF AMERICA, Indian Territory, }
Western   DISTRICT.

I,   J. A. Eubank   , a   Physician   , on oath state that I attended on Mrs.   Mary Elizabeth Choate   , wife of   William F Choate   on the 23   day of August   , 1903; that there was born to her on said date a   male   child; that said child was living March 4, 1905, and is said to have been named Benjamin Paul Choate

JA Eubank M.D.

Witnesses To Mark:
{ G. W. Choate
{ Tobe Taylor

Subscribed and sworn to before me this   24   day of   March   , 1905

My Commission Expires   T. J. Rice
Aug. 1st. 1906
Notary Public.

AFFIDAVIT OF ATTENDING PHYSICIAN OR MIDWIFE

UNITED STATES OF AMERICA
INDIAN TERRITORY
Western   DISTRICT

I,   J.A. Eubank   a   Physician   on oath state that I attended on Mrs.   Mary E Choate   wife of   William F Choate   on the   23   day of Aug   , 190 3 , that there was born to her on said date a .... child, that said child is now living, and is said to have been named   Benjamin Paul Choate

JA Eubank   *M.D.*

Subscribed and sworn to before me this, the   9   day of Feby   190 5

T.J. Rice   Notary Public.

WITNESSETH:
Must be two witnesses   { F.M. Brown
who are citizens   { Will T. Walker

Applications for Enrollment of Choctaw Newborn
Act of 1905 Volume VII

We hereby certify that we are well acquainted with J.A. Eubank a Physician and know him to be reputable and of good standing in the community.

B.F. Hightower   Indianola I.T.

Will T. Walker   Indianola I.T.

NEW-BORN AFFIDAVIT.

Number..............

...Choctaw Enrolling Commission...

IN THE MATTER OF THE APPLICATION FOR ENROLLMENT, as a citizen of the Choctaw Nation, of Benjamin Paul Choate born on the 23" day of August 190 3

Name of father W.F. Choate   a citizen of Choctaw
Nation final enrollment No. 13198
Name of mother Mary E. Choate   a citizen of Choctaw
Nation final enrollment No. 581

Postoffice Indianola IT

AFFIDAVIT OF MOTHER.

UNITED STATES OF AMERICA
INDIAN TERRITORY
Western DISTRICT

I Mary E Choate , on oath state that I am 34 years of age and a citizen by marriage of the Choctaw Nation, and as such have been placed upon the final roll of the Choctaw Nation, by the Honorable Secretary of the Interior my final enrollment number being 581 ; that I am the lawful wife of William F Choate , who is a citizen of the Choctaw Nation, and as such has been placed upon the final roll of said Nation by the Honorable Secretary of the Interior, his final enrollment number being 13198 and that a .... child was born to me on the 23 day of August 190 3; that said child has been named Benjamin Paul Choate , and is now living.

Witnesseth.   Mary E Choate

Must be two ⎫ Christopher C Choate
Witnesses who ⎬
are Citizens. ⎭ G.W. Choate

Applications for Enrollment of Choctaw Newborn
Act of 1905   Volume VII

Subscribed and sworn to before me this   6   day of   Feby   190 5

T.J. Rice
Notary Public.

My commission expires:
My Commission Expires
Aug. 1st. 1906

7-4777

Muskogee, Indian Territory, March 29, 1905.

W. F. Choate,
Indianola, Indian Territory.

Dear Sir:

Receipt is hereby acknowledged of your letter of March 24, 1905, enclosing affidavits of Mary Elizabeth Choate and J. A. Eubanks[sic] to the birth of Benjamin Paul Choate, son of William F. and Mary Elizabeth Choate, August 23, 1903, and the same have been filed with our records as an application for the enrollment of said child.

Respectfully,

Chairman.

Choc New Born 383
Noland Freeman Smith   b. 12-2-02

N.B. 383.
COPY
Muskogee, Indian Territory, April 8, 1905.

Freeman F. Smith,
Canadian, Indian Territory.

Dear Sir:

You are hereby notified that before the application for the enrollment of Noland Freeman Smith can finally be disposed of, it will be necessary that you furnish the Commission either the original or a certified copy of the license and certificate of your marriage to Anna E. Smith.

Applications for Enrollment of Choctaw Newborn
Act of 1905   Volume VII

Please give this matter your immediate attention.

Respectfully,
SIGNED
T. B. Needles.
Commissioner in Charge.

LER 8-18

(COPY)

Canadian, Ind. Ter. 4/11/1905.

Commission to the Five Civilized Tribes,
Muskogee, I. T.

Dear Sirs:

Your favor of the 8st[sic] inst N.B. 383, requiring me to furnish the Commission with "either the original or a certified copy of the license and certificate of my marriage to Anna E. Smith, is received and will say that in 1891 when I married Anna E. Smith that the U. S. Courts would not issue license to marry where both of the contracting parties were Indians by blood, neither would the Indian Courts issue marriage license where both parties were Indians, and as my wife was a Cherokee by blood and I was a Choctaw by blood all that we could get in the way of a license was a certificate from the Minister who performed the ceremony, signed by witnesses who were present when we were married. We secured such a certificate and my wife Anna E. Smith filed it with the Dawes Commission in 1896 with her petition to be enrolled as an intermarried citizen of the Choctaw Nation, and we have never seen it since. I was allowed to filed for my wife, Anna E. Smith and our three children, Arlean, Francis and Fulton Smith and supposed that the records were clear. I am very anxious to have our marriage made a matter of public record as soon as possible, if it is not so now for a great deal may depend on it to my family in the future.

The minister who married us is still here also twenty or thirty of the friends who witnessed our marriage are here. I can furnish you with any kind of a statement from them that you might desire.

Please advise me at once what steps to take in the matter so that the matter may be thoroughly cleared up and our marriage made a matter of record for all time to come.

Very Respectfully Yours,

Freeman R. Smith.

Applications for Enrollment of Choctaw Newborn
Act of 1905   Volume VII

Choctaw N.B. 383

Muskogee, Indian Territory, April 21, 1905

Freeman R. Smith,
Canadian, Indian Territory.

Dear Sir:

    Receipt is hereby acknowledged of your letter of April 11, replying to our communication of April 8, in which you state that the marriage license and certificate between yourself and Anna E. Smith was filed with the Commission at the time Anna E. Smith made application for citizenship in the Choctaw Nation under the Act of Congress approved June 10, 1896, but that if necessary you will furnish affidavits of the minister who married you and any number of witnesses who were present at your marriage.

    In reply to your letter you are informed that the information contained therein has enabled the Commission to identify your wife, Anna E. Smith, as having been enrolled as an intermarried citizen of the Choctaw Nation and it will not, therefore, be necessary for you to furnish the evidence of marriage between yourself and said Anna E. Smith.

Respectfully,

Chairman.

---

7 NB-383

Muskogee, Indian Territory, July 11, 1905.

Freeman R. Smith,
Canadian, Indian Territory.

Dear Sir:

    Receipt is hereby acknowledged of your letter of July 6, 1905, returning certificate sent you by mistake and asking if your son Nowland[sic] Freeman Smith has been approved.

    In reply to your letter you are advised that the name of your son Noland Freeman Smith has been placed upon a schedule of citizens by blood of the Choctaw Nation which has been forwarded the Secretary of the Interior but this office has not yet been advised of Departmental action thereon. You will be notified when his enrollment is approved.

Respectfully,

Commissioner.

Applications for Enrollment of Choctaw Newborn
Act of 1905 Volume VII

BIRTH AFFIDAVIT.

DEPARTMENT OF THE INTERIOR.
COMMISSION TO THE FIVE CIVILIZED TRIBES.

IN RE APPLICATION FOR ENROLLMENT, as a citizen of the Choctaw Nation, of Noland Freeman Smith , born on the 2 day of December , 1902

Name of Father: Freeman R. Smith   a citizen of the Choctaw Nation.
Name of Mother: Anna E. Smith   a citizen of the Choctaw Nation.

Postoffice   Canadian I T

AFFIDAVIT OF MOTHER.

UNITED STATES OF AMERICA, Indian Territory,
   Western   DISTRICT.

I, Anna E Smith , on oath state that I am 36 years of age and a citizen by Intermarriage , of the Choctaw Nation; that I am the lawful wife of Freeman R Smith , who is a citizen, by Blood of the Choctaw Nation; that a male child was born to me on 2 day of Dec , 1902; that said child has been named Noland Freeman Smith , and was living March 4, 1905.

                                         Anna E Smith

Witnesses To Mark:

     Subscribed and sworn to before me this 24th day of Mar , 1905

                                         JD Browder
                                         Notary Public.

AFFIDAVIT OF ATTENDING PHYSICIAN OR MID-WIFE.

UNITED STATES OF AMERICA, Indian Territory,
   Western   DISTRICT.

I, J.A. Adams , a Physician , on oath state that I attended on Mrs. Anna E. Smith , wife of Freeman R Smith on the 2 day of Dec , 1902; that there was born to her on said date a male child; that said child was living March 4, 1905, and is said to have been named Noland Freeman Smith

                                       J.A. Adams M.D.

Applications for Enrollment of Choctaw Newborn
Act of 1905   Volume VII

Witnesses To Mark:

{

    Subscribed and sworn to before me this 24th day of   Mar   , 1905

                                     JD Browder
                                       Notary Public.

<u>Choc New Born 384</u>
    David Franklin Harlan   b. 5-17-03

                                               7-4808

                Muskogee, Indian Territory, March 21, 1905.

Aaron Harlan,
    Paoli, Indian Territory.

Dear Sir:

    Receipt is hereby acknowledged of the affidavits of Marietta Harlan and W. J. Maniss to the birth of David Franklin Harlan son of Aaron and Marietta Harlan, May 17, 1903, and the same have been filed with our records as an application for the enrollment of said child.

                             Respectfully,

                                                 Chairman.

Applications for Enrollment of Choctaw Newborn
Act of 1905   Volume VII

(The letter below does not belong with the current applicant.)

7-NB-348

Muskogee, Indian Territory, November 26, 1906.

Ledbetter & Bledsoe,
    Attorneys at Law,
        Ardmore, Indian Territory.

Gentlemen:

    Receipt is hereby acknowledged of your letter of November 19, 1906, asking the status of the application of Nancy Folsom as a citizen by blood of the Choctaw Nation intermarriage of the Choctaw Nation and requesting to be advised if Nancy Folsom should furnish any other evidence than that already furnished.

    In reply to your letter you are advised that on February 16, 1905, Nancy Folsom appeared at this office for the purpose of testifying relative to her right to enrollment. At that time she was advised that it would be necessary for her to furnish evidence that Daniel Folsom, through whom she claims the right to enrollment, was a recognized Choctaw Indian; also evidence of her marriage to Folsom and evidence of the death of the former wife of Daniel Folsom or his divorce from her prior to his marriage to Nancy Folsom. November 3, 1905, a letter was addressed to you calling your attention to the evidence necessary in this case as recited above, but the same has not yet been furnished and until the evidence requested has been received no action can be taken in the matter of the application for the enrollment of Nancy Folsom as a citizen by blood of the Choctaw Nation intermarriage of the Choctaw Nation.

        Respectfully,

        Commissioner.

BIRTH AFFIDAVIT.

DEPARTMENT OF THE INTERIOR.
COMMISSION TO THE FIVE CIVILIZED TRIBES.

IN RE APPLICATION FOR ENROLLMENT, as a citizen of the Choctaw Nation, of David Franklin Harlan, born on the 17th day of May, 1903

Name of Father: Aron[sic] Harlan   a citizen of the Chocktaw[sic] Nation.
Name of Mother: Mary Etta Harlan   a citizen of the " Nation.

        Postoffice   Paoli I.T.

Applications for Enrollment of Choctaw Newborn
Act of 1905   Volume VII

AFFIDAVIT OF MOTHER.

UNITED STATES OF AMERICA, Indian Territory, }
Southern Judician   DISTRICT.

I, Mary Etta Harlan, on oath state that I am 29 years of age and a citizen by Marriage, of the Chocktaw Nation; that I am the lawful wife of Aaron Harlan, who is a citizen, by Blood of the Choctaw Nation; that a boy child was born to me on 17th day of May, 1903, that said child has been named David Franklin, and is now living.

                                                Mary Etta Harlan

Witnesses To Mark:
{ Leila A Maniss
{ Rosa R Horn

Subscribed and sworn to before me this 16th day of March, 1905.

                                                L. F. Jones
                                                Notary Public.

AFFIDAVIT OF ATTENDING PHYSICIAN OR MID-WIFE.

UNITED STATES OF AMERICA, Indian Territory, }
Southern Judicial   DISTRICT.

I, W.J. Maniss, a Physician, on oath state that I attended on Mrs. Mary Etta Harlan, wife of Aaron Harlan on the 17th day of May, 1903; that there was born to her on said date a boy child; that said child is now living and is said to have been named David Franklin

                                                W.J. Maniss, M.D.

Witnesses To Mark:
{ Leila A Maniss
{ Rosa R Horn

Subscribed and sworn to before me this 16th day of March, 1905.

                                                L. F. Jones
                                               Notary Public.

Applications for Enrollment of Choctaw Newborn
Act of 1905   Volume VII

Choc New Born 385
Catherine Fulton, Jr   b. 5-16-04

BIRTH AFFIDAVIT.

DEPARTMENT OF THE INTERIOR.
COMMISSION TO THE FIVE CIVILIZED TRIBES.

IN RE APPLICATION FOR ENROLLMENT, as a citizen of the   Choctaw   Nation, of Catherine Fulton, Jr   , born on the 16th   day of   May   , 1904

Name of Father: John R. Fulton   a citizen of the   Choctaw   Nation.
Name of Mother: Jessie Fulton   a citizen of the   Choctaw   Nation.

Postoffice   McAlester, I.T.

AFFIDAVIT OF MOTHER.

UNITED STATES OF AMERICA, Indian Territory,
Central   DISTRICT.

I, Jessie Fulton   , on oath state that I am   23   years of age and a citizen ~~by~~ ——, of the   United States   Nation; that I am the lawful wife of   John R. Fulton   , who is a citizen, by blood   of the   Choctaw   Nation; that a   female   child was born to me on   16th   day of   May   , 1904; that said child has been named Catherine Fulton, Jr.   , and was living March 4, 1905.

Jessie Fulton

Witnesses To Mark:

Subscribed and sworn to before me this   21st   day of   March   , 1905

Wirt Franklin
Notary Public.

AFFIDAVIT OF ATTENDING PHYSICIAN OR MID-WIFE.

UNITED STATES OF AMERICA, Indian Territory,
Central   DISTRICT.

I,   Catherin Fulton   , a   mid-wife   , on oath state that I attended on Mrs.   Jessie Fulton   , wife of   John R. Fulton   on the 16th day of May   , 1904; that there was born to her on said date a   female   child; that said child was living March 4, 1905, and is said to have been named Catherine Fulton, Jr.

Applications for Enrollment of Choctaw Newborn
Act of 1905 Volume VII

                                                          her
                                         Catherine x Fulton

Witnesses To Mark: mark
  { Peter Maytubby, Jr
    J M Morrison

Subscribed and sworn to before me this 21st day of   March   , 1905

                                              Wirt Franklin
                                              Notary Public.

Affidavit of Attending Physician or Midwife

UNITED STATES OF AMERICA, }
    INDIAN TERRITORY,
 Central   DISTRICT

                        mother in law to Jessie Fulton
   I,   Catherine Fulton   a   midwife
on oath state that I attended on Mrs. Jessie Fulton   wife of John R. Fulton
on the 16   day of   May , 190 4, that there was born to her on said date a   female child,
that said child is now living, and is said to have been named   Catherine Fulton
                                             her
                                  Catherine x Fulton   M. D.
                                          mark
Subscribed and sworn to before me this the 15   day of   Mark   1905

                                        James Bower
                                            Notary Public.

WITNESSETH:
  Must be two witnesses   { Simpson Folsom
  who are citizens and
  know the child.   W C Bolling

     We hereby certify that we are well acquainted with   Catherine Fulton
a   Midwife   and know her   to be reputable and of good standing in the
community.

                             Must be two citizen { Simpson Folsom
                             witnesses.   W C Bolling

Applications for Enrollment of Choctaw Newborn
Act of 1905   Volume VII

NEW BORN AFFIDAVIT

No _____

CHOCTAW ENROLLING COMMISSION

IN THE MATTER OF THE APPLICATION FOR ENROLLMENT as a citizen of the Choctaw Nation, of   Catherine Fulton   born on the 16   day of   May   190 4

Name of father   John R Fulton   a citizen of   Choctaw   Nation, final enrollment No.   13297
Name of mother   Jessie Fulton   a citizen of   White   Nation, final enrollment No. ——

McAlester I.T.   Postoffice.

AFFIDAVIT OF MOTHER

UNITED STATES OF AMERICA
   INDIAN TERRITORY
DISTRICT   Central

I   Jesse[sic] Fulton   , on oath state that I am   23   years of age and a citizen by   —— of the ——   Nation, and as such have been placed upon the final roll of the   ——   Nation, by the Honorable Secretary of the Interior my final enrollment number being   ....   ; that I am the lawful wife of   John R. Fulton   , who is a citizen of the Choctaw (by blood)   Nation, and as such has been placed upon the final roll of said Nation by the Honorable Secretary of the Interior, his final enrollment number being   13297   and that a   Female   child was born to me on the   16   day of   May   190 4; that said child has been named   Catherine Fulton   , and is now living.

WITNESSETH: Jessie Fulton
Must be two witnesses { Simpson Folsom
who are citizens   { W C Bolling

Subscribed and sworn to before me this, the   15   day of   March   , 190 5

James Bower
Notary Public.

My Commission Expires:
   Sept 23 - 1907

**Applications for Enrollment of Choctaw Newborn
Act of 1905   Volume VII**

No. 3482

Certificate of Record of Marriages.

United States of America,
The Indian Territory, } sct.
Central   District.

I,   E J Fannin   Clerk
of the United States Court, in the Indian Territory and District aforesaid, do hereby CERTIFY, that the License for and Certificate of the Marriage of

Mr. John Fulton   and

M   Jessie Hobbs   was

filed in my office in said Territory and District the 11th day of April A.D., 190 3, and duly recorded in Book 10 of Marriage Record, Page 448

WITNESS my hand and Seal of said Court, at So McAlester this 11th day of April A.D. 190 3

E J Fannin
                              Clerk.
By   W C Donnelly   Deputy.

P. O.

DEPARTMENT OF THE INTERIOR,
COMMISSION TO THE FIVE CIVILIZED TRIBES.
FILED

MAR 23 1905

Tams Bixby   CHAIRMAN.

Applications for Enrollment of Choctaw Newborn
Act of 1905 Volume VII

No. 3482

MARRIAGE LICENSE

United States of America,   The Indian Territory,
                                                   Central District, SS.

To any Person Authorized by Law to Solemnize Marriage, Greeting:

You are hereby commanded to Solemnize the Rite and publish the Banns of Matrimony between Mr.   John Fulton
of   McAlester   in the Indian Territory, aged   19   years,
and M iss   Jessie Hobbs   of   McAlester
in the Indian Territory., aged   17   years, according to law, and do you officially sign and return this License to the parties therein named.

           WITNESS my hand and official seal, this   11th day
           of   April   A. D. 190 3

(Seal)   E. J. Fannin
                             Clerk of the United States Court.

               WC Donnelly   Deputy

Certificate of Marriage.

United States of America, }
    The Indian Territory, } ss.
      Central   District. }   I,   E J Fannin   U S Clerk

Cent Dist I.T.   , do hereby certify, that on the   11th day of   April   A. D. 190 3, I did, duly and according to law, as commanded in the foregoing License, solemnize the Rite and publish the Banns of Matrimony between the parties therein named.

        Witness my hand, this   11th day of   April   A. D. 190 3

My credentials are recorded in the office of the Clerk of
the United States Court in the Indian Territory,
Central District, Book .... , Page ....   EJ Fannin Clerk
                                                    Cent Dist I.T.

Note—This License and Certificate of Marriage must be returned to the Office of the Clerk of the United States Court of the Indian Territory, from whence it was issued, within sixty days from the date thereof, or the party to whom the License was issued will be liable in the amount of the One Hundred Dollars ($100.00)

Applications for Enrollment of Choctaw Newborn
Act of 1905   Volume VII

UNITED STATES OF AMERICA,
INDIAN TERRITORY, CENTRAL DISTRICT.

At South McAlester.

I, E.J. Fannin, Clerk of the United States Court for the Central District of the Indian Territory hereby certify that the within and foregoing is a true and complete copy of "Marriage License" issued to John Fulton and Jessie Hobbs, and the returns made thereon, as the same appears from the records in my office.

In Testimony Whereof I hereunto note my hand and affix the seal of said Court at South McAlester, I.T., this the 21st day of March A.D. 1905.

                E.J. Fannin Clerk of U.S. Court for Central
                District Indian Territory.

                By   JB Rose   Deputy Clerk.

Choc New Born 386
    Florence Fulton b. 5-3-03

(The letter below does not belong with the current applicant.)

                                                             7-2497.

                Muskogee, Indian Territory, April 15, 1903.

Jennie Hill,
    Indianola, Indian Territory.

Dear Madam:

    Receipt is hereby acknowledged of your letter of the 2d inst., stating that you are a citizen by blood of the Choctaw Nation, and have an infant child three months old; and you request to be advised whether said child can be listed for enrollment; and if so, that a blank application for such purpose be sent you.

    Your attention is invited to section 28 of the act of Congress approved July 1, 1902, which was ratified by the citizens of the Choctaw and Chickasaw Nations September 25, 1902, as follows:

Applications for Enrollment of Choctaw Newborn
Act of 1905   Volume VII

"The names of all persons living on the date of the final ratification of this agreement entitled to be enrolled as provided in section 27 hereof shall be placed upon the rolls made by said Commission; and no child born thereafter to a citizen or freedman and no person intermarried thereafter to a citizen shall be entitled to enrollment or to participate in the distribution of the tribal property of the Choctaws and Chickasaws."

Under the above legislation the Commission is without authority to enroll this child. However, a blank application for the enrollment of an infant child is enclosed you herewith.

Respectfully,

Chairman.

(The letter below does not belong with the current applicant.)

7-2497

Muskogee, Indian Territory, May 18, 1905.

Jeff W. Hill,
    Massey, Indian Territory.

Dear Sir:

Referring to the affidavits of Jennie Hill and Francis D. Bush, relative to the birth of Floy May Hill, infant daughter of Jeff W. and Jennie Hill, December 18, 1902, and recently forwarded to this Commission, your attention is invited to Section 28 of the Act of Congress, approved July 1, 1902, (32 Stats., 641), which was ratified by the citizens of the Choctaw and Chickasaw Nations, September 25, 1902, which is as follows:

"The names of all persons living on the date of the final ratification of this agreement entitled to be enrolled as provided in section 27 hereof shall be placed upon the rolls made by said Commission; and no child born thereafter to a citizen or freedman and no person intermarried thereafter to a citizen shall be entitled to enrollment or to participate in the distribution of the tribal property of the Choctaws and Chickasaws."

Under the above legislation the Commission is without authority to enroll infant children born subsequent to September 25, 1902.

Respectfully,

Chairman.

Applications for Enrollment of Choctaw Newborn
Act of 1905 Volume VII

7-4820

Muskogee, Indian Territory, Mach 27, 1905.

Jack Fulton,
    McAlester, Indian Territory.

Dear Sir:

    Receipt is hereby acknowledged of the affidavits of Catherine Fulton and J. C. Grubbs to the birth of Florence Fulton, daughter of Jack and Catherine Fulton, May 3, 1903, and the same have been filed with our records as an application for the enrollment of said child.

Respectfully,

Chairman.

7-NB-386.

Muskogee, Indian Territory, May 25, 1905.

Jack Fulton,
    McAlester, Indian Territory.

Dear Sir:

    There is enclosed you herewith for execution application for the enrollment of your infant child, Florence Fulton.

    In the affidavits filed in this office on March 22, 1905, the date of the applicants[sic] birth is given as May 3, 1903, while in the application filed on the 25th ultimo, the date of birth is given as April 6, 1903. In the enclosed application the date of birth is left blank, in which you will please insert the correct date, and, when the affidavits are properly executed, return the application to this office.

    In having these affidavits executed care should be exercised to see that all names are written in full, as they appear in the body of the affidavit, and in the event that either of the persons signing the affidavit are unable to write, signatures by mark must be attested by two witnesses. Each affidavit must be executed before a Notary Public and the notarial seal and signature of the officer must be attached to each separate affidavit.

Respectfully,

VR 28-2.   Chairman.

Applications for Enrollment of Choctaw Newborn
Act of 1905   Volume VII

7-N.B. 386.

Muskogee, Indian Territory, June 5, 1905.

Jack Fulton,
    McAlester, Indian Territory.

Dear Sir:

    Receipt is hereby acknowledged of the affidavits of Catharine[sic] Fulton and J.O. Grubbs, to the birth of Florence Fulton, daughter of Jack and Catherine Fulton, May 3, 1903, and the same have been filed with our records in the matter of the enrollment of said child.

        Respectfully,

                Commissioner in Charge.

NEW BORN AFFIDAVIT

No ....

CHOCTAW ENROLLING COMMISSION

IN THE MATTER OF THE APPLICATION FOR ENROLLMENT as a citizen of the Choctaw Nation, of Florence Fulton born on the 6[sic] day of April[sic] 190 3

Name of father Jack Fulton   a citizen of Choctaw Nation, final enrollment No. ....
Name of mother Catherine Fulton   a citizen of Choctaw Nation, final enrollment No. 13296

McAlester, I.T.   Postoffice.

AFFIDAVIT OF MOTHER

UNITED STATES OF AMERICA
    INDIAN TERRITORY
DISTRICT   Central

    I Catherine Fulton , on oath state that I am 51 years of age and a citizen by blood of the Choctaw Nation, and as such have been placed upon the final roll of the Choctaw Nation, by the Honorable Secretary of the Interior my

Applications for Enrollment of Choctaw Newborn
Act of 1905   Volume VII

final enrollment number being   13296   ; that I am the lawful wife of   Jack Fulton   , who is a citizen of the   Choctaw   Nation, and as such has been placed upon the final roll of said Nation by the Honorable Secretary of the Interior, his final enrollment number being .... and that a   female   child was born to me on the   6   day of   April   190 3; that said child has been named   Florence Fulton   , and is now living.

WITNESSETH: Catherine x Fulton (her mark)
Must be two witnesses who are citizens { (Name Illegible) / Jack Fulton }

Subscribed and sworn to before me this, the   15   day of   Mrch   , 190 5

James Bower
Notary Public.

My Commission Expires:
Sept 23, 1907

Affidavit of Attending Physician or Midwife

UNITED STATES OF AMERICA,
INDIAN TERRITORY,
Central   DISTRICT

I,   Nancy Nobles   a   ~~Practicing Physician~~   Midwife on oath state that I attended on Mrs.   Catherine Fulton   wife of   Jack Fulton   on the   6[sic]   day of   April[sic]   , 190 3, that there was born to her on said date a   Female   child, that said child is now living, and is said to have been named   Florence Fulton

Nancy x Nobles (her mark)   M. D.

Subscribed and sworn to before me this the   15   day of   Mrch   1905

James Bower
Notary Public.

WITNESSETH:
Must be two witnesses who are citizens and know the child. { America Watson / J M Fulton }

We hereby certify that we are well acquainted with   Nancy Nobles   a   midwife   and know   her   to be reputable and of good standing in the community.

Must be two citizen witnesses. { America Watson / J M Fulton }

Applications for Enrollment of Choctaw Newborn
Act of 1905   Volume VII

BIRTH AFFIDAVIT.

DEPARTMENT OF THE INTERIOR.
COMMISSION TO THE FIVE CIVILIZED TRIBES.

IN RE APPLICATION FOR ENROLLMENT, as a citizen of the Choctaw Nation, of Florence Fulton, born on the 3rd day of May, 1903

Name of Father: Jack Fulton   a citizen of the Choctaw Nation.
Name of Mother: Catherine Fulton   a citizen of the Choctaw Nation.

Postoffice   McAlester, I.T.

AFFIDAVIT OF MOTHER.

UNITED STATES OF AMERICA, Indian Territory,
Central DISTRICT.

I, Catherine Fulton, on oath state that I am 51 years of age and a citizen by blood, of the Choctaw Nation; that I am the lawful wife of Jack Fulton, who is a citizen, by marriage of the Choctaw Nation; that a female child was born to me on 3rd day of May, 1903; that said child has been named Florence Fulton, and was living March 4, 1905.

              her
           Catherine x Fulton
Witnesses To Mark: mark
 Peter Maytubby, Jr
 (Name Illegible)

Subscribed and sworn to before me this 21st day of March, 1905

         Wirt Franklin
          Notary Public.

AFFIDAVIT OF ATTENDING PHYSICIAN OR MID-WIFE.

UNITED STATES OF AMERICA, Indian Territory,
Central DISTRICT.

I, J. O. Grubbs, a Physician, on oath state that I attended on Mrs. Catherine Fulton, wife of Jack Fulton on the 3rd day of May, 1903; that there was born to her on said date a female child; that said child was living March 4, 1905, and is said to have been named Florence Fulton

         J.O. Grubbs

Applications for Enrollment of Choctaw Newborn
Act of 1905 Volume VII

Witnesses To Mark:
{

Subscribed and sworn to before me this 21st day of March, 1905

DW Hopkins
Notary Public.

BIRTH AFFIDAVIT.

DEPARTMENT OF THE INTERIOR.
COMMISSION TO THE FIVE CIVILIZED TRIBES.

IN RE APPLICATION FOR ENROLLMENT, as a citizen of the Choctaw Nation, of Florence Fulton, born on the 3^d day of May, 1903

Name of Father: Jack Fulton — a citizen of the Choctaw Nation.
Name of Mother: Catherine Fulton — a citizen of the Choctaw Nation.

Postoffice McAlester, I.T.

AFFIDAVIT OF MOTHER.

UNITED STATES OF AMERICA, Indian Territory, }
Central DISTRICT. }

I, Catherine Fulton, on oath state that I am 51 years of age and a citizen by Blood, of the Choctaw Nation; that I am the lawful wife of Jack Fulton, who is a citizen, by Intermarriage of the Choctaw Nation; that a Female child was born to me on 3^d day of May, 1903; that said child has been named Florence Fulton, and was living March 4, 1905.

Catherine Fulton
her x mark

Witnesses To Mark:
{ W C Green
  Otto Siler

Subscribed and sworn to before me this 1st day of June, 1905

DW Hopkins
Notary Public.

Applications for Enrollment of Choctaw Newborn
Act of 1905   Volume VII

AFFIDAVIT OF ATTENDING PHYSICIAN OR MID-WIFE.

UNITED STATES OF AMERICA, Indian Territory,
   Central   DISTRICT.

I, J. O. Grubbs, a Physician, on oath state that I attended on Mrs. Catherine Fulton, wife of Jack Fulton on the 3^d day of May, 1903; that there was born to her on said date a Female child; that said child was living March 4, 1905, and is said to have been named Florence Fulton

                        J.O. Grubbs MD

Witnesses To Mark:

    Subscribed and sworn to before me this 1st day of June , 1905

                        DW Hopkins
                            Notary Public.

Choc New Born 387
    Josie Anderson b. 2-8-03
    Joe Anderson b. 2-8-03

                                  7 NB 387

             Muskogee, Indian Territory, June 14, 1905.

Robert Anderson,
    Lehigh, Indian Territory.

Dear Sir:

    Receipt is hereby acknowledged of the affidavits of Rosie Anderson and Margret Pincher to the birth of Josie Anderson, daughter of Robert and Rosie Anderson, February 8, 1903, and the same have been filed in the matter of the enrollment of said child.

                     Respectfully,

                                  Chairman.

Applications for Enrollment of Choctaw Newborn
Act of 1905 Volume VII

7-N.B. 387.

Muskogee, Indian Territory, May 8, 1905.

Robert Anderson,
    Coalgate, Indian Territory.

Dear Sir:

    In the matter of the application for the enrolment[sic] of your infant children, Joe Anderson and Josie Anderson, born February 8, 1903, you should immediately have executed the affidavits forwarded you on April 7, 1905, and return same to the Commission.

    As stated in the Commission's letter of April 7, 1905, the affidavits now on file show that said children were living on March 30, 1903. It is necessary that said children be living on March 4, 1905, in order for them to be finally enrolled. You should, therefore, give this matter your immediate attention.

                    Respectfully,

                                    Commissioner in Charge.

N. B. 387

COPY

Muskogee, Indian Territory, April 7, 1905.

Robert Anderson,   *to Coalgate 5/22/05*
    Lehigh, Indian Territory.

Dear Sir:

    There is inclosed you herewith for execution application for the enrollment of your infant children, Joe Anderson and Josie Anderson, born February 8, 1903.

    The affidavits heretofore filed with the Commission show the child was living on March 30, 1903. It is necessary, for them to be enrolled, that they were living on March 4, 1905. You will please insert age of mother in space provided for the purpose.

    In having these affidavits executed care should be exercised to see that all names are written in full, as they appear in the body of the affidavit, and in the event that either of the persons signing the affidavit are unable to write, signatures by mark must be attested by two witnesses. Each affidavit must be executed before a Notary Public and the notarial seal and signature of the officer must be attached to each separate affidavit.

Applications for Enrollment of Choctaw Newborn
Act of 1905 Volume VII

Respectfully,
SIGNED
T. B. Needles.

LM 7-30. Commissioner in Charge.

BIRTH AFFIDAVIT.

DEPARTMENT OF THE INTERIOR.
COMMISSION TO THE FIVE CIVILIZED TRIBES.

IN RE APPLICATION FOR ENROLLMENT, as a citizen of the Choctaw Nation, of Joe Anderson, born on the 8" day of February, 1903

Name of Father: Robert Anderson   a citizen of the Choctaw Nation.
Name of Mother: Rosie Anderson   a citizen of the Choctaw Nation.

Postoffice   Lehigh, Ind. Ter.

AFFIDAVIT OF MOTHER.

UNITED STATES OF AMERICA, Indian Territory,
Central   DISTRICT.

I, Rosie Anderson, on oath state that I am 23 years of age and a citizen by Intermarriage, of the Choctaw Nation; that I am the lawful wife of Robert Anderson, who is a citizen, by Blood of the Choctaw Nation; that a male child was born to me on 8" day of February, 1903; that said child has been named Joe Anderson, and was living March 4, 1905.

                     her
             Rosie x Anderson
Witnesses To Mark: mark
   { CB Kendrick
     Cline Fowler
Wm Morgan

Subscribed and sworn to before me this 26 day of May, 1905

                 CB Kendrick
                     Notary Public.

Applications for Enrollment of Choctaw Newborn
Act of 1905   Volume VII

AFFIDAVIT OF ATTENDING PHYSICIAN OR MID-WIFE.

UNITED STATES OF AMERICA, Indian Territory,
Central DISTRICT.

I, Margret Pinchen, a Mid wife, on oath state that I attended on Mrs. Rosie Anderson, wife of Robert Anderson on the 8" day of February, 1903; that there was born to her on said date a male child; that said child was living March 4, 1905, and is said to have been named Joe Anderson

PE Wilhelm
Witnesses To Mark:
{ (Name Illegible)
  John Ott

her
Margret x Pinchen
mark

Subscribed and sworn to before me this 27 day of May, 1905

PE. Wilhelm
Notary Public.

NEW-BORN AFFIDAVIT.

Number............

...Choctaw Enrolling Commission...

IN THE MATTER OF THE APPLICATION FOR ENROLLMENT, as a citizen of the Choctaw Nation, of *Joe Amderson*[sic]

born on the 8th day of _February 1903_ 190......

Name of father   Robert Anderson   a citizen of   Choctaw
Nation final enrollment No. 13334
Name of mother   Rosy[sic] Anderson   a citizen of   Choctaw
Nation final enrollment No. 590

Postoffice   Coalgate

AFFIDAVIT OF MOTHER.

UNITED STATES OF AMERICA
INDIAN TERRITORY
Central   DISTRICT

I   Rosie Anderson, on oath state that I am 24 years of age and a citizen by intermarriage of the Choctaw Nation, and as such have been placed upon the final roll of the Choctaw

Applications for Enrollment of Choctaw Newborn
Act of 1905 Volume VII

Nation, by the Honorable Secretary of the Interior my final enrollment number being 590 ; that I am the lawful wife of Robert Anderson , who is a citizen of the Choctaw Nation, and as such has been placed upon the final roll of said Nation by the Honorable Secretary of the Interior, his final enrollment number being 13334 and that a Male child was born to me on the 8th day of Feby 1903 190...... ; that said child has been named Joe Anderson , and is now living.

Witnesseth.   Rosie Anderson

Must be two Witnesses who are Citizens. } James D Ashford
                                                             D.W. Hodges

                                                                                                    195[sic]

Subscribed and sworn to before me this 8 day of Feby XXX

                                                     PE Wilhelm
                                                                Notary Public.

My commission expires:

AFFIDAVIT OF ATTENDING PHYSICIAN OR MIDWIFE

UNITED STATES OF AMERICA
INDIAN TERRITORY
    Central   DISTRICT

I, Margret Pinching a Mid - wife on oath state that I attended on Mrs. Rosie Anderson wife of Robert Anderson on the 8 day of Feby , 190 3, that there was born to her on said date a Female child, that said child is now living, and is said to have been named Josie Anderson

                                          Margaret Pinching   M.D.
Subscribed and sworn to before me this, the 8 day of Feby 190 5

                                                     PE Wilhelm
                                                                Notary Public.

WITNESSETH:

Must be two witnesses who are citizens and know the child. { James D Ashford
                                                                                     D.W. Hodges

We hereby certify that we are well acquainted with Margret Pinching a Mid - wife and know her to be reputable and of good standing in the community.

                                          { James D Ashford
                                             D.W. Hodges

Applications for Enrollment of Choctaw Newborn
Act of 1905 Volume VII

BIRTH AFFIDAVIT.

DEPARTMENT OF THE INTERIOR,
COMMISSION TO THE FIVE CIVILIZED TRIBES.

In Re Application for Enrollment, as a citizen of the Choctaw Nation, of Josie Anderson , born on the 8 day of February , 1903

Name of Father: Robert Anderson   a citizen of the Choctaw Nation.
Name of Mother: Rosa[sic] Anderson   a citizen of the " Nation.
                                                                                           by marriage
                          Post-office ....

AFFIDAVIT OF MOTHER.

UNITED STATES OF AMERICA, }
    INDIAN TERRITORY,
  Central   District.

    I, Rosa Anderson , on oath state that I am twenty years of age and a citizen by marriage , of the Choctaw Nation; that I am the lawful wife of Robert Anderson , who is a citizen, by blood of the Choctaw Nation; that a female child was born to me on 8th day of February , 1903 , that said child has been named Josie Anderson , and is now living.

                                                    her
                                     Rosa x Anderson
WITNESSES TO MARK: mark
{ AD Brown
{ Margret Pinching

    Subscribed and sworn to before me this 30 day of March , 1903

                                        Dwight Brown
                                                   NOTARY PUBLIC.

AFFIDAVIT OF ATTENDING PHYSICIAN OR MID-WIFE.

UNITED STATES OF AMERICA, }
    INDIAN TERRITORY,
  Central   District.

    I, Marguret[sic] Pinching , a mid=wife , on oath state that I attended on Mrs. Rosa Anderson , wife of Robert Anderson on the 8 day of February , 1903 ; that there was born to her on said date a female child; that said child is now living and is said to have been named Josie Anderson

Applications for Enrollment of Choctaw Newborn
Act of 1905 Volume VII

Margret Pinching

WITNESSES TO MARK:

Subscribed and sworn to before me this 30th day of March , 1903

Dwight Brown
NOTARY PUBLIC.

NEW-BORN AFFIDAVIT.

Number..............

...Choctaw Enrolling Commission...

IN THE MATTER OF THE APPLICATION FOR ENROLLMENT, as a citizen of the Choctaw Nation, of *Josie Anderson*

born on the 8th day of *February 1903* 190......

Name of father *Robt Anderson*   a citizen of   *Choctaw*
Nation final enrollment No. *13334*
Name of mother *Rosie Anderson*   a citizen of   *Choctaw*
Nation final enrollment No. *590*

Postoffice   *Coalgate*

AFFIDAVIT OF MOTHER.

UNITED STATES OF AMERICA
INDIAN TERRITORY
Central   DISTRICT

I   *Rosie Anderson*   , on oath state that I am *24* years of age and a citizen by *intermarriage* of the *Choctaw* Nation, and as such have been placed upon the final roll of the *Choctaw* Nation, by the Honorable Secretary of the Interior my final enrollment number being *590* ; that I am the lawful wife of *Robt Anderson* , who is a citizen of the *Choctaw* Nation, and as such has been placed upon the final roll of said Nation by the Honorable Secretary of the Interior, his final enrollment number being *13334* and that a Fe̶Male child was born to me on the *8th* day of *Feby 1903* 190...... ; that said child has been named *Josie Anderson* , and is now living.

Rosie Anderson

Applications for Enrollment of Choctaw Newborn
Act of 1905   Volume VII

Witnesseth.
  Must be two ⎤ James D Ashford
  Witnesses who ⎥
  are Citizens. ⎦ D.W. Hodges

  Subscribed and sworn to before me this 8th   day of   Feby   190 5

                    PE Wilhelm
                            Notary Public.
My commission expires:

AFFIDAVIT OF ATTENDING PHYSICIAN OR MIDWIFE

UNITED STATES OF AMERICA ⎤
INDIAN TERRITORY   ⎬
  Central   DISTRICT   ⎦

  I,   Margret Pinching[sic]   a   Midwife
on oath state that I attended on Mrs.   Rosie Anderson   wife of   Robert Anderson
on the   8   day of   Feby   , 190 3, that there was born to her on said date a   Male
child, that said child is now living, and is said to have been named   Joe Anderson

                    Margaret Pinching   M.D.
  Subscribed and sworn to before me this, the   8 day of   Feby   190 5

                    PE Wilhelm
                            Notary Public.

WITNESSETH:
  Must be two witnesses ⎧ James D Ashford
  who are citizens and ⎨
  know the child.   ⎩ D.W. Hodges

  We hereby certify that we are well acquainted with   Margret Pinching
a   Midwife   and know   her   to be reputable and of good standing in the
community.
                    ⎧ James D Ashford
                    ⎨
                    ⎩ D.W. Hodges

Applications for Enrollment of Choctaw Newborn
Act of 1905   Volume VII

BIRTH AFFIDAVIT.

DEPARTMENT OF THE INTERIOR,
COMMISSION TO THE FIVE CIVILIZED TRIBES.

In Re Application for Enrollment, as a citizen of the Choctaw Nation, of Joe Anderson , born on the 8 day of February , 1903

Name of Father: Robert Anderson   a citizen of the   Choctaw   Nation.
Name of Mother: Rosa[sic] Anderson   a citizen of the   "   Nation.
                                                                 by marriage
                              Post-office   Lehigh

AFFIDAVIT OF MOTHER.

UNITED STATES OF AMERICA, }
  INDIAN TERRITORY,
  Central   District.

    I, Rosa Anderson , on oath state that I am twenty years of age and a citizen by marriage , of the Choctaw Nation; that I am the lawful wife of Robert Anderson , who is a citizen, by blood of the Choctaw Nation; that a male child was born to me on 8th day of February , 1903 , that said child has been named Joe Anderson , and is now living.

                           her
                   Rosa x Anderson
WITNESSES TO MARK: mark
  { AD Brown
    Margret Pinching

    Subscribed and sworn to before me this 30th day of March , 1903

                        Dwight Brown
                          NOTARY PUBLIC.

AFFIDAVIT OF ATTENDING PHYSICIAN OR MID-WIFE.

UNITED STATES OF AMERICA, }
  INDIAN TERRITORY,
  Central   District.

    I, Margurete[sic] Pinching , a mid=wife , on oath state that I attended on Mrs. Rosa Anderson , wife of Robert Anderson on the 8th day of February , 1903 ; that there was born to her on said date a male child; that said child is now living and is said to have been named Joe Anderson

Applications for Enrollment of Choctaw Newborn
Act of 1905   Volume VII

Margret Pinching

WITNESSES TO MARK:
{

Subscribed and sworn to before me this 30th day of March, 1903

Dwight Brown
NOTARY PUBLIC.

BIRTH AFFIDAVIT.

DEPARTMENT OF THE INTERIOR.
COMMISSION TO THE FIVE CIVILIZED TRIBES.

IN RE APPLICATION FOR ENROLLMENT, as a citizen of the   Choctaw   Nation, of Josie Anderson   , born on the 8 day of February, 1903

Name of Father: Robert Anderson   a citizen of the   Choctaw   Nation.
Name of Mother: Rosie Anderson   a citizen of the   Choctaw   Nation.

Postoffice   Lehigh, Ind. Ter.

AFFIDAVIT OF MOTHER.

UNITED STATES OF AMERICA, Indian Territory, }
    Central   DISTRICT.

I,   Rosie Anderson   , on oath state that I am 23   years of age and a citizen by   Intermarriage   , of the   Choctaw   Nation; that I am the lawful wife of Robert Anderson   , who is a citizen, by Blood   of the   Choctaw   Nation; that a   Female   child was born to me on   8" day of   February   , 1903; that said child has been named   Josie Anderson   , and was living March 4, 1905.

                    her
             Rosie x Anderson
Witnesses To Mark: mark
  { CB Kendrick
    Cline Fowler
Wm Morgan

Subscribed and sworn to before me this 26 day of   May   , 1905

CB Kendrick
Notary Public.

Applications for Enrollment of Choctaw Newborn
Act of 1905   Volume VII

AFFIDAVIT OF ATTENDING PHYSICIAN OR MID-WIFE.

UNITED STATES OF AMERICA, Indian Territory, }
   Central   DISTRICT. }

I, Margret Pinchen, a midwife, on oath state that I attended on Mrs. Rosie Anderson, wife of Robert Anderson on the 8" day of February, 1903; that there was born to her on said date a Female child; that said child was living March 4, 1905, and is said to have been named Josie Anderson

                                             her
PE Wilhelm   Margret x Pinchen
Witnesses To Mark: mark
   { John M Ott
   { John Ott

Subscribed and sworn to before me this 29 day of May, 1905

                              PE. Wilhelm
                                Notary Public.

(The following document does not belong with the current applicants.)

                    DEPARTMENT OF THE INTERIOR
Refer in Reply   United States Indian Service
to *Cr Eq 3864*   Five Civilized Tribes

                             Muskogee, Oklahoma, 6/23, 1919

Referring to proof of death and heirship, for $............ per capita payment, due the heirs of *Henry Harry et al* Or Roll No. *386470*, Page No. .... you are advised *It appears that the Notary Public failed to attach her seal to these PgH. Please request her to do so.*

   These proofs should not leave your possession and should be returned as soon as possible.

                              GABE E. PARKER,
               Superintendent for the Five Civilized Tribes,
                                  By   *OCH*

To *Eldon Lowe,*
P. O. *Field Clerk,*
    Sapulpa, Okla.

Applications for Enrollment of Choctaw Newborn
Act of 1905   Volume VII

Choc New Born 388
    Lannes William Schrock b. 2-16-03

BIRTH AFFIDAVIT.

DEPARTMENT OF THE INTERIOR.
COMMISSION TO THE FIVE CIVILIZED TRIBES.

IN RE APPLICATION FOR ENROLLMENT, as a citizen of the   Choctaw   Nation, of   Lannes William Schrock   , born on the 16th day of   February   , 1903

Name of Father: L.L. Schrock   a citizen of the   Choctaw   Nation.
Name of Mother: Frances Schrock   a citizen of the   Choctaw   Nation.

        Postoffice   Tuttle, I.T.

AFFIDAVIT OF MOTHER.

UNITED STATES OF AMERICA, Indian Territory, ⎫
    Southern   DISTRICT. ⎭

    I,   Frances Schrock   , on oath state that I am   26   years of age and a citizen by   blood   , of the   Choctaw   Nation; that I am the lawful wife of   L.L. Schrock   , who is a citizen, by ~~marriage~~ of the   ~~Choctaw~~   Nation; that a male   child was born to me on   16th day of   February   , 1902; that said child has been named   Lannes William Schrock   , and was living March 4, 1905.

                           Frances Schrock
Witnesses To Mark:
{

    Subscribed and sworn to before me this   16th day of   March   , 1905

                           WCGreen
                          Notary Public.
Com expires 10/17-1908

AFFIDAVIT OF ATTENDING PHYSICIAN OR MID-WIFE.

UNITED STATES OF AMERICA, Indian Territory, ⎫
    Central Judicial   DISTRICT. ⎭

    I,   WE Brown   , a   Physician   , on oath state that I attended on   Mrs. Frances Schrock   , wife of   L.L. Schrock   on the   16th day of

Applications for Enrollment of Choctaw Newborn
Act of 1905   Volume VII

February, 1903; that there was born to her on said date a   male   child; that said child was living March 4, 1905, and is said to have been named Lannes William Schrock

                                      W.E. Brown

Witnesses To Mark:

{

    Subscribed and sworn to before me this   14th   day of   March   , 1905

                                John *(Illegible)*
                                        Notary Public.

My Commission expires Feb. 17th 1907.

BIRTH AFFIDAVIT.

Department of the Interior,
COMMISSION TO THE FIVE CIVILIZED TRIBES.

    IN RE APPLICATION FOR ENROLLMENT, as a citizen of the   Choctaw   Nation, of   Lannes William Schrock   , born on the   16   day of   Feb   , 190 3

Name of Father: Lannes L Schrock   a citizen of the ———— Nation.
Name of Mother: Mrs Francis Schrock   a citizen of the   Choctaw   Nation.

                      Post-Office: Tuttle Ind. Ter.

AFFIDAVIT OF MOTHER.

UNITED STATES OF AMERICA, ⎫
    INDIAN TERRITORY,   ⎬
  Southern   District. ⎭

    I, Mrs. Francis Schrock , on oath state that I am 24   years of age and a citizen by   Blood , of the   Choctaw   Nation; that I am the lawful wife of Lannes L. Schrock   , who is a citizen, by ———— of the ———— Nation; that a male   child was born to me on 16 day of Feb. , 190 3, that said child has been named   Lannes William Schrock   , and is now living.

                                Francis Williams Schrock

WITNESSES TO MARK:

{

    Subscribed and sworn to before me this   8th   day of   April   , 190 3

                                    J.H. Carlisle
                                      Notary Public.

Applications for Enrollment of Choctaw Newborn
Act of 1905   Volume VII

AFFIDAVIT OF ATTENDING PHYSICIAN OR MID-WIFE.

UNITED STATES OF AMERICA, }
   INDIAN TERRITORY,
   Southern   District.

    I, W.E. Brown , a Physician , on oath state that I attended on Mrs. Francis Schrock , wife of Lannes L. Schrock on the 16 day of Feb. , 190 3; that there was born to her on said date a male child; that said child is now living and is said to have been named Lannes William Schrock

                                        W.E. Brown M.D.

WITNESSES TO MARK:

    Subscribed and sworn to before me this 8th *day of* April , *1903*

                                        J.H. Carlisle
                                           Notary Public.

                                                      7-5328

                          Muskogee, Indian Territory, March 21, 1905.

L. L. Schrock,
    Tuttle, Indian Territory.

Dear Sir:

    Receipt is hereby acknowledged of your letter of March 16, 1905, enclosing affidavits of Francis Schrock and W. E. Brown to the birth of Lannes William Schrock, son of L. L. and Francis Schrock, February 16, 1903, and the same have been filed with our records as an application for the enrollment of said child.

    Replying to that part of your letter in which you ask if you can wait to file for this child until your wife goes to file the remainder of her allotment, you are advised that no selection of allotment can be made for children born subsequent to September 25, 1902, until their enrollment has been approved by the Secretary of the Interior.

                                    Respectfully,

                                                  Chairman.

Applications for Enrollment of Choctaw Newborn
Act of 1905   Volume VII

Choc New Born 389
Willie Grace Penny   b. 7-21-04

BIRTH AFFIDAVIT.

DEPARTMENT OF THE INTERIOR.
COMMISSION TO THE FIVE CIVILIZED TRIBES.

IN RE APPLICATION FOR ENROLLMENT, as a citizen of the   Choctaw   Nation, of Willie Grace Penney   , born on the 21   day of July   , 1904

Name of Father: O.S. Penney   a citizen of the   Choctaw   Nation.
Name of Mother: Annie L. Penney   a citizen of the   Choctaw   Nation.

Postoffice   South McAlester, Ind. Tery.

AFFIDAVIT OF MOTHER.

UNITED STATES OF AMERICA, Indian Territory,
Central   DISTRICT.

I, Annie L. Penney , on oath state that I am 23   years of age and a citizen by   Blood   , of the   Choctaw   Nation; that I am the lawful wife of   O.S. Penney   , who is a citizen, by .... of the .... Nation; that a   Female child was born to me on   21st day of   July , 1904; that said child has been named Willie Grace Penney   , and was living March 4, 1905.

Annie L. Penny

Witnesses To Mark:
{

Subscribed and sworn to before me this 16th day of   March   , 1905

Frank Smith
Notary Public.

My Commission expires June 20/05

AFFIDAVIT OF ATTENDING PHYSICIAN OR MID-WIFE.

UNITED STATES OF AMERICA, Indian Territory,
Central   DISTRICT.

I,   T.S. Chapman   , a   Physician   , on oath state that I attended on Mrs.   Annie L Penney   , wife of   O.S. Penney   on the 21st day of   July   ,

Applications for Enrollment of Choctaw Newborn
Act of 1905 Volume VII

1904; that there was born to her on said date a   Female   child; that said child was living March 4, 1905, and is said to have been named Willie Grace Penney

T.S. Chapman M.D.

Witnesses To Mark:
{

Subscribed and sworn to before me this 16th day of March , 1905

Frank Smith
Notary Public.

My Commission expires June 20/05

Choc New Born 390
　　Dewry Dewitt Dobson b. 6-12-03

N. B. 390
COPY
Muskogee, Indian Territory, April 7, 1905.

Leonidas Dobson,
　　Cartersville, Indian Territory.

Dear Sir:

　　There is inclosed you herewith for execution application for the enrollment of your infant child, Dewey Dewitt Dobson, born June 12, 1903.

　　The affidavits heretofore filed with the Commission show the child was living on September 3, 1903. It is necessary, for the child to be enrolled, that he was living on March 4, 1905. You will please insert the age of the mother in space provided for that purpose.

　　In having these affidavits executed care should be exercised to see that all names are written in full, as they appear in the body of the affidavit, and in the event that either of the persons signing the affidavit are unable to write, signatures by mark must be attested by two witnesses. Each affidavit must be executed before a Notary Public and the notarial seal and signature of the officer must be attached to each separate affidavit.

Applications for Enrollment of Choctaw Newborn
Act of 1905 Volume VII

LM 7-29

Respectfully,
SIGNED
T. B. Needles.
Commissioner in Charge.

7 NB 390

Muskogee, Indian Territory, April 21, 1905.

Leonidas Dobson,
    Elkin, Indian Territory.

Dear Sir:

    Receipt is hereby acknowledged of your letter of April 15, 1905, stating that you appeared before the enrolling Commission of Bokoshe on April 3, 1905, and made application for the enrollment of your child Dewey Dewitt Dobson and you ask if it will be necessary for you to execute application forwarded in our letter of April 7, 1905.

    In reply to your letter you are advised that the affidavits executed April 3, 1905, have been received and filed with the record in the matter of the application for the enrollment of your child Dewey Dewitt Dobson and it will not be necessary for you to execute those transmitted with our letter of April 7, 1905.

Respectfully,

Chairman.

7 NB 390

Muskogee, Indian Territory, June 6, 1905.

Leonidas Dobson,
    Elkins, Indian Territory.

Dear Sir:

    Receipt is hereby acknowledged of your letter of May 21, 1905, asking if your child Dewey Dewitt Dobson has been approved.

    In reply to your letter you are advised that the name of your child Dewey Dewitt Dobson has been placed upon a schedule of citizens by blood of the Nation which is being prepared for forwarding to the Secretary of the Interior and you will be notified when his enrollment is approved.

Applications for Enrollment of Choctaw Newborn
Act of 1905   Volume VII

That portion of your letter requesting plat of certain land has been made the subject of another communication.

Respectfully,

Chairman.

7-NB-390

Muskogee, Indian Territory, July 31, 1905.

Leonidas Dobson,
Elkins, Indian Territory.

Dear Sir:

Receipt is hereby acknowledged of your letter of July 25, 1905, asking if Dewey DeWitt[sic] Dobson has been approved.

In reply to your letter you are advised that on July 22, 1905, the Secretary of the Interior approved the enrollment of your son Dewey DeWitt Dobson as a citizen by blood of the Choctaw Nation and selection of allotment may now be made in behalf of this child.

Respectfully,

Commissioner.

BIRTH AFFIDAVIT.

DEPARTMENT OF THE INTERIOR,
COMMISSION TO THE FIVE CIVILIZED TRIBES.

In Re Application for Enrollment, as a citizen of the Choctaw Nation, of Dewey Dewitt, born on the 12 day of June, 1903

Name of Father: Leonidas Dobson   a citizen of the Choctaw Nation.
Name of Mother: Mary Dobson   a citizen of the Choctaw Nation.

Post-office   Cartersville, Ind Ter

Applications for Enrollment of Choctaw Newborn
Act of 1905   Volume VII

AFFIDAVIT OF MOTHER.

UNITED STATES OF AMERICA,
   INDIAN TERRITORY,
Central   District.

I, Mary Dobson , on oath state that I am 21 years of age and a citizen by Marriage , of the Choctaw Nation; that I am the lawful wife of Leonidas Dobson , who is a citizen, by Blood of the Choctaw Nation; that a male child was born to me on 12 day of June , 1903 , that said child has been named Dewey Dewitt , and is now living.

                                    her
                                Mary x Dobson

WITNESSES TO MARK: mark
- Lewis Renault Jeffries
- William C. *(Illegible)*

Subscribed and sworn to before me this 28 day of August , 1903

                                EF Jeffries
                                NOTARY PUBLIC.
                      Time expires Sep 18 1903

AFFIDAVIT OF ATTENDING PHYSICIAN OR MID-WIFE.

UNITED STATES OF AMERICA,
   INDIAN TERRITORY,
.... District.

I, F C Parrott , a M.D. , on oath state that I attended on Mrs. Mary Dobson , wife of Lon Dobson on the 12 day of June , 1903 ; that there was born to her on said date a male child; that said child is now living and is said to have been named Dewey Dewitt

                                F C Parrott M.D.

WITNESSES TO MARK:

Subscribed and sworn to before me this 3 day of Sept , 1903

                                EF Jeffries
                                NOTARY PUBLIC.
                      Time expires Sep 18 1903

Applications for Enrollment of Choctaw Newborn
Act of 1905   Volume VII

BIRTH AFFIDAVIT.

DEPARTMENT OF THE INTERIOR.
COMMISSION TO THE FIVE CIVILIZED TRIBES.

IN RE APPLICATION FOR ENROLLMENT, as a citizen of the Choctaw Nation, of Dewey Dewitt Dobson, born on the 12 day of June, 1903

Name of Father: Leonidas Dobson   a citizen of the Choctaw Nation.
Name of Mother: Mary Dobson   a citizen of the Choctaw Nation.

Postoffice   Elkins Ind Ter

AFFIDAVIT OF MOTHER.

UNITED STATES OF AMERICA, Indian Territory,
Central   DISTRICT.

I, Mary Dobson, on oath state that I am 23 years of age and a citizen by intermarriage, of the Choctaw Nation; that I am the lawful wife of Leonidas Dobson, who is a citizen, by blood of the Choctaw Nation; that a male child was born to me on 12 day of June, 1903; that said child has been named Dewey Dewitt Dobson, and was living March 4, 1905.

                                                        her
                                        Mary x Dobson
Witnesses To Mark: mark
    C.B. Ward
    Chas T Difendafer

Subscribed and sworn to before me this 3 day of April, 1905

                                      OL Johnson
                                        Notary Public.

AFFIDAVIT OF ATTENDING PHYSICIAN OR MID-WIFE.

UNITED STATES OF AMERICA, Indian Territory,
Central   DISTRICT.

I, F.C. Parrott, a physician, on oath state that I attended on Mrs. Mary Dobson, wife of Leonidas Dobson on the 12 day of June, 1903; that there was born to her on said date a male child; that said child was living March 4, 1905, and is said to have been named Dewey Dewitt Dobson

                                        F.C. Parrott

Applications for Enrollment of Choctaw Newborn
Act of 1905   Volume VII

Witnesses To Mark:

{

Subscribed and sworn to before me this 3 day of April , 1905

OL Johnson
Notary Public.

Choc New Born 391
Raymond W. Morgan   b. 8-11-03
Louisa Alice Morgan   b. 11-27-04

N. B. 393
COPY
Muskogee, Indian Territory, April 7, 1905.

Robert A. Morgan,
Paoli, Indian Territory.

Dear Sir:

There is inclosed you herewith for execution application for the enrollment of your infant child, Raymond W. Morgan, born August 11, 1903.

The affidavits heretofore filed with the Commission show the child was living on September 10, 1903. It is necessary, for the child to be enrolled, that he was living on March 4, 1905.

In having these affidavits executed care should be exercised to see that all names are written in full, as they appear in the body of the affidavit, and in the event that either of the persons signing the affidavit are unable to write, signatures by mark must be attested by two witnesses. Each affidavit must be executed before a Notary Public and the notarial seal and signature of the officer must be attached to each separate affidavit.

Respectfully,
SIGNED
T. B. Needles.
Commissioner in Charge.

LM 7-28

Applications for Enrollment of Choctaw Newborn
Act of 1905   Volume VII

COMMISSIONERS:
TAMS BIXBY,
THOMAS B. NEEDLES,
C.R. BRECKINBRIDGE.

WM. O. BEALL
Secretary

DEPARTMENT OF THE INTERIOR,
COMMISSIONER TO THE FIVE CIVILIZED TRIBES.

$W^m O.B.$

REFER IN REPLY TO THE FOLLOWING:

7-NB-391.

ADDRESS ONLY THE
COMMISSION TO THE FIVE CIVILIZED TRIBES.

Muskogee, Indian Territory, May 25, 1905.

Robert A. Morgan,
    Paoli, Indian Territory.

Dear Sir:

    There is enclosed you herewith for execution application for the enrollment of your infant child, Raymond W. Morgan.

    In the affidavits of September 10, 1903, heretofore filed in this office, the date of the applicant's birth is given as August 11, 1903, while in those of the 12th ultimo it is given as August 12, 1903. In the enclosed application the date of birth if left blank. Please insert the correct date, and, when the affidavits are properly executed, return the application to this office.

    In having these affidavits executed care should be exercised to see that all names are written in full, as they appear in the body of the affidavit, and in the event that either of the persons signing the affidavit are unable to write, signatures by mark must be attested by two witnesses. Each affidavit must be executed before a Notary Public and the notarial seal and signature of the officer must be attached to each separate affidavit.

                       Respectfully,
                         Tams Bixby
                             Chairman.

VR 25-9.

7-N.B. 391.

Muskogee, Indian Territory, June 5, 1905.

Robert A. Morgan,
    Paoli, Indian Territory.

Dear Sir:

    Receipt is hereby acknowledged of the affidavits of Alice F. Morgan and Louisa W. Morgan to the birth of Raymond W. Morgan, son of Robert A. and Alice F. Morgan,

Applications for Enrollment of Choctaw Newborn
Act of 1905   Volume VII

August 11, 1903, and the same have been filed with our records in the matter of the enrollment of said child.

Respectfully,

Commissioner in Charge.

7-NB-391.

Muskogee, Indian Territory, May 25, 1905.

Robert A. Morgan,
    Paoli, Indian Territory.

Dear Sir:

    There is enclosed you herewith for execution application for the enrollment of your infant child, Raymond W. Morgan.

    In the affidavits of September 10, 1903, heretofore filed in this office, the date of the applicant's birth is given as August 11, 1903, while in those of the 12th ultimo it is given as August 12, 1903. In the enclosed application the date of birth if left blank. Please insert the correct date, and, when the affidavits are properly executed, return the application to this office.

    In having these affidavits executed care should be exercised to see that all names are written in full, as they appear in the body of the affidavit, and in the event that either of the persons signing the affidavit are unable to write, signatures by mark must be attested by two witnesses. Each affidavit must be executed before a Notary Public and the notarial seal and signature of the officer must be attached to each separate affidavit.

Respectfully,

Chairman.

VR 25-9.

Applications for Enrollment of Choctaw Newborn
Act of 1905   Volume VII

BIRTH AFFIDAVIT.

DEPARTMENT OF THE INTERIOR.
COMMISSION TO THE FIVE CIVILIZED TRIBES.

IN RE APPLICATION FOR ENROLLMENT, as a citizen of the Choctaw Nation, of Louisa Alice Morgan, born on the 27 day of Nov, 1904

                    by Intermarriage
Name of Father: Robert A Morgan   a citizen of the Choctaw Nation.
Name of Mother: Alice F. Morgan   a citizen of the Choctaw Nation.

       Postoffice   Paoli I T

AFFIDAVIT OF MOTHER.

UNITED STATES OF AMERICA, Indian Territory, }
  Southern   DISTRICT.

   I, Alice F Morgan, on oath state that I am 35 years of age and a citizen by Blood, of the Choctaw Nation; that I am the lawful wife of Robert A Morgan, who is a citizen, by Intermarriage of the Choctaw Nation; that a Female child was born to me on 27th day of Nov, 1904, that said child has been named Louisa Alice Morgan, and is now living.

            Alice F. Morgan

Witnesses To Mark:
{

   Subscribed and sworn to before me this 12th day of April, 1903

My commission expires Mch 12-1905   AS Kelley
                Notary Public.

AFFIDAVIT OF ATTENDING PHYSICIAN OR MID-WIFE.

UNITED STATES OF AMERICA, Indian Territory, }
  Southern   DISTRICT.

   I, Louisa W Morgan, a Midwife, on oath state that I attended on Mrs. Alice F Morgan, wife of Robert A Morgan on the 27 day of Nov, 1904; that there was born to her on said date a Female child; that said child is now living and is said to have been named Louisa Alice Morgan

            Louisa W. Morgan

Witnesses To Mark:
{

Applications for Enrollment of Choctaw Newborn
Act of 1905   Volume VII

Subscribed and sworn to before me this 12th day of April, 1903

AS Kelley
Notary Public.

BIRTH AFFIDAVIT.

DEPARTMENT OF THE INTERIOR.
COMMISSION TO THE FIVE CIVILIZED TRIBES.

IN RE APPLICATION FOR ENROLLMENT, as a citizen of the Choctaw Nation, of Raymond W Morgan, born on the 11th day of August, 1903

Name of Father: Robt A Morgan   a citizen of the Choctaw Nation.
Name of Mother: Alice F. Morgan   a citizen of the Choctaw Nation.

Postoffice   Paoli I T

AFFIDAVIT OF MOTHER.

UNITED STATES OF AMERICA, Indian Territory,
Southern DISTRICT.

I, Alice F Morgan, on oath state that I am 34 years of age and a citizen by Blood, of the Choctaw Nation; that I am the lawful wife of Robt A Morgan, who is a citizen, by Marriage of the Choctaw Nation; that a male child was born to me on 11th day of August, 1903, that said child has been named Raymond W Morgan, and is now living.

Alice F. Morgan

Witnesses To Mark:

Subscribed and sworn to before me this 10th day of September, 1903

EH McCord
Notary Public.

AFFIDAVIT OF ATTENDING PHYSICIAN OR MID-WIFE.

UNITED STATES OF AMERICA, Indian Territory,
Southern DISTRICT.

I, J.B. Maples, a Physician, on oath state that I attended on Mrs. Alice F Morgan, wife of Robt A Morgan on the 11th day of August,

Applications for Enrollment of Choctaw Newborn
Act of 1905   Volume VII

1903; that there was born to her on said date a   Male   child; that said child is now living and is said to have been named Raymond W. Morgan

J.B. Maples M.D.

Witnesses To Mark:
{

Subscribed and sworn to before me this 10th day of September, 1903

EH McCord
Notary Public.

BIRTH AFFIDAVIT.

DEPARTMENT OF THE INTERIOR.
COMMISSION TO THE FIVE CIVILIZED TRIBES.

IN RE APPLICATION FOR ENROLLMENT, as a citizen of the   Choctaw   Nation, of Raymond Wade Morgan, born on the 12th day of Aug, 1903

by Intermarriage
Name of Father: Robert A Morgan   a citizen of the Choctaw Nation.
Name of Mother: Alice F. Morgan   a citizen of the Choctaw Nation.

Postoffice   Paoli I T

AFFIDAVIT OF MOTHER.

UNITED STATES OF AMERICA, Indian Territory, }
    Southern   DISTRICT.

I, Alice F Morgan, on oath state that I am 35 years of age and a citizen by Blood, of the Choctaw Nation; that I am the lawful wife of Robert A Morgan, who is a citizen, by Intermarriage of the Choctaw Nation; that a male child was born to me on 12th day of August, 1903, that said child has been named Raymond Wade Morgan, and is now living.

Alice F. Morgan

Witnesses To Mark:
{

Subscribed and sworn to before me this 12th day of April, 1905

My Commission expires Mch 12-1908   A.S. Kelley
Notary Public.

Applications for Enrollment of Choctaw Newborn
Act of 1905 Volume VII

AFFIDAVIT OF ATTENDING PHYSICIAN OR MID-WIFE.

UNITED STATES OF AMERICA, Indian Territory,
Southern DISTRICT.

I, Louisa W Morgan, a Midwife, on oath state that I attended on Mrs. Alice F Morgan, wife of Robert A Morgan on the 12 day of August, 1903; that there was born to her on said date a Male child; that said child is now living and is said to have been named Raymond Wade Morgan

Louisa W Morgan

Witnesses To Mark:

Subscribed and sworn to before me this 12th day of April, 1905

A.S. Kelley
Notary Public.

BIRTH AFFIDAVIT.

DEPARTMENT OF THE INTERIOR.
COMMISSION TO THE FIVE CIVILIZED TRIBES.

IN RE APPLICATION FOR ENROLLMENT, as a citizen of the Choctaw Nation, of Raymond W Morgan, born on the 11th day of Aug, 1903

Name of Father: Robert A Morgan   a citizen of the Choctaw Nation.
Name of Mother: Alice F Morgan   a citizen of the Choctaw Nation.

Postoffice   Paoli I.T.

AFFIDAVIT OF MOTHER.

UNITED STATES OF AMERICA, Indian Territory,
Southern DISTRICT.

I, Alice F Morgan, on oath state that I am 34 years of age and a citizen by Blood, of the Choctaw Nation; that I am the lawful wife of Robert A Morgan, who is a citizen, by Intermarriage of the Choctaw Nation; that a male child was born to me on 11th day of Aug, 1903; that said child has been named Raymond W Morgan, and was living March 4, 1905.

Alice F Morgan

Witnesses To Mark:

Applications for Enrollment of Choctaw Newborn
Act of 1905 Volume VII

Subscribed and sworn to before me this 31st day of May, 1905

A.S. Kelley
Notary Public.

AFFIDAVIT OF ATTENDING PHYSICIAN OR MID-WIFE.

UNITED STATES OF AMERICA, Indian Territory, }
Southern DISTRICT. }

I, Louisa W. Morgan, a Midwife, on oath state that I attended on Mrs. Alice F Morgan, wife of Robert A Morgan on the 11th day of Aug, 1903; that there was born to her on said date a male child; that said child was living March 4, 1905, and is said to have been named Raymond W Morgan

Louisa W. Morgan

Witnesses To Mark:
{

Subscribed and sworn to before me this 31st day of May, 1905

A.S. Kelley
Notary Public.

My Commission Expires Mch 12-1908

Choc New Born 392
    Belle Coleman b. 9-26-02

N.B. 392.
COPY
Muskogee, Indian Territory, April 8, 1905.

W.A. Coleman,
    Harris, Indian Territory.

Dear Sir:

    There is enclosed you herewith for execution application for the enrollment of your infant child, Belle M. Coleman, born September 25, 1902.

Applications for Enrollment of Choctaw Newborn
Act of 1905 Volume VII

    The papers heretofore filed with the Commission were incomplete in that they contained neither the affidavit of the mother nor that of the attending physician or midwife. Your affidavit which is on file in this office show that the child was living on November 26, 1902. It is necessary for the child to be enrolled, that she was living on March 4, 1905. You will please insert the age of the mother in the place left blank for that purpose.

    In the event that the mother is dead, or that there was no physician nor mid-wife in attendance, it will be necessary that you procure the affidavits of two persons who have actual knowledge of the fact; that the child was born, that she was living on March 4, 1905 and that Lou Anna Coleman is her mother.

    In having these affidavits executed care should be exercised to see that all names are written in full, as they appear in the body of the affidavit, and in the event that either of the persons signing the affidavit are unable to write, signatures by mark must be attested by two witnesses. Each affidavit must be executed before a Notary Public and the notarial seal and signature of the officer must be attached to each separate affidavit.

                                        Respectfully,
                                          SIGNED
                                          T. B. Needles.
LM 8-17   Commissioner in Charge.

                                                              7-N B-392.

                        Muskogee, Indian Territory, April 24, 1905.

W. A. Coleman,
        Norwood, Indian Territory.

Dear Sir:

    Receipt is hereby acknowledged of the affidavits of Lou Anna Coleman and Laura Smith, to the birth of Belle Coleman, child of W. A. and Lou Anna Coleman, September 26, 1902, and the same have been filed with our records as an application for the enrollment of said child.

                                        Respectfully,

                                                      Chairman.

Applications for Enrollment of Choctaw Newborn
Act of 1905 Volume VII

7-NB-392.

Muskogee, Indian Territory, May 26, 1905.

W. A. Coleman,
    Norwood, Indian Territory.

Dear Sir:

    There is enclosed you herewith for execution application for the enrollment of your infant child.

    In the affidavits filed on the 24th ultimo, the date of the applicant's birth is given as September 26, 1902, and her name is given by her mother as Belle Coleman and by the midwife as Billie Coleman, while in the application filed on the 25th ultimo, the date of birth is given as September 26, 1903, and the name as Belle Coleman. In the enclosed application the name and date of birth are left blank. Please insert the correct name and date of birth, and return the application to this office when properly executed.

    In having these affidavits executed care should be exercised to see that all names are written in full, as they appear in the body of the affidavit, and in the event that either of the persons signing the affidavit are unable to write, signatures by mark must be attested by two witnesses. Each affidavit must be executed before a Notary Public and the notarial seal and signature of the officer must be attached to each separate affidavit.

Respectfully,

WR 25-6.   Chairman.

---

7 NB-392

Muskogee, Indian Territory, June 7, 1905.

W. A. Coleman,
    Norwood, Indian Territory.

Dear Sir:

    Receipt is hereby acknowledged of the affidavits of Lou Anna Coleman and Laura Smith to the birth of Belle Coleman, daughter of W. A. and Lou Anna Coleman, September 25, 1902, and the same have been filed with our records as an application for the enrollment of said child.

Respectfully,

Chairman.

Applications for Enrollment of Choctaw Newborn
Act of 1905 Volume VII

DEPARTMENT OF THE INTERIOR,
Commission to the Five Civilized Tribes.

In re application for Enrollment as a citizen of the Choctaw Nation, of Belle M. Coleman , born on the 26 day of Sept 190 2
Name of Father: W.A. Coleman , a citizen of the Choctaw Nation.
Name of Mother: Lou Anna Coleman , a citizen of the Choctaw Nation.

Post Office: Harris, I.T.
----o----
Father
AFFIDAVIT OF MOTHER.

United States of America,
   Indian Territory,
      Central District.

I, W.A. Coleman , on oath state that I am 40 years of age and a citizen by Marriage of the Choctaw Nation; That I am the lawful ~~wife~~ husband of Lou Anna Coleman , who is a citizen by blood of the Choctaw Nation, that a female child was born to ~~me~~ her on the 26 day of September , 190 2; that said child has been named Belle M. Coleman and is now living.

Witnesses to Mark: WA Coleman

_____

_____

Subscribed and sworn to before me this 26 day of Nov 1902

T.J. Barnes
Notary Public.

NEW-BORN AFFIDAVIT.

Number..................

...Choctaw Enrolling Commission...

IN THE MATTER OF THE APPLICATION FOR ENROLLMENT, as a citizen of the Choctaw Nation, of Belle Coleman born on the 26 day of Sept 190 3

Applications for Enrollment of Choctaw Newborn
Act of 1905 Volume VII

Name of father   W. A. Coleman   a citizen of   Choctaw
Nation final enrollment No.   596
Name of mother   Lou Ann[sic] Coleman   a citizen of   Choctaw
Nation final enrollment No.   13548

                                        Postoffice   Harris I.T.

AFFIDAVIT OF MOTHER.

UNITED STATES OF AMERICA
INDIAN TERRITORY
Central   DISTRICT

      I   Lou Ann[sic] Coleman   , on oath state that I am 36 years of age and a citizen by blood of the Choctaw Nation, and as such have been placed upon the final roll of the Choctaw Nation, by the Honorable Secretary of the Interior my final enrollment number being 13548 ; that I am the lawful wife of W.A. Coleman , who is a citizen of the Choctaw Nation, and as such has been placed upon the final roll of said Nation by the Honorable Secretary of the Interior, his final enrollment number being 596 and that a female child was born to me on the 26 day of Sept 190 3; that said child has been named Belle Coleman, and is now living.

Witnesseth.   Lou Anna Coleman
Must be two Witnesses who are Citizens.   J.B. McFarland
                      H.C. Stanford

Subscribed and sworn to before me this 21 day of Jan 1905

                                    W.A. Shoney
                                            Notary Public.
My commission expires: Jan 10 1909

AFFIDAVIT OF ATTENDING PHYSICIAN OR MIDWIFE

UNITED STATES OF AMERICA
INDIAN TERRITORY
Central   DISTRICT

      I,   Laura Smith   a   midwife on oath state that I attended on Mrs. Lou Ann Coleman wife of W. A. Coleman on the 26th day of Sept , 190 3 , that there was born to her on said date a female child, that said child is now living, and is said to have been named Belle Coleman

                                              her
                                  Laura Smith x
                                      mark

Applications for Enrollment of Choctaw Newborn
Act of 1905 Volume VII

Subscribed and sworn to before me this, the 21 day of Jan 190 5

WITNESSETH: W.A. Shoney   Notary Public.
Must be two witnesses { JB McFarland
who are citizens { H.C. Stanford

We hereby certify that we are well acquainted with   Laura Smith a *midwife* and know her to be reputable and of good standing in the community.

J B McFarland

H.C. Stanford

BIRTH AFFIDAVIT.

DEPARTMENT OF THE INTERIOR.
COMMISSION TO THE FIVE CIVILIZED TRIBES.

IN RE APPLICATION FOR ENROLLMENT, as a citizen of the Choctaw Nation, of Belle Coleman, born on the 26th day of September, 1902

Name of Father: W.A. Coleman   a citizen of the Choctaw Nation.
Name of Mother: Lou Anna Coleman   a citizen of the Choctaw Nation.

Postoffice   Norwood, Ind. Ter.

AFFIDAVIT OF MOTHER.

UNITED STATES OF AMERICA, Indian Territory, }
Central   DISTRICT. }

I, Lou Anna Coleman, on oath state that I am 36 years of age and a citizen by blood, of the Choctaw Nation; that I am the lawful wife of W.A. Coleman, who is a citizen, by marriage of the Choctaw Nation; that a female child was born to me on 26th day of September, 1902; that said child has been named Belle Coleman, and was living March 4, 1905.

Lou Anna Coleman

Witnesses To Mark:
{

Applications for Enrollment of Choctaw Newborn
Act of 1905 Volume VII

Subscribed and sworn to before me this 12th day of April, 1905

Wirt Franklin
Notary Public.

AFFIDAVIT OF ATTENDING PHYSICIAN OR MID-WIFE.

UNITED STATES OF AMERICA, Indian Territory, }
Central   DISTRICT.

I, Larah[sic] Smith, a Midwife, on oath state that I attended on Mrs. Lou Anna Coleman, wife of W.A. Coleman on the 26 day of Sept, 1902; that there was born to her on said date a Female child; that said child was living March 4, 1905, and is said to have been named Belle Coleman

her
Laura x Smith
mark

Witnesses To Mark:
{ S F Scott
{ J B McFarland

Subscribed and sworn to before me this 15 day of April, 1905

N.P. Hutchinson
Notary Public.

BIRTH AFFIDAVIT.

DEPARTMENT OF THE INTERIOR.
COMMISSION TO THE FIVE CIVILIZED TRIBES.

IN RE APPLICATION FOR ENROLLMENT, as a citizen of the Choctaw Nation, of Belle Coleman, born on the 26 day of Sept, 1902

Name of Father: W.A. Coleman   a citizen of the Choctaw Nation.
Name of Mother: Lou Anna Coleman   a citizen of the Choctaw Nation.

Postoffice   Norwood, Ind. Ter.

AFFIDAVIT OF MOTHER.

UNITED STATES OF AMERICA, Indian Territory, }
Central   DISTRICT.

I, Lou Anna Coleman, on oath state that I am 36 years of age and a citizen by blood, of the Choctaw Nation; that I am the lawful wife of

Applications for Enrollment of Choctaw Newborn
Act of 1905   Volume VII

W.A. Coleman, who is a citizen, by intermarriage of the Choctaw Nation; that a female child was born to me on 26 day of Sept, 1902; that said child has been named Belle Coleman, and was living March 4, 1905.

                                          Lou Anna Coleman

Witnesses To Mark:
{

Subscribed and sworn to before me this 31 day of May, 1905

                                          N.P. Hutchinson
                                          Notary Public.

AFFIDAVIT OF ATTENDING PHYSICIAN OR MID-WIFE.

UNITED STATES OF AMERICA, Indian Territory,⎫
    Central   DISTRICT. ⎭

I, Laura Smith, a Midwife, on oath state that I attended on Mrs. Lou Anna Coleman, wife of W.A. Coleman on the 26 day of Sept, 1902; that there was born to her on said date a female child; that said child was living March 4, 1905, and is said to have been named Belle Coleman

                                          her
                                    Laura x Smith
Witnesses To Mark: mark
{ Frank Scott
  E H Williams

Subscribed and sworn to before me this 31 day of May, 1905

                                          N.P. Hutchinson
                                          Notary Public.

Applications for Enrollment of Choctaw Newborn
Act of 1905   Volume VII

Choc New Born 393
Earlie Perteet b. 2-8-04

7-4668

Muskogee, Indian Territory, March 25, 1905.

John Perteet,
　Krebs, Indian Territory.

Dear Sir:

　　Receipt is hereby acknowledged of the affidavits of Lizzie Perteet and M. E. Perteet to the birth of Earlie Perteet, son of John and Lizzie Perteet, February 8, 1904, and the same have been filed with our records as an application for the enrollment of said child.

Respectfully,

Chairman.

BIRTH AFFIDAVIT.

DEPARTMENT OF THE INTERIOR.
COMMISSION TO THE FIVE CIVILIZED TRIBES.

　　IN RE APPLICATION FOR ENROLLMENT, as a citizen of the   Choctaw   Nation, of Earlie Perteet   , born on the 8 day of Feb. , 1904

Name of Father: John Perteet　　　　a citizen of the U.S.　　Nation.
Name of Mother: Lizzie Perteet　　　a citizen of the Choctaw　Nation.

Postoffice   Krebs I.T.

AFFIDAVIT OF MOTHER.

UNITED STATES OF AMERICA, Indian Territory, ⎫
　　Central　　　　　DISTRICT.　　　　　　⎬
　　　　　　　　　　　　　　　　　　　　　⎭

　　I, Lizzie Perteet   , on oath state that I am 22   years of age and a citizen by Blood   , of the   Choctaw   Nation; that I am the lawful wife of   John Perteet , who is a citizen, by Birth   of the   U.S.   Nation; that a   male   child was born to me on   the 8   day of   Feb   , 1904; that said child has been named   Earlie Perteet   , and was living March 4, 1905.

Lizzie Perteet

Applications for Enrollment of Choctaw Newborn
Act of 1905   Volume VII

Witnesses To Mark:
{ Lee Silmon
{ Minnie Oglesby

    Subscribed and sworn to before me this 22 day of   March   , 1905

                                    W.J. Oglesby
                                           Notary Public.

AFFIDAVIT OF ATTENDING PHYSICIAN OR MID-WIFE.

UNITED STATES OF AMERICA, Indian Territory, }
   Central   DISTRICT.

    I, M.E. Perteet   , a   Mid Wife   , on oath state that I attended on Mrs. Lizzie Perteet   , wife of   John Perteet   on the 8 day of   Feb   , 1904; that there was born to her on said date a   male   child; that said child was living March 4, 1905, and is said to have been named Earlie Perteet

                                  M.E. x Perteet

Witnesses To Mark:
{ Lee Silmon
{ Minnie Oglesby

    Subscribed and sworn to before me this 22 day of   March   , 1905

                                      W.J. Oglesby
                                           Notary Public.

Choc New Born 394
    Ruth May Dixon b. 10-16-04

Applications for Enrollment of Choctaw Newborn
Act of 1905   Volume VII

7 D 820-

BIRTH AFFIDAVIT.

DEPARTMENT OF THE INTERIOR.
COMMISSION TO THE FIVE CIVILIZED TRIBES.

IN RE APPLICATION FOR ENROLLMENT, as a citizen of the Choctaw Nation, of Ruth May Dixon, born on the 16th day of Oct, 1904

Name of Father: Wallace Dixon   a citizen of the Choctaw Nation.
Name of Mother: Amber Dixon   a citizen of the Choctaw Nation.

Postoffice   Naples Ind Ter

AFFIDAVIT OF MOTHER.

UNITED STATES OF AMERICA, Indian Territory,
Southern   DISTRICT.

I, Amber Dixon, on oath state that I am 21 years of age and a citizen by birth, of the Choctaw Nation; that I am the lawful wife of Wallace Dixon, who is a citizen, by birth of the Choctaw Nation; that a Female child was born to me on 16th day of October, 1904, that said child has been named Ruth May Dixon, and is now living.

Amber Dixon

Witnesses To Mark:

Subscribed and sworn to before me this 23^d day of November, 1904

James M Gordon
Notary Public.
My Com expires Mch 1907

AFFIDAVIT OF ATTENDING PHYSICIAN OR MID-WIFE.

UNITED STATES OF AMERICA, Indian Territory,
Southern   DISTRICT.

I, Elizabeth James, a mid wife, on oath state that I attended on Mrs. Amber Dixon, wife of Wallace Dixon on the 16 day of October, 1904; that there was born to her on said date a Female child; that said child is now living and is said to have been named Ruth May Dixon

Applications for Enrollment of Choctaw Newborn
Act of 1905 Volume VII

                                                     her
                                      Elizabeth x James
Witnesses To Mark: mark
  { *(Name Illegible)* Dibble I.T.
    R.G. Hendrix

      Subscribed and sworn to before me this   23^d day of November , 1904

                                        James M Gordon
                                              Notary Public.
             My Com expires Mch 1907

BIRTH AFFIDAVIT.
                       DEPARTMENT OF THE INTERIOR.
                COMMISSION TO THE FIVE CIVILIZED TRIBES.

      IN RE APPLICATION FOR ENROLLMENT, as a citizen of the   Choctaw   Nation, of Ruthie[sic] May Dixon   , born on the 16th day of November[sic] , 1904

Name of Father: Wallace Dixon   a citizen of the Choctaw   Nation.
Name of Mother: Amber Dixon   a citizen of the Choctaw   Nation.

                        Postoffice   Naples, I.T.

                      AFFIDAVIT OF MOTHER.

UNITED STATES OF AMERICA, Indian Territory, }
     Southern   **DISTRICT.** }

     I, Amber Dixon   , on oath state that I am 23   years of age and a citizen by marriage , of the Choctaw   Nation; that I am the lawful wife of Wallace Dixon , who is a citizen, by blood of the   Choctaw   Nation; that a   female   child was born to me on 16th day of November   , 1904; that said child has been named Ruthie May Dixon   , and was living March 4, 1905.

                                        Amber Dixon
Witnesses To Mark:
  {

      Subscribed and sworn to before me this 6th day of April   , 1905

                                      JE Williams
                                        Notary Public.

Applications for Enrollment of Choctaw Newborn
Act of 1905   Volume VII

AFFIDAVIT OF ATTENDING PHYSICIAN OR MID-WIFE.

UNITED STATES OF AMERICA, Indian Territory, }
 Southern   DISTRICT.

    I, Betty[sic] James , a mid-wife , on oath state that I attended on Mrs. Amber Dixon , wife of Wallace Dixon on the 16th day of November , 1904; that there was born to her on said date a female child; that said child was living March 4, 1905, and is said to have been named Ruthie May Dixon

                                         Bettie James

Witnesses To Mark:
{

    Subscribed and sworn to before me this 6th day of April , 1905

                                         JE Williams
                                            Notary Public.

BIRTH AFFIDAVIT.

DEPARTMENT OF THE INTERIOR.
COMMISSION TO THE FIVE CIVILIZED TRIBES.

    IN RE APPLICATION FOR ENROLLMENT, as a citizen of the   Choctaw   Nation, of Ruthie May Dixon , born on the 16th day of Oct , 1904

Name of Father: Wallace Dixon   a citizen of the Choctaw Nation.
Name of Mother: Amber Dixon   a citizen of the Choctaw Nation.

                            Postoffice   Naples, I.T.

AFFIDAVIT OF MOTHER.

UNITED STATES OF AMERICA, Indian Territory, }
   19   DISTRICT.

    I, Amber Dixon , on oath state that I am .... years of age and a citizen by intermarriage , of the Choctaw Nation; that I am the lawful wife of Wallace Dixon , who is a citizen, by blood of the Choctaw Nation; that a female child was born to me on 16th   day of Oct , 1904; that said child has been named Ruth May Dixon , and was living March 4, 1905.

                                       Amber Dixon

Witnesses To Mark:
{

Applications for Enrollment of Choctaw Newborn
Act of 1905   Volume VII

Subscribed and sworn to before me this   13   day of   April   , 1905

My Commission expires
on the 18 March 1909

James B Pilgrim
Notary Public.

AFFIDAVIT OF ATTENDING PHYSICIAN OR MID-WIFE.

UNITED STATES OF AMERICA, Indian Territory, }
  19   DISTRICT. }

I,   Bettie James   , a   mid-wife   , on oath state that I attended on Mrs.   Amber Dixon   , wife of   Wallace Dixon   on the   16   day of   Oct   , 1904; that there was born to her on said date a   female   child; that said child was living March 4, 1905, and is said to have been named   Ruth May Dixon

Bettie James

Witnesses To Mark:
{

Subscribed and sworn to before me this   13   day of   April   , 1905

My Commission expires
on the 18 March 1909

James B Pilgrim
Notary Public.

7-4670

Muskogee, Indian Territory, November 28, 1904.

Wallace Dixon,
    Naples, Indian Territory.

Dear Sir:

Receipt is hereby acknowledged of the affidavits of Amber Dixon and Elizabeth James relative to the birth of Ruth May Dixon October 16, 1904, which it is presumed have been forwarded to this Commission as an application for enrollment of said child as a citizen by blood of the Choctaw Nation.

The Act of Congress approved July 1, 1902, which was ratified by the citizens of the Choctaw and Chickasaw Nations September 25, 1902, among other things provides that no child born to a citizen of the Choctaw or Chickasaw Nations[sic] subsequent to the date of said ratification shall be entitled to enrollment or to participate in the distribution of the tribal property of the Choctaw and Chickasaws.

Applications for Enrollment of Choctaw Newborn
Act of 1905 Volume VII

Respectfully,

Commissioner in Charge.

N. B. 394

Muskogee, Indian Territory, April 7, 1905.

Wallace Dixon,
    Naples, Indian Territory.

Dear Sir:

    There is inclosed you herewith for execution application for the enrollment of your infant child, Ruth May Dixon, born October 16, 1904.

    The affidavits heretofore filed with the Commission show the child was living on November 23, 1904. It is necessary, for the child to be enrolled, that she was living on March 4, 1905. You will please insert the mother's age in space left blank for that purpose.

    In having these affidavits executed care should be exercised to see that all names are written in full, as they appear in the body of the affidavit, and in the event that either of the persons signing the affidavit are unable to write, signatures by mark must be attested by two witnesses. Each affidavit must be executed before a Notary Public and the notarial seal and signature of the officer must be attached to each separate affidavit.

Respectfully,

LM 7-15.   Commissioner in Charge.

Choctaw N.B. 394.

Muskogee, Indian Territory, April 19, 1905.

Wallace Dixon,
    Naples, Indian Territory.

Dear Sir:

    Receipt is hereby acknowledged of the affidavits of Amber Dixon and Bettie James to the birth of Ruth May Dixon, daughter of Wallace and Amber Dixon, October 16, 1904, and the same have been filed with our records in the matter of the enrollment of said child.

Applications for Enrollment of Choctaw Newborn
Act of 1905   Volume VII

Respectfully,

Chairman.

7 NB 394

Muskogee, Indian Territory, June 20, 1905.

W. L. Dixon,
    Naples, Indian Territory.

Dear Sir:

    Receipt is hereby acknowledged of your letter of June 12, 1905, asking if the name of Ruth May Dixon has been approved so that you can file on her land.

    In reply to your letter you are advised that the name of Ruth may Dixon has been placed upon a schedule of citizens by blood of the Choctaw Nation prepared for forwarding to the Secretary of the Interior, but her enrollment has not yet been approved by him and until her enrollment has been so approved no selection of allotment can be made in her behalf.

Respectfully,

Chairman.

Choc New Born 395
    Madora Jane Martin   b. 2-7-05

BIRTH AFFIDAVIT.

DEPARTMENT OF THE INTERIOR.
COMMISSION TO THE FIVE CIVILIZED TRIBES.

    IN RE APPLICATION FOR ENROLLMENT, as a citizen of the Choctaw Nation, of Madora Jane Martin, born on the 7 day of February, 1905

Name of Father: Henry J. Martin   a citizen of the United States Nation.
Name of Mother: Eliza Martin (nee Mathis)   a citizen of the Choctaw Nation.

Postoffice   Antioch I.T.

Applications for Enrollment of Choctaw Newborn
Act of 1905 Volume VII

AFFIDAVIT OF MOTHER.

UNITED STATES OF AMERICA, Indian Territory,
Southern DISTRICT.

I, Eliza Martin (enrolled as Eliza Mathis), on oath state that I am 22 years of age and a citizen by blood, of the Choctaw Nation; that I am the lawful wife of Henry J Martin, who is a citizen, by .... of the United States ~~Nation~~; that a female child was born to me on 7 day of February, 1905; that said child has been named Madora Jane Martin, and was living March 4, 1905.

Eliza Martin

Witnesses To Mark:
{

Subscribed and sworn to before me this 27th day of April, 1905

My Commission D C Cook
Expires Nov 21st 1906 Notary Public.

AFFIDAVIT OF ATTENDING PHYSICIAN OR MID-WIFE.

UNITED STATES OF AMERICA, Indian Territory,
Southern DISTRICT.

I, Annie Woodard, a Midwife, on oath state that I attended on Mrs. Eliza Martin, wife of Henry J. Martin on the 7 day of February, 1905; that there was born to her on said date a female child; that said child was living March 4, 1905, and is said to have been named Madora Jane Martin

Annie Woodard

Witnesses To Mark:
{

Subscribed and sworn to before me this 27th day of April, 1905

My Commission D C Cook
Expires Nov 21st 1906 Notary Public.

Applications for Enrollment of Choctaw Newborn
Act of 1905 Volume VII

BIRTH AFFIDAVIT.

 IN RE-APPLICATION FOR ENROLLMENT, as a citizen of the   Choctaw   Nation, of Madora Jane Martin , born on the 7"   day of   Feb , 1905

Name of Father: Henry J Martin   a citizen of the   United States   Nation.
Name of Mother: Eliza Martin Nee Mathis   a citizen of the   Choctaw   Nation.

        Postoffice   Antioch I.T.

AFFIDAVIT OF MOTHER.

UNITED STATES OF AMERICA, INDIAN TERRITORY,
   Southern   District.

 I,   Eliza Martin , on oath state that I am   22   years of age and a citizen by blood , of the   Choctaw   Nation; that I am the lawful wife of   Henry J. Martin , who is a citizen, by   birth   of the   United States   ~~Nation~~; that a   female   child was born to me on   7"   day of   February , 1905 , that said child has been named   Madora Jane , and is now living.

            Eliza Martin
Witnesses To Mark: (nee Eliza Mathis)

 Subscribed and sworn to before me this   9th   day of   March , 1905.

           C J Davenport
             Notary Public.

AFFIDAVIT OF ATTENDING PHYSICIAN OR MID-WIFE.

UNITED STATES OF AMERICA, INDIAN TERRITORY,
   Southern   District.

 I,   Price Patterson , a   Physician , on oath state that I attended on Mrs.   Eliza Martin , wife of   Henry J Martin   on the 7"   day of   Feb , 190 5; that there was born to her on said date a   female   child; that said child is now living and is said to have been named   Madora Jane

          Price Patterson, M.D.
Witnesses To Mark:

 Subscribed and sworn to before me this   27th day of   Feb , 1905.

           T J Austin
             Notary Public.

Applications for Enrollment of Choctaw Newborn
Act of 1905   Volume VII

BIRTH AFFIDAVIT.

DEPARTMENT OF THE INTERIOR.
COMMISSION TO THE FIVE CIVILIZED TRIBES.

IN RE APPLICATION FOR ENROLLMENT, as a citizen of the Choctaw Nation, of Madora Jane Martin, born on the 7 day of February, 1905

Name of Father: Henry J. Martin a citizen of the U.S. Nation.
Name of Mother: Eliza Martin nee Mathis a citizen of the Choctaw Nation.

Postoffice Antioch I.T.

AFFIDAVIT OF MOTHER.

UNITED STATES OF AMERICA, Indian Territory, } DISTRICT.

I, Eliza Martin, on oath state that I am 22 years of age and a citizen by blood, of the Choctaw Nation; that I am the lawful wife of Henry J Martin, who is a citizen, ~~by~~ of the U. S. Nation; that a female child was born to me on 7 day of February, 1905; that said child has been named Madora Jane Martin, and was living March 4, 1905.

Eliza Martin

Witnesses To Mark:
{

Subscribed and sworn to before me this 25th day of April, 1905

C J Davenport
Notary Public.

AFFIDAVIT OF ATTENDING PHYSICIAN OR MID-WIFE.

UNITED STATES OF AMERICA, Indian Territory, } DISTRICT.

I, Price Patterson, a Physician, on oath state that I attended on Mrs. Eliza Martin, wife of Henry J. Martin on the 7 day of February, 1905; that there was born to her on said date a female child; that said child was living March 4, 1905, and is said to have been named Madora Jane Martin

Price Patterson

Applications for Enrollment of Choctaw Newborn
Act of 1905   Volume VII

Witnesses To Mark:
{ GW Curtiss
  JJ Ryan

    Subscribed and sworn to before me this 29" day of   April   , 1905

                              John Guinn
                                    Notary Public.

                                  7-4573

                Muskogee, Indian Territory, March 15, 1905.

Henry J. Martin,
    Pauls Valley, Indian Territory.

Dear Sir:

    Receipt is hereby acknowledged of your letter of March 9, 1905, enclosing the affidavits of Eliza Martin nee Mathis and Brice[sic] Patterson to the birth of Madora Jane Martin, Infant[sic] daughter of Henry J. and Eliza Martin, February 7, 1905, and the same have been filed with our records as an application for the enrollment of said child.

                Respectfully,

                                      Chairman.

                                    N. B. 395

                        COPY
                Muskogee, Indian Territory, April 7, 1905.

Henry J. Martin,
    Antioch, Indian Territory.

Dear Sir:

    There is inclosed you herewith for execution application for the enrollment of your infant child, Madora Jane Martin, born February 7, 1905.

    In the application heretofore filed with the Commission, the affidavit of the physician shows the child was living on February 27, 1905. It will be necessary, for the child to be enrolled, that said affidavit show she was living on March 4, 1905.

    In having these affidavits executed care should be exercised to see that all names are written in full, as they appear in the body of the affidavit, and in the event that either

Applications for Enrollment of Choctaw Newborn
Act of 1905   Volume VII

of the persons signing the affidavit are unable to write, signatures by mark must be attested by two witnesses. Each affidavit must be executed before a Notary Public and the notarial seal and signature of the officer must be attached to each separate affidavit.

Respectfully,
SIGNED
T. B. Needles.
Commissioner in Charge.

LM 7-21

Choctaw N.B. 395.
Muskogee, Indian Territory, April 21, 1905.

H. J. Martin,
    Pauls Valley, Indian Territory.

Dear Sir:

    Receipt is hereby acknowledged of your letter of April 17, in which you state that sometime ago you forwarded application for the enrollment of your child, Madora Jane Martin, daughter of yourself and Eliza Martin, formerly Mathies[sic]; that you are informed that it will be necessary for you to forward certified copy of your marriage, and you ask if this will be necessary.

    In reply to your letter you are informed that your wife being an enrolled citizen by blood of the Choctaw Nation, it will not be necessary for you to forward either your marriage license or certificate in the matter of the enrollment of your child above named.

Respectfully,

Chairman.

7 NB 395
Muskogee, Indian Territory, May 1, 1905.

H. J. Martin,
    Lock Box 601,
        Pauls Valley, Indian Territory.

Dear Sir:

    Receipt is hereby acknowledged of your letter of April 25, 1905, stating that you are holding the affidavit recently forwarded you in the matter of the enrollment of the

Applications for Enrollment of Choctaw Newborn
Act of 1905   Volume VII

infant child of Eliza Mathis now Martin for the reason that the physician is out of the country and it needs his affidavit that the child was living on March 4, 1905.

In reply to your letter you are informed that if you will forward the affidavits of two disinterested persons who know of the birth of Madora Jane Martin and that she is the child of your wife Eliza Martin, and that she was living on March 4, 1905, the same will receive consideration in the matter of the enrollment of your child.

Respectfully,

Chairman.

---

7 NB 395

Muskogee, Indian Territory, May 5, 1905.

Henry J. Martin,
    Pauls Valley, Indian Territory.

Dear Sir:

Receipt is hereby acknowledged of your letter of April 27, 1905, enclosing affidavits of Eliza Martin and Annie Woodard to the birth of Madora Jane Martin daughter of Henry J. and Eliza Martin, February 7, 1905, and the same have been filed with our records as an application for the enrollment of said child.

Respectfully,

Commissioner in Charge.

---

7 N.B. 395.

Muskogee, Indian Territory, May 10, 1905.

Henry J. Martin,
    Lock Box 601,
        Pauls Valley, Indian Territory.

Dear Sir:

Receipt is hereby acknowledged of your letter of May 6, stating that you have heretofore forwarded the affidavits of the mother and the physician and attendants at the birth of your child, Madora May Martin, and you ask if the records are now complete in this case.

Applications for Enrollment of Choctaw Newborn
Act of 1905   Volume VII

In reply to your letter you are advised that if further evidence is necessary to enable us to determine the right of your child, Madora May Martin, to enrollment as a citizen by blood of the Choctaw Nation, you will be advised.

The matter of the relinquishments mentioned in your letter will be made the subject of a separate communication.

Respectfully,

Chairman.

7--N.B. 395.

Muskogee, Indian Territory, May 6, 1905.

Henry J. Martin,
    Pauls Valley, Indian Territory.

Dear Sir:

Receipt is hereby acknowledged of your letter of May 2, enclosing the affidavits of Eliza Martin and Price Patterson to the birth of Madora Jane Martin, daughter of Henry J. and Eliza Martin, February 7, 1905, and the same have been filed with our records in the matter of the enrollment of said child.

Respectfully,

Commissioner in Charge.

7-NB-395

Muskogee, Indian Territory, July 8, 1905.

Henry J. Martin,
    Lock Box 601,
        Pauls Valley, Indian Territory.

Dear Sir:

Receipt is hereby acknowledged of your letter of July 5, 1905, asking if your daughter Madora Jane Martin has been approved.

In reply to your letter you are advised that the name of Madora Jane Martin has been placed upon a schedule of citizens by blood of the Choctaw Nation which has been

Applications for Enrollment of Choctaw Newborn
Act of 1905 Volume VII

forwarded the Secretary of the Interior but this office has not yet been advised of Departmental action. You will be notified when her enrollment is approved.

Respectfully,

Commissioner.

<u>Choc New Born 396</u>
    George W. Beams b. 9-27-04
    Ada Olive Beams b. 10-26-02

Choctaw 4675

Muskogee, Indian Territory, November 24, 1902.

George W. Beams,
    South McAlester, Indian Territory.

Dear Sir:-

    Receipt is hereby acknowledged of your letter of November 15, relative to the enrollment of your child, Ada Olive Beams, born October 26, 1902.

    Replying to your letter you are informed that the Commission is without authority to enroll this child as a citizen of the Choctaw Nation, it appearing that said child was born October 26, 1902, subsequent to the ratification by the citizens of the Choctaw and Chickasaw Nations on September 25, 1902, of the act of Congress approved July 1, 1902.

    Section twenty eight thereof provides as follows:

    "The names of all persons living on the date of the final ratification of this agreement entitled to be enrolled as provided in section 27 hereof shall be placed upon the rolls made by said Commission; and no child born thereafter to a citizen or freedman and no person intermarried thereafter to a citizen shall be entitled to enrollment or to participate in the distribution of the tribal property of the Choctaws and Chickasaws."

Respectfully,

(End of letter)

Applications for Enrollment of Choctaw Newborn
Act of 1905 Volume VII

BIRTH AFFIDAVIT.

DEPARTMENT OF THE INTERIOR.
COMMISSION TO THE FIVE CIVILIZED TRIBES.

IN RE APPLICATION FOR ENROLLMENT, as a citizen of the Choctaw Nation, of Ada Olive Beams, born on the 26th day of October, 1902

Name of Father: George W. Beams   a citizen of the Choctaw Nation.
Name of Mother: Sallie Beams   a citizen of the Choctaw Nation.

Postoffice   South McAlester, I.T.

AFFIDAVIT OF MOTHER.

UNITED STATES OF AMERICA, Indian Territory, }
Central   DISTRICT. }

I, Sallie Beams, on oath state that I am 26 years of age and a citizen by marriage, of the Choctaw Nation; that I am the lawful wife of George W. Beams, who is a citizen, by blood of the Choctaw Nation; that a female child was born to me on 26th day of October, 1902; that said child has been named Ada Olive Beams, and was living March 4, 1905.

                                    Sallie Beams

Witnesses To Mark:
{

Subscribed and sworn to before me this 20th day of March, 1905

                                    Wirt Franklin
                                    Notary Public.

AFFIDAVIT OF ATTENDING PHYSICIAN OR MID-WIFE.

UNITED STATES OF AMERICA, Indian Territory, }
Central   DISTRICT. }

I, Mattie Creswell, a mid-wife, on oath state that I attended on Mrs. Sallie Beams, wife of George W Beams on the 26th day of October, 1902; that there was born to her on said date a female child; that said child was living March 4, 1905, and is said to have been named Ada Olive Beams

                                    Mattie Creswell

Witnesses To Mark:
{

Applications for Enrollment of Choctaw Newborn
Act of 1905 Volume VII

Subscribed and sworn to before me this 20th day of March , 1905

Wirt Franklin
Notary Public.

BIRTH AFFIDAVIT.

DEPARTMENT OF THE INTERIOR.
COMMISSION TO THE FIVE CIVILIZED TRIBES.

IN RE APPLICATION FOR ENROLLMENT, as a citizen of the Choctaw Nation, of George W. Beams, Jr , born on the 27th day of September , 1904

Name of Father: George W. Beams   a citizen of the Choctaw Nation.
Name of Mother: Sallie Beams   a citizen of the Choctaw Nation.

Postoffice South McAlester, I.T.

AFFIDAVIT OF MOTHER.

UNITED STATES OF AMERICA, Indian Territory, }
   Central   DISTRICT. }

     I, Sallie Beams , on oath state that I am 26 years of age and a citizen by marriage , of the Choctaw Nation; that I am the lawful wife of George W. Beams , who is a citizen, by blood of the Choctaw Nation; that a male child was born to me on 27th day of September , 1904; that said child has been named George W Beams, Jr , and was living March 4, 1905.

Sallie Beams

Witnesses To Mark:
{

Subscribed and sworn to before me this 20th day of March , 1905

Wirt Franklin
Notary Public.

AFFIDAVIT OF ATTENDING PHYSICIAN OR MID-WIFE.

UNITED STATES OF AMERICA, Indian Territory, }
   Central   DISTRICT. }

     I, Mattie Creswell , a mid-wife , on oath state that I attended on Mrs. Sallie Beams , wife of George W Beams on the 27th day of

Applications for Enrollment of Choctaw Newborn
Act of 1905   Volume VII

September, 1904; that there was born to her on said date a   male   child; that said child was living March 4, 1905, and is said to have been named   George W. Beams, Jr

Mattie Creswell

Witnesses To Mark:

{ Subscribed and sworn to before me this   20th   day of   March   , 1905

Wirt Franklin
Notary Public.

Choc New Born 397
    Buelah[sic] Lois Mackey   b. 11-19-02
    James W. Mackey   b. 10-14-04

    No. 1   Dismissed 10-6-05

DEPARTMENT OF THE INTERIOR,
COMMISSIONER TO THE FIVE CIVILIZED TRIBES.

Record in the matter of the application for enrollment as a citizen by blood of the Choctaw Nation of:

    JAMES W. MACKEY   7-NB-397.

7-NB-397.

Muskogee, Indian Territory, May 22, 1905.

Ben P. Mackey,
    Savanna, Indian Territory.

Dear Sir:

    Referring to the application for the enrollment of your infant child, James W. Mackey, born October 14, 1904, it is noted in the affidavits heretofore filed in this office that the applicant is dead.

    In order that this fact may be made a matter of record you will kindly execute the enclosed proof of death, and when properly executed return it to this office.

Applications for Enrollment of Choctaw Newborn
Act of 1905   Volume VII

Respectfully,

Chairman.

Encl. D-C.

7-N.B. 397.

Muskogee, Indian Territory, June 2, 1905.

Benjamin P. Mackey,
    Savanna, Indian Territory.

Dear Sir:

    Receipt is hereby acknowledged of your letter of May 27, enclosing affidavits to the death of James W. Mackey, October 19, 1904.

    Replying to that portion of your letter in which you ask if you can file for your children now being enrolled, you are advised that the name of your child Beulah Lois Mackey has been placed upon a schedule of new born citizens by blood of the Choctaw Nation, and you will be advised when her enrollment is approved by the Secretary of the Interior. Pending the enrollment of this child, however, no selection of allotment can be made in her behalf.

    Referring to the application for the enrollment of your child, James W. Mackey you are informed that by the provisions of the act of Congress approved March 3, 1905, the Commission was authorized to enroll children born to citizens by by[sic] blood of the Choctaw and Chickasaw Nations between September 25, 1901, and March 4, 1905, and living on the latter date.

    You will therefore see that the Commission is without authority to enroll children born subsequent to September 25, 1902, who were not living on March 4, 1905.

Respectfully,

(End of letter)

Applications for Enrollment of Choctaw Newborn
Act of 1905 Volume VII

7-NB-397.

Muskogee, Indian Territory, June 6, 1905.

Ben P. Mackey,
    Savanna, Indian Territory.

Dear Sir:

    There is enclosed herewith for execution death certificate in the matter of the death of James W. Mackey.

    In the proof of death heretofore filed in this office you, in your affidavit, state that James W. Mackey died on October 14, 1904, while the affidavit of Lela E. Dawson, an acquaintance, gives the date of his death as October 19, 1905. The former is apparently correct.

    In order that the correct date may appear upon the records of the Commission you are requested to kindly have the death certificate above referred to executed and return to this office.

    In having these affidavits executed care should be exercised to see that all names are written in full, as they appear in the body of the affidavit, and in the event that either of the persons signing the affidavit are unable to write, signatures by mark must be attested by two witnesses. Each affidavit must be executed before a Notary Public and the notarial seal and signature of the officer must be attached to each separate affidavit.

Respectfully,

Incl. D-C.   Commissioner in Charge.

---

7 NB 397

Muskogee, Indian Territory, June 19, 1905.

Benjamin P. Mackey,
    Savanna, Indian Territory.

Dear Sir:

    Receipt is hereby acknowledged of the affidavits of Benjamin P. Mackey and Lela E. Dawson to the death of James W. Mackey, which occurred October 19, 1904, and the same have been filed with our records as evidence of the death of the above named citizen.

Respectfully,

Chairman.

Applications for Enrollment of Choctaw Newborn
Act of 1905   Volume VII

BIRTH AFFIDAVIT.

DEPARTMENT OF THE INTERIOR.
COMMISSION TO THE FIVE CIVILIZED TRIBES.

IN RE APPLICATION FOR ENROLLMENT, as a citizen of the   Choctaw   Nation, of James W. Mackey   , born on the   14   day of   Oct   , 1904

Name of Father: Ben P. Mackey   a citizen of the   Choctaw   Nation.
Name of Mother: Belle Mackey   a citizen of the   Choctaw   Nation.

Postoffice   Savanna

AFFIDAVIT OF MOTHER.

UNITED STATES OF AMERICA, Indian Territory, }
Central   DISTRICT.

I, Belle Mackey   , on oath state that I am 23 years of age and a citizen by Inter M   , of the   Choctaw   Nation; that I am the lawful wife of   Ben P Mackey, who is a citizen, by   blood   of the   Choctaw   Nation; that a   male child was born to me on   14th day of   Oct   , 1902, that said child has been named James W Mackey   , and is now living.

Belle Mackey

Witnesses To Mark:
{ Effie D. Gorman
{ Katie Culbertson

Subscribed and sworn to before me this   16th day of   January   , 1905

W.T. Culbertson
Notary Public.

AFFIDAVIT OF ATTENDING PHYSICIAN OR MID-WIFE.

UNITED STATES OF AMERICA, Indian Territory, }
Central   DISTRICT.

I,   S.P. Ross   , a   Physician   , on oath state that I attended on Mrs. Belle Mackey   , wife of   Ben P Mackey   on the   14th day of Oct , 1905; that there was born to her on said date a   male   child; that said child is now living and is said to have been named   James W Mackey

Applications for Enrollment of Choctaw Newborn
Act of 1905   Volume VII

S.P. Ross M.D.

Witnesses To Mark:
- Katie Culbertson
- Effie D. Gorman

Subscribed and sworn to before me this 16th day of January, 1905

W.T. Culbertson
Notary Public.

DEPARTMENT OF THE INTERIOR.
COMMISSION TO THE FIVE CIVILIZED TRIBES.

In the matter of the death of James W Mackey a citizen of the Choctaw Nation, who formerly resided at or near Savanna, Ind. Ter., and died on the 19th day of October, 1904

AFFIDAVIT OF RELATIVE.

UNITED STATES OF AMERICA, Indian Territory,
Central   DISTRICT.

I, Benjamin P. Mackey, on oath state that I am 24 years of age and a citizen by blood, of the Choctaw Nation; that my postoffice address is Savanna, Ind. Ter.; that I am The father of James W Mackey who was a citizen, by blood, of the Choctaw Nation and that said James W Mackey died on the 19th day of October, 1904

Benjamin P Mackey

Witnesses To Mark:
- Beulah A Mackey
- David M Mackey

Subscribed and sworn to before me this 27th day of May, 1905.

W T Culbertson
Notary Public.

AFFIDAVIT OF ACQUAINTANCE.

UNITED STATES OF AMERICA, Indian Territory,
Central   DISTRICT.

I, Lela E Dawson, on oath state that I am 52 years of age, and a citizen by blood of the Choctaw Nation; that my postoffice address is Savanna, Ind. Ter.;

Applications for Enrollment of Choctaw Newborn
Act of 1905   Volume VII

that I was personally acquainted with   James W Mackey   who was a citizen, by blood, of the Choctaw Nation; and that said   James W Mackey   died on the 19th day of October   , 1905[sic]

Lela E Dawson

Witnesses To Mark:
  { Maggie E Harper
  { Beulah A Mackey

Subscribed and sworn to before me this   27th day of   May   , 1905.

W T Culbertson
Notary Public.

DEPARTMENT OF THE INTERIOR.
COMMISSION TO THE FIVE CIVILIZED TRIBES.

In the matter of the death of   James W Mackey   a citizen of the   Choctaw Nation, who formerly resided at or near   Savanna   , Ind. Ter., and died on the   19th day of   October   , 1904

AFFIDAVIT OF RELATIVE.

UNITED STATES OF AMERICA, Indian Territory, }
  Central   DISTRICT. }

I,   Benjamin P. Mackey   , on oath state that I am   24   years of age and a citizen by blood   , of the Choctaw   Nation; that my postoffice address is   Savanna   , Ind. Ter.; that I am   Father   of   James W Mackey   who was a citizen, by blood   , of the Choctaw   Nation and that said   James W Mackey   died on the   19th day of October   , 1904

Benjamin P Mackey

Witnesses To Mark:
  { Mrs Maggie Harper
  { Beulah A Mackey

Subscribed and sworn to before me this   7th day of   June   , 1905.

W T Culbertson
Notary Public.

Applications for Enrollment of Choctaw Newborn
Act of 1905   Volume VII

AFFIDAVIT OF ACQUAINTANCE.

UNITED STATES OF AMERICA, Indian Territory, }
Central   DISTRICT.

I, Lela E Dawson, on oath state that I am 52 years of age, and a citizen by blood of the Choctaw Nation; that my postoffice address is Savanna, Ind. Ter.; that I was personally acquainted with James W Mackey who was a citizen, by blood, of the Choctaw Nation; and that said James W Mackey died on the 19th day of October, 1904

Lela E Dawson

Witnesses To Mark:
{ Mrs. Maggie Harper
{ Beulah A Mackey

Subscribed and sworn to before me this 7th day of June, 1905.

W T Culbertson
Notary Public.

W.F.
7-NB-397.

DEPARTMENT OF THE INTERIOR,
COMMISSIONER TO THE FIVE CIVILIZED TRIBES.

In the matter of the application for the enrollment of James W. Mackey as a citizen by blood of the Choctaw Nation.

----oOo----

It appears from the record herein that on March 17, 1905 there was filed with the Commission to the Five Civilized Tribes an application for the enrollment of James W. Mackey as a citizen by blood of the Choctaw Nation.

It further appears from the record herein and the records of this office that the applicant was born October 14, 1904; that he is a son of Benjamin P. Mackey, a recognized and enrolled citizen by blood of the Choctaw Nation whose name appears opposite number 12923 upon the final roll of citizens by blood of the Choctaw Nation, approved by the Secretary of the Interior March 6, 1903, and Belle Mackey, a recognized and enrolled citizen by intermarriage of the Choctaw Nation; and that said applicant died October 19, 1904.

The Act of Congress approved March 3, 1905 (Public No. 212) among other things provided:

"That the Commission to the Five Civilized Tribes is authorized for sixty days after the date of the approval of this act to receive and consider applications for enrollments of children born subsequent to September twenty-fiftj, nineteen hundred and two, and prior to March fourth, nineteen hundred and five, and who were living on said latter date, to citizens by blood of the Choctaw and Chickasaw

Applications for Enrollment of Choctaw Newborn
Act of 1905   Volume VII

tribes whose enrollment has been approved by the Secretary of the Interior prior to the date of the approval of this act; and to enroll and make allotments to such children."

It is, therefore, hereby ordered that the application for the enrollment of James W. Mackey as a citizen by blood of the Choctaw Nation be dismissed.

Tams Bixby   Commissioner.

Muskogee, Indian Territory.
OCT 6- 1905

7-NB-397.

COPY

Muskogee, Indian Territory, October 6, 1905.

Benjamin P. Mackey,
    Savanna, Indian Territory.

Dear Sir:

Inclosed herewith you will find a copy of the order of the Commissioner to the Five Civilized Tribes, dated October 6, 1905, dismissing the application for the enrollment of James W. Mackey as a citizen by blood of the Choctaw Nation.

Respectfully,
SIGNED
Tams Bixby
Commissioner.

Register.
7-NB-397.

7-NB-397.

COPY

Muskogee, Indian Territory, October 6, 1905.

Mansfield, McMurray & Cornish,
    Attorneys for Choctaw and Chickasaw Nations,
        South McAlester, Indian Territory.

Gentlemen:

Inclosed herewith you will find a copy of the order of the Commissioner to the Five Civilized Tribes, dated October 6, 1905, dismissing the application for the enrollment of James W. Mackey as a citizen by blood of the Choctaw Nation.

Applications for Enrollment of Choctaw Newborn
Act of 1905 Volume VII

7-NB-397.

Choctaw
BIRTH AFFIDAVIT.

Respectfully,
SIGNED

Tams Bixby
Commissioner.

DEPARTMENT OF THE INTERIOR.
COMMISSION TO THE FIVE CIVILIZED TRIBES.

IN RE APPLICATION FOR ENROLLMENT, as a citizen of the Choctaw Nation, of Bula[sic] Lois Mackey, born on the 19th day of November, 1902

Name of Father: Benjamin P. Mackey   a citizen of the Choctaw Nation.
Name of Mother: Belle Mackey   a citizen of the Choctaw Nation.

Postoffice   Savanna, Ind. Ter.

AFFIDAVIT OF MOTHER.

UNITED STATES OF AMERICA, Indian Territory,
Central   DISTRICT.

I, Belle Mackey, on oath state that I am 23 years of age and a citizen by intermarriage, of the Choctaw Nation; that I am the lawful wife of Benjamin P. Mackey, who is a citizen, by blood of the Choctaw Nation; that a female child was born to me on 19th day of November, 1902; that said child has been named Bula Lois Mackey, and was living March 4, 1905.

Belle Mackey

Witnesses To Mark:

Subscribed and sworn to before me this 1st day of May, 1905

OL Johnson
Notary Public.

Applications for Enrollment of Choctaw Newborn
Act of 1905   Volume VII

AFFIDAVIT OF ATTENDING PHYSICIAN OR MID-WIFE.

UNITED STATES OF AMERICA, Indian Territory,
Central   DISTRICT.

I,   Elizabeth H. Mackey   , a   midwife   , on oath state that I attended on Mrs.   Belle Mackey   , wife of   Benjamin P. Mackey   on the 19th day of November   , 1902; that there was born to her on said date a   female   child; that said child was living March 4, 1905, and is said to have been named   Bula Lois Mackey

Elizabeth H Mackey

Witnesses To Mark:

Subscribed and sworn to before me this   1st day of   May   , 1905

OL Johnson
Notary Public.

BIRTH AFFIDAVIT.

DEPARTMENT OF THE INTERIOR,
COMMISSION TO THE FIVE CIVILIZED TRIBES.

IN RE Application for Enrollment, as a citizen of the   Choctaw   Nation, of   Bulah Lois Mackey   , born on the   19   day of   Nov   , 1902

Name of Father: Ben P Mackey   a citizen of the   Choctaw   Nation.
Name of Mother: Belle Mackey   a citizen of the   Choctaw   Nation.

Post-Office: Savanna I.T.

AFFIDAVIT OF MOTHER.

UNITED STATES OF AMERICA,
   INDIAN TERRITORY.
Central   District.

I,   Belle Mackey   , on oath state that I am   21   years of age and a citizen by   marriage   , of the Choctaw Nation; that I am the lawful wife of   Ben P Mackey   , who is a citizen, by   blood   of the Choctaw Nation; that a   female   child was born to me on   19th day of   Nov   , 1902 , that said child has been named   Bulah Lois Mackey   , and is now living.

Belle Mackey

Applications for Enrollment of Choctaw Newborn
Act of 1905   Volume VII

WITNESSES TO MARK:
{ W W Mackey

Subscribed and sworn to before me this 22 day of Dec , 1902

W.T. Culbertson
NOTARY PUBLIC.

AFFIDAVIT OF ATTENDING PHYSICIAN OR MID-WIFE.

UNITED STATES OF AMERICA, }
INDIAN TERRITORY.
Central   District.

I, S.P. Ross , a Physician , on oath state that I attended on Mrs. Belle Mackey , wife of Ben Mackey on the 19th day of Nov , 1902 ; that there was born to her on said date a female child; that said child is now living and is said to have been named Bulah Lois

S.P. Ross M.D.

WITNESSES TO MARK:
{ J.W. Culbertson

Subscribed and sworn to before me this 22 day of Dec , 1902

W.T. Culbertson
NOTARY PUBLIC.

NEW-BORN AFFIDAVIT.

Number............

...Choctaw Enrolling Commission...

IN THE MATTER OF THE APPLICATION FOR ENROLLMENT, as a citizen of the Choctaw   Nation, of   Buelah[sic] Lois Mackey

born on the 19 day of November 190 2

Name of father Ben P Mackey   a citizen of   Choctaw
Nation final enrollment No. 12923
Name of mother Belle Mackey   a citizen of   Choctaw
Nation final enrollment No. 848

Applications for Enrollment of Choctaw Newborn
Act of 1905   Volume VII

Postoffice   Savanna

AFFIDAVIT OF MOTHER.

UNITED STATES OF AMERICA
INDIAN TERRITORY
Central   DISTRICT

I   Belle Mackey   , on oath state that I am   23   years of age and a citizen by   Inter M   of the   Choctaw   Nation, and as such have been placed upon the final roll of the   Choctaw   Nation, by the Honorable Secretary of the Interior my final enrollment number being   848 ; that I am the lawful wife of   Ben P. Mackey   , who is a citizen of the   Choctaw   Nation, and as such has been placed upon the final roll of said Nation by the Honorable Secretary of the Interior, his final enrollment number being   12923   and that a   Female   child was born to me on the   19th day of   November   190 2; that said child has been named   Buelah Lois Mackey   , and is now living.

Belle Mackey

Witnesseth.

Must be two Witnesses who are Citizens. } Effie D Gorman

Elizbeth[sic] Mackey

Subscribed and sworn to before me this   ??   day of   Jan   190 5

W.T. Culbertson
Notary Public.

My commission expires:
Sept - 1907

AFFIDAVIT OF ATTENDING PHYSICIAN OR MIDWIFE

UNITED STATES OF AMERICA
INDIAN TERRITORY
Central   DISTRICT

I,   SP Ross   a   Physician   on oath state that I attended on Mrs.   Belle Mackey   wife of   Ben P Mackey   on the   19th day of   November   , 190 2, that there was born to her on said date a   Female   child, that said child is now living, and is said to have been named   Buelah Lois Mackey

S. P. Ross   M.D.

Subscribed and sworn to before me this, the   ??   day of January   190 5

W.T. Culbertson   Notary Public.

Applications for Enrollment of Choctaw Newborn
Act of 1905 Volume VII

WITNESSETH:
Must be two witnesses
who are citizens
{ L. E. Dawson
  Elizabeth Mackey

We hereby certify that we are well acquainted with S.P. Ross a Physician and know him to be reputable and of good standing in the community.

Katie Culbertson   J.W. Culbertson

_____   Elizabeth Mackey

BIRTH AFFIDAVIT.

DEPARTMENT OF THE INTERIOR.
COMMISSION TO THE FIVE CIVILIZED TRIBES.

IN RE APPLICATION FOR ENROLLMENT, as a citizen of the Choctaw Nation, of Beulah Lois Mackey, born on the 19 day of November, 1902

Name of Father: Benj P. Mackey   a citizen of the Choctaw Nation.
Name of Mother: Belle Mackey   a citizen of the Choctaw Nation.

Postoffice   Savanna, I.T.

AFFIDAVIT OF MOTHER.

UNITED STATES OF AMERICA, Indian Territory,
Central DISTRICT.

I, Belle Mackey, on oath state that I am 23 years of age and a citizen by Marriage, of the Choctaw Nation; that I am the lawful wife of Benj P. Mackey, who is a citizen, by blood of the Choctaw Nation; that a female child was born to me on 19 day of November, 1902; that said child has been named Beulah Lois Mackey, and was living March 4, 1905.

                                Belle Mackey

Witnesses To Mark:
{ Mrs Maggie Harper
  L E Dawson

Applications for Enrollment of Choctaw Newborn
Act of 1905   Volume VII

Subscribed and sworn to before me this .... day of ...., 190....

>   ....
>   Notary Public.

AFFIDAVIT OF ATTENDING PHYSICIAN OR MID-WIFE.

UNITED STATES OF AMERICA, Indian Territory, }
.... DISTRICT. }

I,   S.P. Ross   , a   Physician   , on oath state that I attended on Mrs.   Belle Mackey   , wife of   Benj P. Mackey   on the   19 day of   Nov   , 1902; that there was born to her on said date a   Female   child; that said child was living March 4, 1905, and is said to have been named   Beulah Lois Mackey

>   S.P. Ross M.D.

Witnesses To Mark:
{ Mrs Maggie Harper
{ L E Dawson

Subscribed and sworn to before me this   14th   day of   March   , 1905

< Seal >   *(Name Illegible)*
                                               Notary Public.
My commission expires Dec 16th 1906

BIRTH AFFIDAVIT.

DEPARTMENT OF THE INTERIOR.
COMMISSION TO THE FIVE CIVILIZED TRIBES.

IN RE APPLICATION FOR ENROLLMENT, as a citizen of the   Choctaw   Nation, of Buelah[sic] L Mackey   , born on the   19th   day of Nov   , 1902

Name of Father: Ben P Mackey   a citizen of the   Choctaw   Nation.
Name of Mother: Belle Mackey   a citizen of the   Choctaw   Nation.

Postoffice   Savanna

Applications for Enrollment of Choctaw Newborn
Act of 1905   Volume VII

AFFIDAVIT OF MOTHER.

UNITED STATES OF AMERICA, Indian Territory, }
Central   DISTRICT.

    I, Belle Mackey, on oath state that I am 23 years of age and a citizen by Inter M, of the Choctaw Nation; that I am the lawful wife of Ben P Mackey, who is a citizen, by blood of the Choctaw Nation; that a Female child was born to me on 19th day of November, 1902, that said child has been named Buelah[sic] Lois Mackey, and is now living.

                                      Belle Mackey

Witnesses To Mark:
{ Effie D Gorman
{ Katie Culbertson

    Subscribed and sworn to before me this 16th day of January, 1905.

                                        W.T. Culbertson
                                        Notary Public.

AFFIDAVIT OF ATTENDING PHYSICIAN OR MID-WIFE.

UNITED STATES OF AMERICA, Indian Territory, }
Central   DISTRICT.

    I, SP Ross, a Physician, on oath state that I attended on Mrs. Belle Mackey, wife of Ben P Mackey on the 19th day of Nov, 1902; that there was born to her on said date a .... child; that said child is now living and is said to have been named Buelah[sic] L Mackey

                                        S.P. Ross MD

Witnesses To Mark:
{ Katie Culbertson
{ T. J. Ryan

    Subscribed and sworn to before me this 16th day of January, 1905.

                                        W.T. Culbertson
                                        Notary Public.

Applications for Enrollment of Choctaw Newborn
Act of 1905   Volume VII

BIRTH AFFIDAVIT.

DEPARTMENT OF THE INTERIOR,
COMMISSION TO THE FIVE CIVILIZED TRIBES.

IN RE *Application for Enrollment,* as a citizen of the Choctaw Nation, of Beulah Lois Mackey, born on the 19 day of November, 1902

Name of Father: Ben P Mackey   a citizen of the Choctaw Nation.
Name of Mother: Belle Mackey   a citizen of the Choctaw Nation.

Post-Office: Savanna Ind. Ter.

AFFIDAVIT OF MOTHER.

UNITED STATES OF AMERICA,
   INDIAN TERRITORY.
Central District.

I, Belle Mackey, on oath state that I am 21 years of age and a citizen by Marriage, of the Choctaw Nation; that I am the lawful wife of Benj P. Mackey, who is a citizen, by blood of the Choctaw Nation; that a female child was born to me on 19th day of November, 1902, that said child has been named Beulah Lois Mackey, and is now living.

                                      Belle Mackey

WITNESSES TO MARK:

Subscribed and sworn to before me this 22 day of December, 1902

                                      T.C. Humphrey
                                         NOTARY PUBLIC.

Applications for Enrollment of Choctaw Newborn
Act of 1905 Volume VII

7-4622.

Muskogee, Indian Territory, December 22, 1902.

Ben P. Mackey,
    Savanna, Indian Territory.

Dear Sir:

    Receipt is hereby acknowledged of the application for enrollment as a citizen of the Choctaw Nation of Bulah Lois Mackey, infant daughter of Ben P. and Belle Mackey, born November 19, 1902.

    You are advised that the Commission is without authority to enroll this child as a citizen of the Choctaw Nation, it appearing that said child was born November 19, 1902, subsequent to the ratification by the citizens of the Choctaw an Chickasaw Nations September 25, 1902, of an act of Congress approved July 1, 1902 (32 Stats., 641).

    Section twenty-eight thereof provides as follows:

    "The names of all persons living on the date of the final ratification of this agreement entitled to be enrolled as provided in section 27 hereof shall be placed upon the rolls made by said Commission; and no child born thereafter to a citizen or freedman and no person intermarried thereafter to a citizen shall be entitled to enrollment or to participate in the distribution of the tribal property of the Choctaws and Chickasaws."

Respectfully,

Acting Chairman.

7-4682

Muskogee, Indian Territory, January 23, 1905.

Ben P. Mackey,
    Savanna, Indian Territory.

Dear Sir:

    Receipt is hereby acknowledged of the affidavits of Belle Mackey and S. P. Ross to the birth of Beulah L. Mackey and James W. Mackey, minor children of Ben P. and Belle Mackey November 19, 1902, and October 14, 1904, respectively, which it is presumed have been forwarded as applications for enrollment of the above named children.

Applications for Enrollment of Choctaw Newborn
Act of 1905   Volume VII

You are advised that under the provisions of the act of Congress approved July 1, 1902, no children born to citizens of the Choctaw and Chickasaw Nations subsequent to the date of the ratification of said act, are entitled to enrollment and allotment in the Choctaw and Chickasaw Nations.

Respectfully,

Chairman.

7-4682

Muskogee, Indian Territory, March 20, 1905.

B. P. Mackey,
    Savanna, Indian Territory.

Dear Sir:

Receipt is hereby acknowledged of your letter of March 15, 1905, enclosing affidavits of Belle Mackey and S. P. Ross, M.D., to the birth of Beulah Lois Mackey daughter of Benjamin P. and Belle Mackey, November 19, 1902, and the same have been filed with our records as an application for the enrollment of said child.

Respectfully,

Chairman.

N. B. 397
COPY
Muskogee, Indian Territory, April 7, 1905.

Benjamin P. Mackey,
    Savanna, Indian Territory.

Dear Sir:

There is inclosed you herewith for execution application for the enrollment of your infant children, Beulah Lois Mackey and James W. Mackey, born November 19, 1902, and October 14, 1904, respectively.

The affidavits heretofore filed with the Commission show James W. Mackey was living on January 16, 1905. It will be necessary for the child to be enrolled, that he was living on March 4, 1905.

In having these affidavits executed care should be exercised to see that all names are written in full, as they appear in the body of the affidavit, and in the event that either

Applications for Enrollment of Choctaw Newborn
Act of 1905   Volume VII

of the persons signing the affidavit are unable to write, signatures by mark must be attested by two witnesses. Each affidavit must be executed before a Notary Public and the notarial seal and signature of the officer must be attached to each separate affidavit.

Respectfully,

SIGNED

LM 7-22

T. B. Needles.
Commissioner in Charge.

---

7))4682.

Muskogee, Indian Territory, May 9, 1905.

Benjamin P. Mackey,
    Savanna, Indian Territory.

Dear Sir:

    Receipt is hereby acknowledged of the affidavits of Belle Mackey and Elizabeth H. Mackey to the birth of Bula[sic] Lois Mackey, daughter of Benjamin P. and Belle Mackey, November 19, 1902, and the same have been filed with our records as an application for the enrollment of said child.

Respectfully,

Commissioner in Charge.

Choc New Born 398
    Clyde R. Coleman   b. 11-18-02

Applications for Enrollment of Choctaw Newborn
Act of 1905 Volume VII

NEW BORN
CHOCTAW
ENROLLMENT

CLYDE R. COLEMAN

(BORN November 18, 1902)

As Citizen of the
CHOCTAW NATION
Act of Congress
Approved March 3, 1905

REFUSED FEBRUARY 21, 1907
RECORD FORWARDED DEPARTMENT. FEBRUARY 21, 1907

ACTION APPROVED BY SECRETARY OF INTERIOR.
MARCH 4, 1907

NOTICE OF DEPARTMENTAL ACTION FORWARDED
ATTORNEYS FOR CHOCTAW AND CHICKASAW NATIONS
APRIL 15, 1907

NOTICE OF DEPARTMENTAL ACTION MAILED
APPLICANT. APRIL 15, 1907

Applications for Enrollment of Choctaw Newborn
Act of 1905 Volume VII

BIRTH AFFIDAVIT.

DEPARTMENT OF THE INTERIOR.
COMMISSION TO THE FIVE CIVILIZED TRIBES.

IN RE APPLICATION FOR ENROLLMENT, as a citizen of the Choctaw Nation, of Clyde R. Coleman, born on the 18 day of Nov., 1902

Name of Father: Riley L. Coleman   a citizen of the Chickasaw Nation.
Name of Mother: Sarah Jane Coleman   a citizen of the Chickasaw Nation.

Postoffice   Stigler, Ind. Ter.

AFFIDAVIT OF MOTHER.

UNITED STATES OF AMERICA, Indian Territory,
Central   DISTRICT.

I, Sarah Jane Coleman, on oath state that I am 22 years of age and a citizen by Blood, of the Chickasaw Nation; that I am the lawful wife of Riley L. Coleman, who is a citizen, by Marriage of the Chickasaw Nation; that a male child was born to me on 18 day of Nov., 1902, that said child has been named Clyde R. Coleman, and is now living.

Sarah Jane Coleman

Witnesses To Mark:

Subscribed and sworn to before me this 11 day of Dec., 1902

J. S. Stigler

(SEAL)   Notary Public.

AFFIDAVIT OF ATTENDING PHYSICIAN OR MID-WIFE.

UNITED STATES OF AMERICA, Indian Territory,
Central   DISTRICT.

I, Dr. L. K. Stephens, a Physician, on oath state that I attended on Mrs. Sarah J. Coleman, wife of Rily[sic] L. Coleman on the 18 day of Nov., 1902; that there was born to her on said date a male child; that said child is now living and is said to have been named Clyde R. Coleman

Dr. L. K. Stephens

Witnesses To Mark:

Applications for Enrollment of Choctaw Newborn
Act of 1905   Volume VII

Subscribed and sworn to before me this 11 day of Dec. , 1902

J. S. Stigler
(SEAL)   Notary Public.

---

7 N. B. 398.

Muskogee, Indian Territory, April 11, 1905.

Riley L. Coleman,
    Stigler, Indian Territory.

Dear Sir:

    There is inclosed you herewith for execution application for the enrollment of your infant child, Clyde R. Coleman, born November 18, 1902.

    In The affidavits heretofore filed with the Commission you make application for the enrollment of your child as a Chickasaw, stating that both yourself and your wife are Chickasaws by blood.

    The records of the Commission show a Sarah Caddy Coleman, Choctaw, and Riley L. Coleman, her husband, a non-citizen. If this description is that of you and your wife it will be necessary that you make application for the enrollment of your child as a Choctaw. The inclosed application is prepared in compliance with the above mentioned record.

    In having these affidavits executed care should be exercised to see that all names are written in full, as they appear in the body of the affidavit, and in the event that either of the persons signing the affidavit are unable to write, signatures by mark must be attested by two witnesses. Each affidavit must be executed before a Notary Public and the notarial seal and signature of the officer must be attached to each separate affidavit.

Respectfully,
(Signed) T. B. Needles,
Commissioner in Charge.

LM 11-26.

Applications for Enrollment of Choctaw Newborn
Act of 1905   Volume VII

7-NB-398.

Muskogee, Indian Territory, May 25, 1905.

Riley L. Coleman,
    Stigler, Indian Territory.

Dear Sir:

    There is enclosed you herewith for execution application for the enrollment of your infant child, Clyde R. Coleman, born November 18, 1902.

    Your attention is called to the Commission's letter of the 11th ultimo, in which was enclosed an application similar to the one above mentioned. The affidavits heretofore filed with the Commission show the child was living on December 11, 1902. It is necessary, for the child to be enrolled, that he was living on March 4, 1905. From these affidavits it appears that your wife, Sarah Jane Coleman, is a Chickasaw; and the application for the enrollment of Clyde R. Coleman is made out in the Chickasaw nation, while the records of the Commission show Sarah Gaddy Coleman, who appears to be the same as Sarah Jane Coleman, to be a Choctaw and you to be a non-citizen.

    The enclosed application is made out in compliance with the records of the Commission which will be necessary for you to have executed before this matter can be finally determined.

    In having these affidavits executed care should be exercised to see that all names are written in full, as they appear in the body of the affidavit, and in the event that either of the persons signing the affidavit are unable to write, signatures by mark must be attested by two witnesses. Each affidavit must be executed before a Notary Public and the notarial seal and signature of the officer must be attached to each separate affidavit.

Respectfully,

VR 25-5.   Chairman.

7-NB-398

Muskogee, Indian Territory, July 29, 1905.

Riley L. Coleman,
    Stigler, Indian Territory.

Dear Sir:

    Your attention is called to communications addressed to you by the Commission to the Five Civilized Tribes under dates of April 1, and May 25, 1905, with which there

Applications for Enrollment of Choctaw Newborn
Act of 1905   Volume VII

was inclosed for execution application for the enrollment of your infant child, Clyde R. Coleman, born November 18, 1902.

In said letter you were advised that The affidavits heretofore filed in this office show that the child was living on December 11, 1902, and that it was necessary for the enrollment of the child, that he was living on March 4, 1905. You were also advised that it appeared from said affidavits that the name of your wife was given as Sarah Jane Coleman, a citizen by blood of the Chickasaw Nation, while the records of the Commission to the Five Civilized Tribes show her correct name as being Sarah Gaddy Coleman, a citizen by blood of the Choctaw Nation.

You were requested to have the affidavits properly executed and return to this office, no reply to this letter has been received.

In the event that your said child died prior to March March[sic] 4, 1905, you are requested to erase the words, "was living March 4, 1905", and insert instead the date of her[sic] death, if the child is living at this time you are requested to have the application heretofore forwarded you properly executed and return to this office immediately, as no further action can be taken relative to the enrollment of your said child, until the evidence requested is supplied.

Respectfully,

Commissioner.

7-NB-398

Muskogee, Indian Territory, January 4, 1906.

Riley L. Coleman,
    Stigler, Indian Territory.

Dear Sir:

There is inclosed you herewith for execution application for the enrollment of your infant child, Clyde R. Coleman born November 18, 1902.

Your attention is invited to the fact that communications have heretofore been addressed to you on several different occasions requesting additional evidence in the matter of the application for the enrollment of your child Clyde R. Coleman and until the affidavits of the mother and the attending physician or midwife, showing the date of the birth of the child and that it was living on March 4, 1905, are executed and returned to this office, no further action can be taken in the matter of the enrollment of said child.

This matter should receive your immediate attention.

Applications for Enrollment of Choctaw Newborn
Act of 1905 Volume VII

Respectively,

Commissioner.

7-NB-398

Muskogee, Indian Territory, April 30, 1906.

Riley L. Coleman,
Stigler, Indian Territory.

Dear Sir:

Your attention is again invited to office letter of January 4, 1906, inclosing for execution application for the enrollment of your infant child Clyde R. Coleman born November 18, 1902.

You are requested to give this matter immediate attention and if this child is not now living please state the date of his death.

Respectfully,

Commissioner.

7-NB-398. O.L.J.

DEPARTMENT OF THE INTERIOR,
COMMISSIONER TO THE FIVE CIVILIZED TRIBES.

In the matter of the application for the enrollment of Clyde R. Coleman as a citizen by blood of the Choctaw Nation.

DECISION.

It appears from the record herein that on March 4, 1905 application was made to the Commission to the Five Civilized Tribes for the enrollment of Clyde R. Coleman as a citizen by blood of the Choctaw Nation under the provisions of the Act of Congress approved March 3, 1905 (33 Stats., 1060).

It further appears from the record herein and from the records in the possession of this office that said applicant was born on November 18, 1902, and is the son of Riley L. Coleman, a non-citizen, and Sarah Jane Coleman, whose name (as Sarah Gaddy Coleman) appears opposite No. 13651 upon the final roll of citizens by blood of the Choctaw Nation approved by the Secretary of the Interior March 19, 1903.

Applications for Enrollment of Choctaw Newborn
Act of 1905   Volume VII

Although ample opportunity has been afforded the parents of said applicant to show that the latter was living on March 4, 1905, they have failed to do so.

I am, therefore, of the opinion that the application for the enrollment of Clyde R. Coleman as a citizen by blood of the Choctaw Nation should be denied, under the provisions of the Act of Congress approved March 3, 1905 (33 Stats., 1060). and it is so ordered.

Tams Bixby   Commissioner.

Muskogee, Indian Territory,
   FEB 21 1907

7-NB-398.

COPY

Muskogee, Indian Territory, February 21, 1907.

Riley L. Coleman,
   Stigler, Indian Territory.

Dear Sir:

Inclosed herewith you will find a copy of the decision of the Commissioner to the Five Civilized Tribes, rendered February 21, 1907, denying the application for the enrollment of Clyde R. Coleman as a citizen by blood of the Choctaw Nation.

The decision, with the record of proceedings in the case, is this day transmitted to the Secretary of the Interior for review. The final decision of the Secretary will be made known to you as soon as this office is informed of the same.

Respectfully,
SIGNED

Tams Bixby
Commissioner.

Registered.
Incl. 7-NB-398.

Applications for Enrollment of Choctaw Newborn
Act of 1905   Volume VII

7-NB-398.

COPY

Muskogee, Indian Territory, February 21, 1907.

Mansfield, McMurray & Cornish,
    Attorneys for Choctaw and Chickasaw Nations,
        South McAlester, Indian Territory.

Gentlemen:

    Inclosed herewith you will find a copy of the decision of the Commissioner to the Five Civilized Tribes, rendered February 21, 1907, denying the application for the enrollment of Clyde R. Coleman as a citizen by blood of the Choctaw Nation.

    The decision, with the record of proceedings in the case, is this day transmitted to the Secretary of the Interior for review. The final decision of the Secretary will be made known to you as soon as this office is informed of the same.

                      Respectfully,
                      SIGNED
                      Tams Bixby
                      Commissioner.

Incl. 7-NB-398.

COPY

Muskogee, Indian Territory, February 21, 1907.

The Honorable,
    The Secretary of the Interior.

Sir:

    There is transmitted herewith record of proceedings in the matter of the application for the enrollment of Clyde R. Coleman as a citizen by blood of the Choctaw Nation, including the decision of the Commissioner to the Five Civilized Tribes, dated February 21, 1907, denying said application.

                      Respectfully,
                      SIGNED
                      Tams Bixby
                      Commissioner.

2 Incl. 7-NB-398.
Through the
    Commissioner of Indian Affairs.

Applications for Enrollment of Choctaw Newborn
Act of 1905   Volume VII

D. C. 12854-1907.

I. T. D.
4398, 5188, 6184, 6928,
6952, 7112, 7450, 7452,
7456, 7464, 7494, 7496,
7664, 7688, 7692, 7706,
7710, 7722, 7726, 7732,
7740, 7750, 7756, 7818,
     7570, 7832,--1907.
LRS?[sic]
DIRECT.

JP.
W.H.M.

DEPARTMENT OF THE INTERIOR,
WASHINGTON.   March 4, 1907.

Commissioner to the Five Civilized Tribes,
    Muskogee, Indian Territory.

Sir:

    Your decisions in the following Choctaw citizenship cases, adverse to the applicants, are hereby affirmed. Copies of Indian Office letters, submitting your reports and recommending that the decisions be affirmed, are enclosed herewith:

Title of Case.	Date of your letter of transmittal.
Carlton Smith (Miss. Choc.)	January 21, 1907.
Mattie McFarland (intermarriage),	October 19, 1906.
Elmer Meadows (freedman),	February 13, 1907.
Daniel Oscar Sledge, et al., (by blood),	February 14, 1907.
Bula Lewis (freedman),	February 14, 1907.
Henry Adams (freedman)	February 14, 1907.
Mattie Doak (intermarriage),	February 13, 1907.
Clyde R. Coleman (by blood),	February 21, 1907.
Alice Chatman (freedman)	February 21, 1907.
Jim Brown (freedman),	February 21, 1907.
John Frankling[sic] Brewer (by blood),	February 21, 1907.
Cordelia Frazier, et al., (freedman),	February 21, 1907.
John Herbert LeFlore (freedman),	February 23, 1907.
Mabel M. Jones, et al. (by blood),	February 21, 1907.
Charles H. Hopkins, et al (Choctaw or Chickasaw Freedman)	February 23, 1907.
T. L. Reid, Jr., et al, (by blood),	February 26, 1907.
Albert Jones (by blood),	February 26, 1907.
Arella Colbert, et al. (as citizens),	February 26. 1907.
John D. Fleming (by blood),	February 26, 1907.

Applications for Enrollment of Choctaw Newborn
Act of 1905 Volume VII

Edmund Macco Cohee (freedman),	February 26, 1907.
Temperence Caroline Batty (by blood),	February 26, 1907.
Amos Lewis (freedman),	February 26, 1907.
Mary A. Crowder (intermarriage),	February 26, 1907.
Cally Reives[sic] (freedman),	February 26, 1907.
W. J. Miller, et al. (Miss. Choc.),	February 7, 1903.
Henry Pruitt, et al.,	February 25, 1907.

A copy hereof and all the papers in the above mentioned cases have been sent to the Indian Office.

Respectfully,
E. A. Hitchcock,
Secretary.

26 enclosures, and
63 enclosures to Ind. Of.,
    with copy hereof.
WCF. 3-4-07.

Refer in reply to the following:
Land: 19643-1907.   Copy

DEPARTMENT OF THE INTERIOR,
OFFICE OF INDIAN AFFAIRS?[sic]
WASHINGTON, March 1, 1907.

The Honorable,
    The Secretary of the Interior.

Sir:

There is enclosed a report from Commissioner Bixby dated February 21, 1907, transmitting the record relative to the application for the enrollment of Clyde R. Coleman as a citizen by blood of the Choctaw Nation. On February 21, 1907, the Commissioner held that the applicant was not entitled to enrollment. The record shows that the action of the Commissioner is correct and the approval thereof is recommended.

Very respectfully,
C.F. Larrabee,
Acting Commissioner.

GAW-GH.

Applications for Enrollment of Choctaw Newborn
Act of 1905   Volume VII

7-NB-398

Muskogee, Indian Territory, April 15, 1907.

Riley L. Coleman,
    Stigler, Indian Territory.

Dear Sir:

You are hereby advised that on March 4, 1907, the Secretary of the Interior affirmed the decision of this office of February 21, 1907, denying the application for the enrollment of Clyde R. Coleman as a citizen by blood of the Choctaw Nation.

Respectfully,

Commissioner.

7-NB-398

Muskogee, Indian Territory, April 15, 1907.

Mansfield, McMurray & Cornish,
    Attorneys for Choctaw and Chickasaw Nations,
        South McAlester, Indian Territory.

Gentlemen:

You are hereby advised that on March 4, 1907, the Secretary of the Interior affirmed the decision of this office of February 21, 1907, denying the application for the enrollment of Clyde R. Coleman as a citizen by blood of the Choctaw Nation.

Respectfully,

Commissioner.

Applications for Enrollment of Choctaw Newborn
Act of 1905   Volume VII

7-NB-398

Muskogee, Indian Territory, February 9, 1907.

Sarah Jane Coleman,
% Riley L. Coleman,
Stigler, Indian Territory.

Dear Madam:

In the matter of the application for the enrollment of your child, Clyde R. Coleman, as a new born citizen of the Choctaw Nation under the Act of Congress approved March 3, 1905, you are advised that it will be necessary for you to forward at once affidavits of the mother and the physician or midwife in attendance at the birth of this child, showing that said child was living March 4, 1905.

This evidence has heretofore been requested on several previous occasions and the same has not been received. If Clyde R. Coleman is not now living you are requested to state the date of his death and forward proof of the death on the blank enclosed herewith.

This matter should receive immediate attention.

Respectfully,

BC.
DC.
Env.

Commissioner.

JP.

D. C. 12854-1907.   W.H.M.
DEPARTMENT OF THE INTERIOR,
WASHINGTON.   March 4, 1907.

I. T. D.
4398, 5188, 6184, 6928,
6952, 7112, 7450, 7452,
7456, 7464, 7494, 7496,
7664, 7688, 7692, 7706,
7710, 7722, 7726, 7732,
7740, 7750, 7756, 7818,
    7570, 7832,--1907.
LRS?[sic]
<u>DIRECT.</u>

Commissioner to the Five Civilized Tribes,
Muskogee, Indian Territory.

Applications for Enrollment of Choctaw Newborn
Act of 1905   Volume VII

Sir:

    Your decisions in the following Choctaw citizenship cases, adverse to the applicants, are hereby affirmed. Copies of Indian Office letters, submitting your reports and recommending that the decisions be affirmed, are enclosed herewith:

Title of Case.	Date of your letter of transmittal.
Carlton Smith (Miss. Choc.)	January 21, 1907.
Mattie McFarland (intermarriage),	October 19, 1906.
Elmer Meadows (freedman),	February 13, 1907.
Daniel Oscar Sledge, et al., (by blood),	February 14, 1907.
Bula Lewis (freedman),	February 14, 1907.
Henry Adams (freedman)	February 14, 1907.
Mattie Doak (intermarriage),	February 13, 1907.
Clyde R. Coleman (by blood),	February 21, 1907.
Alice Chatman (freedman)	February 21, 1907.
Jim Brown (freedman),	February 21, 1907.
John Frankling[sic] Brewer (by blood),	February 21, 1907.
Cordelia Frazier, et al., (freedman),	February 21, 1907.
John Herbert LeFlore (freedman),	February 23, 1907.
Mabel M. Jones, et al. (by blood),	February 21, 1907.
Charles H. Hopkins, et al (Choctaw or Chickasaw Freedman)	February 23, 1907.
T. L. Reid, Jr., et al, (by blood),	February 26, 1907.
Albert Jones (by blood),	February 26, 1907.
Arella Colbert, et al. (as citizens),	February 26. 1907.
John D. Fleming (by blood),	February 26, 1907.
Edmund Macco Cohee (freedman),	February 26, 1907.
Temperence Caroline Batty (by blood),	February 26, 1907.
Amos Lewis (freedman),	February 26, 1907.
Mary A. Crowder (intermarriage),	February 26, 1907.
Cally Reives[sic] (freedman),	February 26, 1907.
W. J. Miller, et al. (Miss. Choc.),	February 7, 1903.
Henry Pruitt, et al.,	February 25, 1907.

    A copy hereof and all the papers in the above mentioned cases have been sent to the Indian Office.

                          Respectfully,
                          E. A. Hitchcock,
                                  Secretary.

26 enclosures, and
63 enclosures to Ind. Of.,
    with copy hereof.
WCF. 3-4-07.

Applications for Enrollment of Choctaw Newborn
Act of 1905   Volume VII

Refer in reply to the following:
Land: 19643-1907.

Copy

DEPARTMENT OF THE INTERIOR,
OFFICE OF INDIAN AFFAIRS?[sic]
WASHINGTON, March 1, 1907.

The Honorable,
The Secretary of the Interior.

Sir:

There is enclosed a report from Commissioner Bixby dated February 21, 1907, transmitting the record relative to the application for the enrollment of Clyde R. Coleman as a citizen by blood of the Choctaw Nation. On February 21, 1907, the Commissioner held that the applicant was not entitled to enrollment. The record shows that the action of the Commissioner is correct and the approval thereof is recommended.

Very respectfully,
C.F. Larrabee,
Acting Commissioner.

GAW-GH.

REFER IN REPLY TO THE FOLLOWING:	(COPY)	
Land 19645-1907.	**DEPARTMENT OF THE INTERIOR,** OFFICE OF INDIAN AFFAIRS, WASHINGTON.	

March 1, 1907.

Refer in reply to the following:
Land: 19643-1907.

Copy

DEPARTMENT OF THE INTERIOR,
OFFICE OF INDIAN AFFAIRS?[sic]
WASHINGTON, March 1, 1907.

The Honorable,
The Secretary of the Interior.

Sir:

There is enclosed a report from Commissioner Bixby dated February 21, 1907, transmitting the record relative to the application for the enrollment of Clyde R. Coleman as a citizen by blood of the Choctaw Nation. On February 21, 1907, the Commissioner

Applications for Enrollment of Choctaw Newborn
Act of 1905   Volume VII

held that the applicant was not entitled to enrollment. The record shows that the action of the Commissioner is correct and the approval thereof is recommended.

Very respectfully,
C.F. Larrabee,
Acting Commissioner.

GAW-GH.

Choc New Born 399
    Lelia L. McDaniel   b. 1-22-04

7-5394

Muskogee, Indian Territory, March 23, 1905.

Marvin McDaniel,
    Durant, Indian Territory.

Dear Sir:

    Receipt is hereby acknowledged of the affidavits of Cammie McDaniel and James M. Shuler to the birth of Lelia L. McDaniel daughter of Marvin and Cammie McDaniel, January 22, 1904, and the same have been filed with our records as an application for the enrollment of said child.

Respectfully,

Chairman.

N. B. 399

Muskogee, Indian Territory, April 7, 1905.

Marvin McDaniel,
    Durant, Indian Territory.

Dear Sir:

    You are hereby advised that before the application for the enrollment of your infant child, Lelia L. McDaniel, can be finally disposed of, it will be necessary for you to furnish the Commission either the original or a certified copy of the license and certificate of marriage of yourself and Cammie McDaniel.

Applications for Enrollment of Choctaw Newborn
Act of 1905　Volume VII

Please give this matter your immediate attention.

Respectfully,

Commissioner in Charge.

Choctaw N.B. 399.

Muskogee, Indian Territory, April 18, 1905.

Marvin McDaniel,
    Durant, Indian Territory.

Dear Sir:

    Receipt is hereby acknowledged of the Marriage license and certificate between B. M. McDaniel and Miss Cammie Todd which you offer in support of the application for the enrollment of your child, Lena[sic] McDaniel, and the same have been filed with our records in this case.

Respectfully,

Chairman.

9--N.B. 399.

Muskogee, Indian Territory, May 26, 1905.

B. M. McDaniel,
    Durant, Indian Territory.

Dear Sir:

    Receipt is hereby acknowledged of your letter of May 22, asking if you can have land set aside for allotment of Lela[sic] L. McDaniel in order that she may file on same when approved.

    In reply to your letter you are advised that no reservation of land or selection of allotment can be made for children enrolled under the provisions of the act of Congress approved March 3, 1905, until their enrollment has been approved by the Secretary of the Interior.

Respectfully,

Chairman.

Applications for Enrollment of Choctaw Newborn
Act of 1905 Volume VII

(The letter below does not belong with the current applicant.)

7-5397

Muskogee, Indian Territory, July 18, 1903.

E. A. Hickman,
    Cartersville, Indian Territory.

Dear Sir:

    Receipt is hereby acknowledged of the affidavits of Lucy Hickman and Farley C. Parrott relative to the birth of Houston Hickman, infant son of E. A. and Lucy Hickman, May 8, 1903, which it is presumed has been forwarded to this office as an application for enrollment, as a citizen by blood of the Choctaw Nation, of the above named child.

    Your attention is invited to Section 28 of the Act of Congress approved July 1, 1902 which is as follows:

> "The names of all persons living on the date of the final ratification of this agreement entitled to be enrolled as provided in section 27 hereof shall be placed upon the rolls made by said Commission; and no child born thereafter to a citizen or freedman and no person intermarried thereafter to a citizen shall be entitled to enrollment or to participate in the distribution of the tribal property of the Choctaws and Chickasaws."

the[sic] said act of Congress was ratified by the citizens of the Choctaw and Chickasaw Nations September 25, 1902, and you will therefore understand that the Commission is now without authority to enroll infant children born to citizens of the Choctaw or Chickasaw Nations subsequent to September 25, 1902.

    Respectfully,

    Commissioner in Charge.

7-NB-399

Muskogee, Indian Territory, August 3, 1905.

Marvin McDaniel,
    Durant, Indian Territory.

Dear Sir:

    Receipt is hereby acknowledged of your letter of July 28, 1905, asking why Lelia L. McDaniel has not been approved.

Applications for Enrollment of Choctaw Newborn
Act of 1905   Volume VII

In reply to your letter you are advised that on July 22, 1905, the Secretary of the Interior approved the enrollment of your child Lelia L. McDaniel as a citizen by blood of the Choctaw Nation.

Respectfully,

Commissioner.

CERTIFICATE OF RECORD.

United States of America,
    INDIAN TERRITORY, } *ss.*
    Western District.

I, **ROBERT P. HARRISON**, Clerk of the United States Court in the Western District, Indian Territory, do hereby certify that the instrument hereto attached was filed for record in my office the   16   day of   Sept.   1902 at   8 a M., and duly recorded in Book   N   , Marriage Record, Page   215

WITNESS my hand and seal of said Court at Muscogee, in said Territory, this   16   day of   Sept.   A. D. 1902

R P Harrison   Clerk.

By R.A. Bayne   Deputy.

MARRIAGE LICENSE.

United States of America,
    INDIAN TERRITORY, } *ss.*   *No.* **244**
    Western District.

To Any Person Authorized by Law to Solemnize Marriage---Greeting:

You are Hereby Commanded to Solemnize the Rite and Publish the Banns of Matrimony between Mr.   B. M. McDaniel   of   Cowlington   , in the Indian Territory, aged   19   years and M iss Cammie Todd   of   Muskogee   in the Indian Territory aged   19   years according to law, and do you officially sign and return this License to the parties therein named.

WITNESS my hand and official seal at Muscogee Indian Territory this   13th   day of September   A.D. 190 2

R.P. Harrison
Clerk of the U.S. Court

By   C. E. Wilcox   Deputy

Applications for Enrollment of Choctaw Newborn
Act of 1905 Volume VII

CERTIFICATE OF MARRIAGE.
•••••

United States of America, }
   INDIAN TERRITORY,   } ss.
   Western District.

   I, Thos. F Brewer, *a Minister of the Gospel, DO HEREBY CERTIFY that on the* 14th *day of* Sep. *A. D.* 1902, *I did duly and according to law as commanded in the foregoing License, solemnize the Rite and publish the Banns of Matrimony between the parties therein named.*

   WITNESS *my hand this* 15" *day of* Sept *A. D.* 1902

   My credentials are recorded in the office of the Clerk of the United States Court, Indian Territory, Western District, Book ...., Page ....

                                       Thos F. Brewer
                                       A Minister of the Gospel

Note—This License and Certificate of Marriage must be returned to the Office of the Clerk of the United States Court in the Northern District, Indian Territory, from whence it was issued, within sixty days from the date thereof, or the party to whom the license was issued will be liable in the amount of the One Hundred Dollars ($100.00)

BIRTH AFFIDAVIT.

DEPARTMENT OF THE INTERIOR.
COMMISSION TO THE FIVE CIVILIZED TRIBES.

   IN RE APPLICATION FOR ENROLLMENT, as a citizen of the   Choctaw   Nation, of Lelia L. McDaniel   , born on the 22nd   day of January   , 1904

Name of Father: Marvin McDaniel   a citizen of the   Choctaw   Nation.
Name of Mother: Cammie McDaniel   a citizen of the   Choctaw   Nation.

                            Postoffice   Durant, I.T.

AFFIDAVIT OF MOTHER.

UNITED STATES OF AMERICA, Indian Territory, }
    Central   DISTRICT.

   I,   Cammie McDaniel   , on oath state that I am   22   years of age and a citizen by   Intermarriage   , of the   Choctaw   Nation; that I am the lawful wife of   Marvin McDaniel   , who is a citizen, by blood   of the   Choctaw   Nation; that a   Female   child was born to me on   22nd   day of   January   ,

Applications for Enrollment of Choctaw Newborn
Act of 1905 Volume VII

1904; that said child has been named   Lelia L. McDaniel   , and was living March 4, 1905.

Cammie McDaniel

Witnesses To Mark:
{

Subscribed and sworn to before me this 20th day of March , 1905

Com Ex Feb 8th 1908

Charles A Phillips
Notary Public.
Central District I.T.

AFFIDAVIT OF ATTENDING PHYSICIAN OR MID-WIFE.

UNITED STATES OF AMERICA, Indian Territory, }
  Central   DISTRICT.

I, Jas L Shuler , a Physician , on oath state that I attended on Mrs. Cammie McDaniel , wife of Marvin McDaniel on the 22nd day of January , 1904; that there was born to her on said date a Female child; that said child was living March 4, 1905, and is said to have been named Lelia L. McDaniel

Jas L. Shuler

Witnesses To Mark:
{

Subscribed and sworn to before me this 20th day of March , 1905

Charles A Phillips
Notary Public.
Com Ex Feb 8th 1908   Central District I.T.

Choc New Born 400
  Houston Hickman   b. 5-8-03
  Katherine R. Hickman   b. 11-4-04

Applications for Enrollment of Choctaw Newborn
Act of 1905   Volume VII

7-605   7-13672
BIRTH AFFIDAVIT.

DEPARTMENT OF THE INTERIOR.
COMMISSION TO THE FIVE CIVILIZED TRIBES.

IN RE APPLICATION FOR ENROLLMENT, as a citizen of the   Choctaw   Nation, of Houston Eugene Hickman   , born on the   8 day of   May , 1903

Name of Father: Eugene A. Hickman   a citizen of the   Choctaw   Nation.
Name of Mother: Lucy Hickman   a citizen of the   Choctaw   Nation.

Postoffice   Cartersville I.T.

AFFIDAVIT OF MOTHER.

UNITED STATES OF AMERICA, Indian Territory,
Central   DISTRICT.

I, Lucy Hickman , on oath state that I am 38 years of age and a citizen by blood , of the Choctaw Nation; that I am the lawful wife of Eugene A Hickman , who is a citizen, by intermarriage of the Choctaw Nation; that a male child was born to me on 8th day of May , 1903; that said child has been named Houston Eugene Hickman , and was living March 4, 1905.

Lucy Hickman

Witnesses To Mark:
{

Subscribed and sworn to before me this 4th day of   April , 1905

OL Johnson
Notary Public.

AFFIDAVIT OF ATTENDING PHYSICIAN OR MID-WIFE.

UNITED STATES OF AMERICA, Indian Territory,
.... DISTRICT.

I,   F C Parrott   , a   physician   , on oath state that I attended on Mrs. Lucy Hickman , wife of Eugene A Hickman on the 8th day of May , 1903; that there was born to her on said date a   male   child; that said child was living March 4, 1905, and is said to have been named Houston Eugene Hickman

F C Parrott

Applications for Enrollment of Choctaw Newborn
Act of 1905 Volume VII

Witnesses To Mark:
{

    Subscribed and sworn to before me this 4 day of April , 1905

OL Johnson
Notary Public.

7-605 - 7 - 13672
BIRTH AFFIDAVIT.

DEPARTMENT OF THE INTERIOR.
COMMISSION TO THE FIVE CIVILIZED TRIBES.

    IN RE APPLICATION FOR ENROLLMENT, as a citizen of the Choctaw Nation, of Katherine R Hickman , born on the 4th day of November , 1904

Name of Father: Eugene A. Hickman   a citizen of the Choctaw Nation.
Name of Mother: Lucy Hickman   a citizen of the Choctaw Nation.

    Postoffice   Cartersville I.T.

AFFIDAVIT OF MOTHER.

UNITED STATES OF AMERICA, Indian Territory, }
    Central   DISTRICT. }

    I, Lucy Hickman , on oath state that I am 38 years of age and a citizen by blood , of the Choctaw Nation; that I am the lawful wife of Eugene A Hickman , who is a citizen, by intermarriage of the Choctaw Nation; that a female child was born to me on 4th day of November , 1904; that said child has been named Katherine R. Hickman , and was living March 4, 1905.

Lucy Hickman

Witnesses To Mark:
{

    Subscribed and sworn to before me this 4th day of April , 1905

OL Johnson
Notary Public.

Applications for Enrollment of Choctaw Newborn
Act of 1905   Volume VII

AFFIDAVIT OF ATTENDING PHYSICIAN OR MID-WIFE.

UNITED STATES OF AMERICA, Indian Territory,
    Central   DISTRICT.

    I, L J Smith   , a   physician   , on oath state that I attended on Mrs. Lucy Hickman   , wife of Eugene A Hickman   on the 4th day of November , 1904; that there was born to her on said date a female child; that said child was living March 4, 1905, and is said to have been named Katherine R Hickman

                            L J Smith MD

Witnesses To Mark:
{

    Subscribed and sworn to before me this 5 day of   April   , 1905

                          EF Jeffries
                          Notary Public.
                        Com Expires Sep 18 1906

BIRTH AFFIDAVIT.

DEPARTMENT OF THE INTERIOR,
COMMISSION TO THE FIVE CIVILIZED TRIBES.

    In Re Application for Enrollment, as a citizen of the   Choctaw   Nation, of Houston , born on the   8   day of May   , 1903

Name of Father: E A Hickman   a citizen of the   Choctaw   Nation.
Name of Mother: Lucy Hickman   a citizen of the   Choctaw   Nation.

                      Post-office   Cartersville Ind Ter

AFFIDAVIT OF MOTHER.

UNITED STATES OF AMERICA,
    INDIAN TERRITORY,
    Central   District.

    I, Lucy Hickman , on oath state that I am 36   years of age and a citizen by Blood , of the   Choctaw   Nation; that I am the lawful wife of E A Hickman , who is a citizen, by Marriage of the   Choctaw   Nation; that a   Male   child was born to me on   8 day of May   , 1903 , that said child has been named   Houston , and is now living.

                            Lucy Hickman

Applications for Enrollment of Choctaw Newborn
Act of 1905   Volume VII

WITNESSES TO MARK:
{ Annie Keese
{ Thomas I Towns

Subscribed and sworn to before me this 3 day of June , 1903

E F Jeffries
NOTARY PUBLIC.
Com Expires Sep 18 1906

AFFIDAVIT OF ATTENDING PHYSICIAN OR MID-WIFE.

UNITED STATES OF AMERICA,
INDIAN TERRITORY,
Central   District.

I,   Farley C Parrott   , a   Physician   , on oath state that I attended on Mrs. Lucy Hickman , wife of E A Hickman on the 8 day of May , 1903 ; that there was born to her on said date a   Male   child; that said child is now living and is said to have been named Houston

Farley C Parrott MD

WITNESSES TO MARK:
{ Annie Keese
{ Thomas I Towns

Subscribed and sworn to before me this 3 day of June , 1903

E F Jeffries
NOTARY PUBLIC.
Com Expires Sep 18 1906

Applications for Enrollment of Choctaw Newborn
Act of 1905 Volume VII

NEW-BORN AFFIDAVIT.

Number..............

...Choctaw Enrolling Commission...

IN THE MATTER OF THE APPLICATION FOR ENROLLMENT, as a citizen of the Choctaw Nation, of Houston E Hickman

born on the 8 day of __May__ 190 3

Name of father   Eugene A Hickman   a citizen of   Choctaw
Nation final enrollment No.   605
Name of mother   Lucy Hickman   a citizen of   Choctaw
Nation final enrollment No.   13672

                              Postoffice   Cartersville I T

AFFIDAVIT OF MOTHER.

UNITED STATES OF AMERICA
INDIAN TERRITORY
   Central   DISTRICT

I   Lucy Hickman   , on oath state that I am 38 years of age and a citizen by Blood of the Choctaw Nation, and as such have been placed upon the final roll of the Choctaw Nation, by the Honorable Secretary of the Interior my final enrollment number being   13672 ; that I am the lawful wife of   Eugene A Hickman   , who is a citizen of the   Choctaw   Nation, and as such has been placed upon the final roll of said Nation by the Honorable Secretary of the Interior, his final enrollment number being   605   and that a   Male   child was born to me on the   8   day of   May   190 3; that said child has been named   Houston E Hickman   , and is now living.

Witnesseth.   Lucy Hickman
   Must be two   ⎫ (Name Illegible)
   Witnesses who ⎬
   are Citizens. ⎭ (Name Illegible)

Subscribed and sworn to before me this   11   day of   Feb   190 5

                              EF Jeffries
                                    Notary Public.
My commission expires:
   Sept 18 1905[sic]

Applications for Enrollment of Choctaw Newborn
Act of 1905   Volume VII

AFFIDAVIT OF ATTENDING PHYSICIAN OR MIDWIFE

UNITED STATES OF AMERICA
INDIAN TERRITORY
   Central   DISTRICT

I, F C Parrott a Physician on oath state that I attended on Mrs. Lucy Hickman wife of Eugene A Hickman on the 8 day of May , 190 3 , that there was born to her on said date a Male child child, that said child is now living, and is said to have been named Houston E Hickman

Subscribed and sworn to before me this, the 1ˢᵗ day of February 190 5

WITNESSETH: ET Jeffries   Notary Public.
Must be two witnesses { *(Name Illegible)*   Com Expires Sep 18 1906
who are citizens   { *(Name Illegible)*

We hereby certify that we are well acquainted with F C Parrott a Physician and know him to be reputable and of good standing in the community.

(Name Illegible)   Iron Bridge IT

(Name Illegible)   Cartersville IT

N. B. 400
COPY
Muskogee, Indian Territory, April 7, 1905.

Eugene A. Hickman,
    Carterville, Indian Territory.

Dear Sir:

    There is inclosed you herewith for execution application for the enrollment of your infant child, Houston Hickman, born May 8, 1903.

    The affidavits heretofore filed with the Commission show the child was living on June 3, 1903. It is necessary, for the child to be enrolled, that he was living on March 4, 1905. You will please insert the age of the mother in space left blank for that purpose.

    In having these affidavits executed care should be exercised to see that all names are written in full, as they appear in the body of the affidavit, and in the event that either of the persons signing the affidavit are unable to write, signatures by mark must be

Applications for Enrollment of Choctaw Newborn
Act of 1905   Volume VII

attested by two witnesses. Each affidavit must be executed before a Notary Public and the notarial seal and signature of the officer must be attached to each separate affidavit.

Respectfully,
SIGNED

T. B. Needles.

Commissioner in Charge.

LM 7-13.

COMMISSIONERS: TAMS BIXBY, THOMAS B. NEEDLES, C.R. BRECKINBRIDGE. WM. O. BEALL Secretary	**DEPARTMENT OF THE INTERIOR,** **COMMISSIONER TO THE FIVE CIVILIZED TRIBES.**	*Wm O.B.* REFER IN REPLY TO THE FOLLOWING: Choctaw 5397.

ADDRESS ONLY THE
COMMISSION TO THE FIVE CIVILIZED TRIBES.

Muskogee, Indian Territory, April 18, 1905.

Eugene A. Hickman,
    Centerville, Indian Territory.

Dear Sir:

    Receipt is hereby acknowledged of the affidavits of Lucy Hickman and L. J. Smith to the birth of Katherine R. Hickman, daughter of Eugene A. and Lucy Hickman, November 4, 1904, and the same have been filed with our records as an application for the enrollment of said child.

Respectfully,

Tams Bixby Chairman.

NEW-BORN AFFIDAVIT.

        Number............

...Choctaw Enrolling Commission...

    IN THE MATTER OF THE APPLICATION FOR ENROLLMENT, as a citizen of the Choctaw   Nation, of   Katherine K[sic] Hickman

born on the 4 day of _November_   190 4

Name of father   Eugene A Hickman   a citizen of   Choctaw
Nation final enrollment No. 605

Applications for Enrollment of Choctaw Newborn
Act of 1905 Volume VII

Name of mother   Lucy Hickman   a citizen of   Choctaw
Nation final enrollment No. 13672

                                      Postoffice   Cartersville I T

AFFIDAVIT OF MOTHER.

UNITED STATES OF AMERICA
INDIAN TERRITORY
   Central   DISTRICT

I   Lucy Hickman   , on oath state that I am 38   years of age and a citizen by Blood   of the   Choctaw   Nation, and as such have been placed upon the final roll of the   Choctaw   Nation, by the Honorable Secretary of the Interior my final enrollment number being   13672 ; that I am the lawful wife of   Eugene A Hickman   , who is a citizen of the   Choctaw   Nation, and as such has been placed upon the final roll of said Nation by the Honorable Secretary of the Interior, his final enrollment number being   605   and that a   Girl   child was born to me on the   4   day of   November   190 4; that said child has been named   Katherine K[sic] Hickman   , and is now living.

Witnesseth.   Lucy Hickman
  Must be two   } (Name Illegible)
  Witnesses who }
  are Citizens.   (Name Illegible)

      Subscribed and sworn to before me this   11   day of   Feb   190 5

                                      EF Jeffries
                                              Notary Public.
My commission expires:
   Sept 18 1906

AFFIDAVIT OF ATTENDING PHYSICIAN OR MIDWIFE

UNITED STATES OF AMERICA
INDIAN TERRITORY
   Central   DISTRICT

I,   Lee J Smith   a   Physician on oath state that I attended on Mrs.   Lucy Hickman   wife of   Eugene A Hickman on the   4   day of   November   , 190 4, that there was born to her on said date a   Girl   child, that said child is now living, and is said to have been named   Katherine R Hickman

         Subscribed and sworn to before me this, the   1st day of   February   190 5
                                   ET Jeffries   Notary Public.
                                   Com Expires Sep 18 1906

Applications for Enrollment of Choctaw Newborn
Act of 1905   Volume VII

WITNESSETH:
Must be two witnesses { *(Name Illegible)*
who are citizens   { *(Name Illegible)*

We hereby certify that we are well acquainted with   Lee J Smith
a   Physician   and know   him   to be reputable and of good standing in the community.

(Name Illegible)   Iron Bridge IT

(Name Illegible)   Cartersville IT

Choc New Born 401
            Alvin Airington b. 2-9-05

NEW BORN AFFIDAVIT

No ....

CHOCTAW ENROLLING COMMISSION

IN THE MATTER OF THE APPLICATION FOR ENROLLMENT as a citizen of the Choctaw Nation, of   Alvin Airington   born on the 9   day of   February   190 5

Name of father   Noah Airington   a citizen of   Choctaw   Nation, final enrollment No.   13574
Name of mother   Ellen Airington   a citizen of   Choctaw   Nation, final enrollment No.   602

Caddo, I.T.   Postoffice.

Applications for Enrollment of Choctaw Newborn
Act of 1905 Volume VII

AFFIDAVIT OF MOTHER

UNITED STATES OF AMERICA }
INDIAN TERRITORY }
DISTRICT Central

I Ellen Airington , on oath state that I am 22 years of age and a citizen by marriage of the Choctaw Nation, and as such have been placed upon the final roll of the Choctaw Nation, by the Honorable Secretary of the Interior my final enrollment number being 602 ; that I am the lawful wife of Noah Airington , who is a citizen of the Choctaw Nation, and as such has been placed upon the final roll of said Nation by the Honorable Secretary of the Interior, his final enrollment number being 13574 and that a Male child was born to me on the 9 day of February 190 5; that said child has been named Alvin Airington , and is now living.

WITNESSETH: Ellen Airington
Must be two witnesses { J.T. Jackson
who are citizens   { Lena Jackson

Subscribed and sworn to before me this, the 15 day of February , 190 5

J.T. Jackson
Notary Public.

My Commission Expires: April 19th 1907

Affidavit of Attending Physician or Midwife

UNITED STATES OF AMERICA, }
INDIAN TERRITORY, }
Central DISTRICT

I, H E Rappolee a Practicing Physician on oath state that I attended on Mrs. Ella[sic] Airington wife of Noah Airington on the 9th day of Feb , 190 5, that there was born to her on said date a male child, that said child is now living, and is said to have been named Alvin Airington

H E Rappolee M. D.

Subscribed and sworn to before me this the 16 day of February 1905

J.T. Jackson
Notary Public.

WITNESSETH:
Must be two witnesses { J.T. Jackson
who are citizens and {
know the child.   { Lena Jackson

Applications for Enrollment of Choctaw Newborn
Act of 1905   Volume VII

We hereby certify that we are well acquainted with   H.E. Rappolee a   Physician   and know   him   to be reputable and of good standing in the community.

Must be two citizen ⎰ J. T. Jackson
witnesses.   ⎱ Lena Jackson

BIRTH AFFIDAVIT.

DEPARTMENT OF THE INTERIOR.
COMMISSION TO THE FIVE CIVILIZED TRIBES.

IN RE APPLICATION FOR ENROLLMENT, as a citizen of the   Choctaw   Nation, of Alvin Airington   , born on the 9th   day of   Feb   , 1905

Name of Father: Noah Airington   a citizen of the   Choctaw   Nation.
Name of Mother: Ellen Airington   a citizen of the   Choctaw   Nation.

Postoffice   Caddo Indian Territory

AFFIDAVIT OF MOTHER.

UNITED STATES OF AMERICA, Indian Territory, ⎱
   Central   **DISTRICT.** ⎰

I,   Ellen Airington   , on oath state that I am   22   years of age and a citizen by   marriage   , of the   Choctaw   Nation; that I am the lawful wife of   Noah Airington   , who is a citizen, by blood   of the   Choctaw   Nation; that a male   child was born to me on   9th   day of   Feb.   , 1905; that said child has been named   Alvin Airington   , and was living March 4, 1905.

Ellen Airington

Witnesses To Mark:
{

Subscribed and sworn to before me this 25th   day of   March   , 1905

J L Rappolee
Notary Public.

Applications for Enrollment of Choctaw Newborn
Act of 1905 Volume VII

AFFIDAVIT OF ATTENDING PHYSICIAN OR MID-WIFE.

UNITED STATES OF AMERICA, Indian Territory, }
Central   DISTRICT.

I, H. E. Rappolee, a Physician, on oath state that I attended on Mrs. Ellen Airington, wife of Noah Airington on the 9th day of Feb, 1905; that there was born to her on said date a Male child; that said child was living March 4, 1905, and is said to have been named Alvin Airington

                                      H.E. Rappolee

Witnesses To Mark:
{

Subscribed and sworn to before me this 25th day of March, 1905

                                      J L Rappolee
                                      Notary Public.

Choc New Born 402
    Annie Marie Snow b. 10-29-04

BIRTH AFFIDAVIT.

DEPARTMENT OF THE INTERIOR.
COMMISSION TO THE FIVE CIVILIZED TRIBES.

IN RE APPLICATION FOR ENROLLMENT, as a citizen of the Choctaw Nation, of Annie Marie Snow, born on the 29th day of October, 1904

Name of Father: George Snow   a citizen of the ———Nation.
Name of Mother: Nancy C Snow (nee Moore)   a citizen of the Choctaw Nation.

                        Postoffice   Purcell Ind Ter

AFFIDAVIT OF MOTHER.

UNITED STATES OF AMERICA, Indian Territory, }
    Southern District   DISTRICT.

I, Nancy C Snow (nee Moore), on oath state that I am Twenty-two years of age and a citizen by Blood, of the Choctaw Nation; that I am the lawful

Applications for Enrollment of Choctaw Newborn
Act of 1905   Volume VII

wife of   George Snow   , who is a citizen, by   ———of the ——— Nation; that a female   child was born to me on   29th   day of   October   , 1904, that said child has been named   Annie Marie Snow   , and is now living.

Nancy C Snow (nee Moore)

Witnesses To Mark:

{

Subscribed and sworn to before me this   21st   day of   December   , 1904

B.H. Lane
Notary Public.

AFFIDAVIT OF ATTENDING PHYSICIAN OR MID-WIFE.

UNITED STATES OF AMERICA, Indian Territory,
Southern District   DISTRICT.

I,   JS Childs MD   , a   Physician   , on oath state that I attended on Mrs.   Nancy C Snow (nee Moore)   , wife of   George Snow   on the 29th   day of Oct , 1904; that there was born to her on said date a   Female   child; that said child is now living and is said to have been named Annie Maria Snow

JS Childs MD

Witnesses To Mark:

{

Subscribed and sworn to before me this   21st   day of   December   , 1904

B.H. Lane
Notary Public.

DEPARTMENT OF THE INTERIOR,
COMMISSION TO THE FIVE CIVILIZED TRIBES.
---o-o--

IN RE APPLICATION FOR ENROLLMENT, as a citizen of the Choctaw Nation, of Annie Marie Snow, born on the 29th day of October, 1904,
Name of Father: George Snow, a citizen of the United States.
Name of Mother: Nancy C. Snow (Enrolled as Nancy C. Moore), a citizen of the Choctaw Nation, now dead.
Postoffice of Husband, Purcell, Indian Territory.

---o-o--

Applications for Enrollment of Choctaw Newborn
Act of 1905 Volume VII

AFFIDAVIT OF SARAH E. SNOW AND KATIE CRAWFORD.

UNITED STATES OF AMERICA, |
INDIAN TERRITORY, | SS.
SOUTHERN DISTRICT. |

We, Sarah E. Snow and Katie Crawford, on oath state that we are 65 and 27 years of age respectively, and are each citizens of the United States; that we were well acquainted with Mrs. Nancy C. Snow, (Maiden name, Nancy C. Moore) and knew her to be the lawful wife of George Snow; that we are informed that the said Nancy C. Snow was a citizen by blood of the Choctaw Nation; that the said Nancy C. Snow died at Purcell, Indian Territory, January 31, 1905; that on the 29th day of October, 1904, a female child was born to the said Nancy C. Snow; that said child has been named Annie Marie Snow and was living March 4, 1905, and is now living with its father near Purcell, Indian Territory in the Chickasaw Nation, Indian Territory,; that we were each present on the date of the birth of said child and assisted in the tending of said Mrs. Nancy C. Snow, the wife of George Snow, and that Dr. J. S. Childs, or[sic] Purcell, Indian Territory, a regularly practicing physician was also in attendance on Mrs. Nancy C. Snow on the occasion of the birth of[sic] of said child.

Sarah E Snow
Katie Crawford

Witnesses to signature:
 JF Sharp
 George Snow

Subscribed and sworn to before me, this April 3, 1905.

O.H. Loomis
Notary Public, Ind. Ter., So. Dist.

---o-o---
AFFIDAVIT OF ATTENDING PHYSICIAN.

UNITED STATES OF AMERICA, |
INDIAN TERRITORY, | SS.
SOUTHERN DISTRICT. |

I, J. S. Childs, a Physician, on oath state that I attended on Mrs. Nancy C. Snow, wife of George Snow, on the 29th day of October, 1904; that there was born to her on said date a female child; that said child was living March 4, 1905, and is said to have been named Annie Marie Snow. Affiant further states that Mrs. Nancy C. Snow died Near Purcell, Indian Territory, on the 31st day of January, 1905, that I attended on deceased during her last illness and know her to be dead.

J.S. Childs MD

Applications for Enrollment of Choctaw Newborn
Act of 1905 Volume VII

Witnesses to Signature.
    JF Sharpe
    OH Loomis

Subscribed and sworn to before me this 3rd day of April, 1905.

                            OH Loomis
                        Notary Public, So. Dist. I. T.

N. B. 402

Muskogee, Indian Territory, April 7, 1905.

George Snow,
    Purcell, Indian Territory.

Dear Sir:

    There is inclosed you herewith for execution application for the enrollment of your infant child, Annie Marie Snow, born October 29, 1904.

    The affidavits heretofore filed with the Commission show the child was living on December 21, 1904. It is necessary, for the child to be enrolled, that she was living on March 4, 1905. You will please insert the mother's age in space left blank for that purpose.

    In having these affidavits executed care should be exercised to see that all names are written in full, as they appear in the body of the affidavit, and in the event that either of the persons signing the affidavit are unable to write, signatures by mark must be attested by two witnesses. Each affidavit must be executed before a Notary Public and the notarial seal and signature of the officer must be attached to each separate affidavit.

                            Respectfully,

LM 7-12   Commissioner in Charge.

Applications for Enrollment of Choctaw Newborn
Act of 1905   Volume VII

Choctaw 5387.

Muskogee, Indian Territory, April 10, 1905.

J. F. Sharp,
    Attorney at Law,
        Purcell, Indian Territory.

Dear Sir:

Receipt is hereby acknowledged of your letter of April 3, transmitting the affidavit of J. S. Childs and the joint affidavit of Sarah E. Snow and Katie Crawford to the birth of Annie Marie Snow, daughter of George and Nancy C. Snow, October 29, 1904, and the same have been filed with our records as an application for the enrollment of said child.

        Respectfully,

        Commissioner in Charge.

Choctaw N.B. 402.

Muskogee, Indian Territory, April 28, 1905.

J. F. Sharp, Indian Territory
    Attorney at Law,
        Purcell, Indian Territory.

Dear Sir:

Receipt is hereby acknowledged of your letter of April 24, relative to the application for the enrollment of Annie Marie Snow in which you ask if the affidvits recently forwarded by you are sufficient for the enrollment of this child or if it will be necessary for Mr. Snow to have the blank recently forwarded him from this office executed.

In reply to your letter you are advised that the affidavits heretofore forwarded by you in the matter of the enrollment of Annie Marie Snow are in proper form and it will not be necessary for Mr. Snow to have these forwarded with our letter of April 7 executed and returned to this office.

        Respectfully,

        Chairman.

Applications for Enrollment of Choctaw Newborn
Act of 1905 Volume VII

Choc New Born 403
Unis[sic] Fay Folsom   b. 4-27-03

BIRTH AFFIDAVIT.

DEPARTMENT OF THE INTERIOR,
COMMISSION TO THE FIVE CIVILIZED TRIBES.

In Re Application for Enrollment, as a citizen of the   Choctaw   Nation, of Unis Fay Folsom , born on the   27   day of April   , 1903

Name of Father: Walter Folsom   a citizen of the   Choctaw   Nation.
                                       intermarried
Name of Mother: Leora B. Folsom   a^citizen of the   Choctaw   Nation.

Post-office   Cowlington, Ind. Ter.

AFFIDAVIT OF MOTHER.

UNITED STATES OF AMERICA, }
  INDIAN TERRITORY,
  Central   District.

I, Leora B. Folsom , on oath state that I am   24   years of age and a citizen by marriage , of the   Choctaw   Nation; that I am the lawful wife of   Walter Folsom , who is a citizen, by Blood of the   Choctaw   Nation; that a   Female   child was born to me on 27 day of April , 1903, that said child has been named Unis Fay Folsom , and is now living.

Leora B Folsom

WITNESSES TO MARK:

Subscribed and sworn to before me this   2 day of June   , 1903

Francis D. Bush
NOTARY PUBLIC.

My term expires Feb. 13, 1906

Applications for Enrollment of Choctaw Newborn
Act of 1905   Volume VII

AFFIDAVIT OF ATTENDING PHYSICIAN OR MID-WIFE.

UNITED STATES OF AMERICA,
INDIAN TERRITORY,
Central   District.

I,   F.D. Bush   , a   physician   , on oath state that I attended on Mrs.   Leora B. Folsom , wife of   Walter Folsom   on the   27 day of April , 1903 ; that there was born to her on said date a   Female   child; that said child is now living and is said to have been named   Unis Fay Folsom

Francis D. Bush, M.D.

WITNESSES TO MARK:

Subscribed and sworn to before me this   3   day of   June   , 1903

(Name Illegible)
NOTARY PUBLIC.

Commission expires 8 day of February 1907

7-1043   7   13645
BIRTH AFFIDAVIT.

DEPARTMENT OF THE INTERIOR.
COMMISSION TO THE FIVE CIVILIZED TRIBES.

IN RE APPLICATION FOR ENROLLMENT, as a citizen of the   Choctaw   Nation, of   Unis Fay Folsom   , born on the   27   day of   April   , 1903

Name of Father: Walter W. Folsom   a citizen of the   Choctaw   Nation.
Name of Mother: Leora Folsom   a citizen of the   Choctaw   Nation.

Postoffice   Cowlington Ind Ter

AFFIDAVIT OF MOTHER.

UNITED STATES OF AMERICA, Indian Territory,
Central   DISTRICT.

I,   Leora Folsom   , on oath state that I am   26   years of age and a citizen by intermarriage   , of the   Choctaw   Nation; that I am the lawful wife of   Walter W Folsom   , who is a citizen, by   blood   of the   Choctaw   Nation; that a   female   child was born to me on 27th day of   April   , 1903; that said child has been named   Unis Fay Folsom   , and was living March 4, 1905.

166

Applications for Enrollment of Choctaw Newborn
Act of 1905 Volume VII

Leora Folsom

Witnesses To Mark:
{

Subscribed and sworn to before me this 10 day of April , 1905

My Commission James F. Bridges
expires 4-11-1908 Notary Public.

AFFIDAVIT OF ATTENDING PHYSICIAN OR MID-WIFE.

UNITED STATES OF AMERICA, Indian Territory,
  Central DISTRICT.

I, F.D. Bush , a physician , on oath state that I attended on Mrs. Leora Folsom , wife of Walter W. Folsom on the 27th day of April , 1903; that there was born to her on said date a female child; that said child was living March 4, 1905, and is said to have been named Unis Fay Folsom

F.D. Bush M.D

Witnesses To Mark:
{

Subscribed and sworn to before me this 10 day of April , 1905

My Commission James F. Bridges
expires 4-11-1908 Notary Public.

AFFIDAVIT OF ATTENDING PHYSICIAN OR MIDWIFE

UNITED STATES OF AMERICA
INDIAN TERRITORY
  Central DISTRICT

I, F.D. Bush, M.D. a Physician & Surgeon on oath state that I attended on Mrs. Leora Folsom wife of Walter W. Folsom on the 27 day of April , 190 3 , that there was born to her on said date a Female child, that said child is now living, and is said to have been named Unis Fay Folsom

F.D. Bush M.D.

Subscribed and sworn to before me this, the 1 day of February 190 5

My Commission expires James F. Bridges Notary Public.
4-11-1908.

Applications for Enrollment of Choctaw Newborn
Act of 1905 Volume VII

WITNESSETH:
Must be two witnesses { W W Folsom
who are citizens { Nathan Folsom

We hereby certify that we are well acquainted with Dr. F. D. Bush a Physician & Surgeon and know him to be reputable and of good standing in the community.

W.W. Folsom   P.O. Cowlington I.T.

Nathan Folsom   P.O. Cowlington I.T.

NEW-BORN AFFIDAVIT.

Number..................

...Choctaw Enrolling Commission...

IN THE MATTER OF THE APPLICATION FOR ENROLLMENT, as a citizen of the Choctaw Nation, of Unis Fay Folsom

born on the 27 day of __April__ 190 3

Name of father   Walter W. Folsom   a citizen of   Choctaw
Nation final enrollment No. 13645
Name of mother   Leora Folsom   a citizen of   Choctaw
Nation final enrollment No. 1043

Postoffice   Cowlington I.T.

AFFIDAVIT OF MOTHER.

UNITED STATES OF AMERICA
INDIAN TERRITORY
Central   DISTRICT

I Leora Folsom , on oath state that I am 26 years of age and a citizen by intermarriage of the Choctaw Nation, and as such have been placed upon the final roll of the Choctaw Nation, by the Honorable Secretary of the Interior my final enrollment number being 1043 ; that I am the lawful wife of Walter W Folsom , who is a citizen of the Choctaw Nation, and as such has been placed upon the final roll of said Nation by the Honorable Secretary of the Interior, his final enrollment number being 13645 and that a female child was born to me on the 27 day of April 190 3; that said child has been named Unis Fay Folsom , and is now living.

Applications for Enrollment of Choctaw Newborn
Act of 1905   Volume VII

Leora Folsom

Witnesseth.

Must be two } W W Folsom
Witnesses who
are Citizens.   Nathan Folsom

Subscribed and sworn to before me this   1   day of   Feb   190 5

James F. Bridges
Notary Public.

My commission expires: 4-11-1908

7-5390

Muskogee, Indian Territory, March 20, 1905.

Walter W. Folsom,
    Cowlington, Indian Territory.

Dear Sir:

    Receipt is hereby acknowledged of your letter of March 12, 1905, in which you state that you have forwarded affidavits to the birth of your daughter Eunus[sic] Fay Fulsom[sic], and you ask if this is all that is necessary or if you should make personal appearance in the matter of the enrollment of your child.

    In reply to your letter you are informed that the affidavits heretofore filed to the birth of Eunus Fay Fulsom daughter of Walter W. and Lenora[sic] Fulsom April 27, 1903, have been filed with our records as an application for the enrollment of said child, and it will not be necessary for you to appear in person before the Commission for the purpose of enrolling this child unless you so desire.

    In event further evidence is necessary to determine the right of your child to enrollment you will be duly notified.

Respectfully,

Chairman.

Applications for Enrollment of Choctaw Newborn
Act of 1905 Volume VII

N. B. 403

Muskogee, Indian Territory, April 7, 1905.

Walter W. Folsom,
Cowlington, Indian Territory.

Dear Sir:

There is inclosed you herewith for execution application for the enrollment of your infant child, Unis Fay Folsom, born April 27, 1903.

The affidavits heretofore filed with the Commission show the child was living on June 3, 1903. It is necessary, for the child to be enrolled, that he was living on March 4, 1905. You will please insert the age of the mother in space provided for the purpose.

In having these affidavits executed care should be exercised to see that all names are written in full, as they appear in the body of the affidavit, and in the event that either of the persons signing the affidavit are unable to write, signatures by mark must be attested by two witnesses. Each affidavit must be executed before a Notary Public and the notarial seal and signature of the officer must be attached to each separate affidavit.

Respectfully,

LM 7-11

Commissioner in Charge.

Choctaw 5390.

Muskogee, Indian Territory, April 15, 1905.

Walter W. Folsom,
Cowlington, Indian Territory.

Dear Sir:

Receipt is hereby acknowledged of the affidavits of Leora Folsom and F. D Bush to the birth of Unis Fay Folsom, daughter of Walter W. and Leora Folsom, April 27, 1903, and the same have been filed with our records as an application for the enrollment of said child.

Respectfully,

Chairman.

Applications for Enrollment of Choctaw Newborn
Act of 1905   Volume VII

Choc New Born 404
    Elizabeth Mary Burgevin   b. 3-8-04

Choctaw 5419

Muskogee, Indian Territory, March 30, 1905.

Josephine G. Burgevin,
    Box 54, Spiro, Indian Territory.

Dear Madam:

    Receipt is hereby acknowledged of your letter of March 25, inclosing affidavits of Josephine G. Burgevin and C. E. Jones to the birth of Elizabeth Mary Burgevin, daughter of Frances E. and Josephine G. Burgevin, March 8, 1904, and the same have been filed with our records as an application for the enrollment of said child.

Respectfully,

Chairman.

BIRTH AFFIDAVIT.

DEPARTMENT OF THE INTERIOR.
COMMISSION TO THE FIVE CIVILIZED TRIBES.

IN RE APPLICATION FOR ENROLLMENT, as a citizen of the Choctaw Nation, of Elizabeth Mary Burgevin, born on the 8th day of March, 1904

Name of Father: Frances E Burgevin   a citizen of the United States Nation.
Name of Mother: Josephine G. Burgevin   a citizen of the Choctaw Nation.

Postoffice   Spiro, Indian Territory

AFFIDAVIT OF MOTHER.

UNITED STATES OF AMERICA, Indian Territory,
    Central   DISTRICT.

    I, Josephine G. Burgevin, on oath state that I am 28 years of age and a citizen by Blood, of the Choctaw Nation; that I am the lawful wife of Frances E. Burgevin, who is a citizen, by .... of the United States Nation; that a female child was born to me on the 8th day of March, 1904, that said child has been named Elizabeth Mary Burgevin, and is now living.

Applications for Enrollment of Choctaw Newborn
Act of 1905   Volume VII

                                      Josephine G. Burgevin

Witnesses To Mark:
{

    Subscribed and sworn to before me this   25   day of   March   , 1905.

                                J. Wesley Smith

My Com Ex Oct 24, 1905   Notary Public.

AFFIDAVIT OF ATTENDING PHYSICIAN OR MID-WIFE.

State of Arkansas
~~UNITED STATES OF AMERICA, Indian Territory,~~
County of Washington   ~~DISTRICT.~~

    I,   C. E. Jones   , a   physician   , on oath state that I attended on Mrs.   Josephine G. Burgevin   , wife of   Frances E Burgevin   on the   8 day of March   , 1904; that there was born to her on said date a   female   child; that said child is now living and is said to have been named Elizabeth Mary Burgevin

                                  C.E. Jones M.D.

Witnesses To Mark:
{

    Subscribed and sworn to before me this 22th[sic] day of   March   , 1905.

                                  J.H. Smith
                                  Notary Public.

NEW-BORN AFFIDAVIT.

                Number..................

...Choctaw Enrolling Commission...

    IN THE MATTER OF THE APPLICATION FOR ENROLLMENT, as a citizen of the Choctaw   Nation, of   Elizabeth M. Burgevin

born on the   8th day of   March   190 4

Name of father   Francis[sic] E Burgevin   a citizen of   Choctaw
Nation final enrollment No. —
Name of mother   Josephine G. Burgevin   a citizen of   Choctaw
Nation final enrollment No. 13737

Applications for Enrollment of Choctaw Newborn
Act of 1905 Volume VII

Postoffice   Spiro, I.T.

AFFIDAVIT OF MOTHER.

UNITED STATES OF AMERICA
INDIAN TERRITORY
................................DISTRICT

I   Josephine G. Burgevin   , on oath state that I am 28 years of age and a citizen by blood of the Choctaw Nation, and as such have been placed upon the final roll of the Choctaw Nation, by the Honorable Secretary of the Interior my final enrollment number being   13737 ; that I am the lawful wife of   Francis[sic] E. Burgevin   , who is a citizen of the   U. S.   Nation, and as such has been placed upon the final roll of said Nation by the Honorable Secretary of the Interior, his final enrollment number being .... and that a   Female   child was born to me on the 8th day of   March   190 4; that said child has been named   Elizabeth M. Burgevin   , and is now living.

Witnesseth.   Josephine G Burgevin

Must be two Witnesses who are Citizens.   EO Moore

(Name Illegible)

Subscribed and sworn to before me this 9th day of   Jan   190 5

Edwin L Hickman
Notary Public.

My commission expires: February 19 1905

AFFIDAVIT OF ATTENDING PHYSICIAN OR MIDWIFE

UNITED STATES OF AMERICA
INDIAN TERRITORY
................................DISTRICT

I,   C.E. Jones   a   Physician   on oath state that I attended on Mrs.   Josephine G. Burgevin   wife of   Francis E Burgevin   on the 8th day of   March   , 190 4, that there was born to her on said date a   Female   child, that said child is now living, and is said to have been named   Elizabeth M. Burgevin

C. E. Jones MD

Subscribed and sworn to before me this, the 9th day of   Jan   190 5

(Name Illegible)   Notary Public.

WITNESSETH:
Must be two witnesses who are citizens   { EL Hickman
EA Moore

Applications for Enrollment of Choctaw Newborn
Act of 1905   Volume VII

We hereby certify that we are well acquainted with Dr C.E. Jones a Physician and know him to be reputable and of good standing in the community.

E L Hickman   *(Name Illegible)*

E A Moore   A J Moore

Choc New Born 405
    Alvin Floid Mullens   b. 5-3-04

Choctaw 5451

Muskogee, Indian Territory, March 30, 1905.

Jasper Mullens,
    Durant, Indian Territory.

Dear Sir:

    Receipt is hereby acknowledged of the affidavits of Tempy Mullens and Robt. A. Lively, to the birth of Alvin Floid Mullens, son of Jasper and Tempy Mullens, May 3, 1904, and the same have been filed with our records as an application for the enrollment of said child.

    Respectfully,

    Chairman.

BIRTH AFFIDAVIT.

DEPARTMENT OF THE INTERIOR.
COMMISSION TO THE FIVE CIVILIZED TRIBES.

IN RE APPLICATION FOR ENROLLMENT, as a citizen of the Choctaw Nation, of Alvin Floid Mullens, born on the 3rd day of May, 1904

Name of Father: Jasper Mullens   a citizen of the Intermarried Choctaw Nation.
Name of Mother: Tempy Mullens   a citizen of the Choctaw Nation.

    Postoffice   Durant, Indian Territory.

Applications for Enrollment of Choctaw Newborn
Act of 1905 Volume VII

AFFIDAVIT OF MOTHER.

UNITED STATES OF AMERICA, Indian Territory, }
Central DISTRICT. }

I, Tempy Mullens, on oath state that I am 25 years of age and a citizen by Blood, of the Chocktaw[sic] Nation; that I am the lawful wife of Jasper Mullens, ~~who is a citizen, by~~ Intermarried of the Chocktaw[sic] Nation; that a Male child was born to me on 3rd day of May, 1904; that said child has been named Alvin Floid Mullens, and was living March 4, 1905.

                                                Tempy Mullens

Witnesses To Mark:
{

Subscribed and sworn to before me this 25th day of March, 1905

Com Ex   Charles A Phillips
Feb 8th 1908   Notary Public.

AFFIDAVIT OF ATTENDING PHYSICIAN OR MID-WIFE.

UNITED STATES OF AMERICA, Indian Territory, }
Central DISTRICT. }

I, Robt A. Lively, a physician, on oath state that I attended on Mrs. Tempy Mullens, wife of Jasper Mullens on the 3rd day of May, 1904; that there was born to her on said date a Male child; that said child was living March 4, 1905, and is said to have been named Alvin Floid Mullens

                                            Robt A Lively MD

Witnesses To Mark:
{

Subscribed and sworn to before me this 25th day of March, 1905

Com Ex   Charles A Phillips
Feb 8th 1908   Notary Public.

Applications for Enrollment of Choctaw Newborn
Act of 1905 Volume VII

Choc New Born 406
    Jennette Sittel b. 11-8-03

7-5487

Muskogee, Indian Territory, March 31, 1905.

Fritz Sittel,
    Arpealer[sic], Indian Territory.

Dear Sir:

    Receipt is hereby acknowledged of the affidavits of Malvina Sittel and Hamer[sic] Johnson to the birth of Jennette Sittel daughter of Fritz and Malvina Sittel, November 8, 1903, and the same have been filed with our records as an application for the enrollment of said child.

    Respectfully,

    Chairman.

BIRTH AFFIDAVIT.
DEPARTMENT OF THE INTERIOR.
COMMISSION TO THE FIVE CIVILIZED TRIBES.

    IN RE APPLICATION FOR ENROLLMENT, as a citizen of the Choctaw Nation, of Jennette Sittel, born on the 8th day of November, 1903

Name of Father: Fritz Sittel   a citizen of the Choctaw Nation.
Name of Mother: Malvina Sittel   a citizen of the Choctaw Nation.

Postoffice   Arpelar, I.T.

AFFIDAVIT OF MOTHER.

UNITED STATES OF AMERICA, Indian Territory, ⎫
    Central   DISTRICT. ⎭

    I, Malvina Sittel, on oath state that I am 36 years of age and a citizen by blood, of the Choctaw Nation; that I am the lawful wife of Fritz Sittel, who is a citizen, by marriage of the Choctaw Nation; that a female child was born to me on 8th day of November, 1903; that said child has been named Jennette Sittel, and was living March 4, 1905.

    Malvina Sittel

Applications for Enrollment of Choctaw Newborn
Act of 1905 Volume VII

Witnesses To Mark:

Subscribed and sworn to before me this 20th day of March , 1905

Wirt Franklin
Notary Public.

AFFIDAVIT OF ATTENDING PHYSICIAN OR MID-WIFE.

UNITED STATES OF AMERICA, Indian Territory,
Central DISTRICT.

I, Harriet Johnson , a mid-wife , on oath state that I attended on Mrs. Malvina Sittel , wife of Fritz Sittel on the 8th day of November , 1903; that there was born to her on said date a female child; that said child was living March 4, 1905, and is said to have been named Jennette Sittel

Her
Harriet x Johnson
mark

Witnesses To Mark:
 Susie Anderson
 (Illegible) Cabell

Subscribed and sworn to before me this 25th day of March , 1905

E. Allan Boyd
Notary Public.

Choc New Born 407
 Cilliney Harlen b. 9-30-02

Applications for Enrollment of Choctaw Newborn
Act of 1905   Volume VII

7-2923
7-5513

Muskogee, Indian Territory, April 15, 1903.

Logan Harlen,
    Hartshorne, Indian Territory.

Dear Sir:

    Referring to the application for enrollment as a citizen of the Choctaw Nation of Cilliney Harlen, infant daughter of Logan and Sallie Harlen, born September 30, 1902, which was recently forwarded to this office; your attention is invited to section 28 of the act of Congress approved July 1, 1902, which was ratified by the citizens of the Choctaw and Chickasaw Nations September 25, 1902, as follows:

    "The names of all persons living on the date of the final ratification of this agreement entitled to be enrolled as provided in section 27 hereof shall be placed upon the rolls made by said Commission; and no child born thereafter to a citizen or freedman and no person intermarried thereafter to a citizen shall be entitled to enrollment or to participate in the distribution of the tribal property of the Choctaws and Chickasaws."

    Under the above legislation the Commission is without authority to enroll this child.

    Respectfully,

Chairman.

$W^m O.B.$

COMMISSIONERS:
TAMS BIXBY,
THOMAS B. NEEDLES,
C.R. BRECKINRIDGE.

DEPARTMENT OF THE INTERIOR,
COMMISSIONER TO THE FIVE CIVILIZED TRIBES.

REFER IN REPLY TO THE FOLLOWING:

N. B. 407

WM. O. BEALL
Secretary

ADDRESS ONLY THE
COMMISSION TO THE FIVE CIVILIZED TRIBES.

Muskogee, Indian Territory, April 7, 1905.

Logan Harlen,
    Hartshorne, Indian Territory.

Dear Sir:

    There is inclosed you herewith for execution application for the enrollment of your infant child, Cilliney Harlen, born September 30, 1902.

Applications for Enrollment of Choctaw Newborn
Act of 1905   Volume VII

The affidavits heretofore filed with the Commission show the child was living on April 10, 1903. It is necessary, for the child to be enrolled, that she was living on March 4, 1905. You will please insert the age of the mother in space provided for the purpose.

In having these affidavits executed care should be exercised to see that all names are written in full, as they appear in the body of the affidavit, and in the event that either of the persons signing the affidavit are unable to write, signatures by mark must be attested by two witnesses. Each affidavit must be executed before a Notary Public and the notarial seal and signature of the officer must be attached to each separate affidavit.

Respectfully,

LM 7-10

T.B. Needles
Commissioner in Charge.

(The above letter given again.)

7-5513

Muskogee, Indian Territory, May 2, 1905.

Logan Harlen,
    Wilburton, Indian Territory.

Dear Sir:

Receipt is hereby acknowledged of the affidavits of Sila[sic] Harlen and Mutsie[sic] Jones to the birth of Silany[sic] Harlen daughter of Logan and Sila Harlen, October 30, 1902, and the same have been filed with our records as an application for the enrollment of said child.

Respectfully,

Chairman.

Applications for Enrollment of Choctaw Newborn
Act of 1905   Volume VII

$W^m O.B.$

COMMISSIONERS:
TAMS BIXBY,
THOMAS B. NEEDLES,
C.R. BRECKINBRIDGE.

WM. O. BEALL
Secretary

DEPARTMENT OF THE INTERIOR,
COMMISSIONER TO THE FIVE CIVILIZED TRIBES.

REFER IN REPLY TO THE FOLLOWING:

7-NB-407.

ADDRESS ONLY THE
COMMISSION TO THE FIVE CIVILIZED TRIBES.

Muskogee, Indian Territory, May 24, 1905.

Logan Harlen,
    Wilburton, Indian Territory.

Dear Sir:

    There is enclosed you herewith for execution application for the enrollment of your infant child, Cilliney Harlen, born September 30, 1902.

    The affidavit of April 10, 1903, show that the child was living on that date, while those of April 19, 1905, state that the child is now living. For the child to be enrolled it is necessary that she was living on March 4, 1905. Please execute and return to this office the enclosed affidavits. If the applicant is dead you will please execute the enclosed proof of death, in order that this fact may be made a matter of record.

    In having these affidavits executed care should be exercised to see that all names are written in full, as they appear in the body of the affidavit, and in the event that either of the persons signing the affidavit are unable to write, signatures by mark must be attested by two witnesses. Each affidavit must be executed before a Notary Public and the notarial seal and signature of the officer must be attached to each separate affidavit.

    Respectfully,

Encl. D-C.
VR 24-2.

    Tams Bixby Chairman.

(The above letter given again.)

Applications for Enrollment of Choctaw Newborn
Act of 1905 Volume VII

7-N.B.407.

Muskogee, Indian Territory, June 5, 1905.

Logan Harlen,
    Wilburton, Indian Territory.

Dear Sir:

    Receipt is hereby acknowledged of the affidavits of Sila[sic] Harlen and Mulsie Jones to the birth of Cilliney Harlen, daughter of Logan and Sila[sic] Harlen, September 30, 1902, and the same have been filed with our records in the matter of the enrollment of said child.

Respectfully,

Commissioner in Charge.

BIRTH AFFIDAVIT.

DEPARTMENT OF THE INTERIOR.
COMMISSION TO THE FIVE CIVILIZED TRIBES.

IN RE APPLICATION FOR ENROLLMENT, as a citizen of the Choctaw Nation, of Cilliney Harlen, born on the 30th day of September, 1902

Name of Father: Logan Harlen   a citizen of the Choctaw Nation.
Name of Mother: Sila Harlen   a citizen of the Choctaw Nation.

Postoffice   Hartshorne Ind. Terr.

AFFIDAVIT OF MOTHER.

UNITED STATES OF AMERICA, Indian Territory,
.... DISTRICT.

    I, Sila Harlen, on oath state that I am .... years of age and a citizen by blood, of the Choctaw Nation; that I am the lawful wife of Logan Harlen, who is a citizen, by blood of the Choctaw Nation; that a female child was born to me on 30th day of September, 1902; that said child has been named Cilliney Harlen, and was living March 4, 1905.

Witnesses To Mark:

Applications for Enrollment of Choctaw Newborn
Act of 1905   Volume VII

Subscribed and sworn to before me this .... day of ...., 1905.

....
Notary Public.

_____

AFFIDAVIT OF ATTENDING PHYSICIAN OR MID-WIFE.

UNITED STATES OF AMERICA, Indian Territory, }
.... DISTRICT. }

  I, ..., a ...., on oath state that I attended on Mrs. Sila Harlen , wife of Logan Harlen on the 30th day of September , 1902; that there was born to her on said date a female child; that said child was living March 4, 1905, and is said to have been named Cilliney Harlen

Witnesses To Mark:
{ ....
  ....

Subscribed and sworn to before me this .... day of ...., 1905.

....
Notary Public.

_____

BIRTH AFFIDAVIT.

DEPARTMENT OF THE INTERIOR,
COMMISSION TO THE FIVE CIVILIZED TRIBES.

_____

  IN RE Application for Enrollment, as a citizen of the Choctaw Nation, of Cilliney Harlin[sic] , born on the 30th day of September , 1902

Name of Father: Logan Harlin   a citizen of the Choctaw Nation.
Name of Mother: Sallie Harlin   a citizen of the Choctaw Nation.

     Post-Office: Hartshorne, Ind. Ter.

_____

Applications for Enrollment of Choctaw Newborn
Act of 1905   Volume VII

AFFIDAVIT OF MOTHER.

UNITED STATES OF AMERICA,
   INDIAN TERRITORY.
   Central   District.

I, Sallie Harlin, on oath state that I am about 30 years of age and a citizen by blood, of the Choctaw Nation; that I am the lawful wife of Logan Harlin, who is a citizen, by blood of the Choctaw Nation; that a girl child was born to me on 30th day of September, 1902, that said child has been named Cilliney Harlin, and is now living.

                                            her
                                      Sallie x Harlin
WITNESSES TO MARK: mark
   { Alfred Seeley
     Lon Novick

Subscribed and sworn to before me this 10th *day of* April, *1903*

                                 Wm J. Hulsey, Mayor
                                    NOTARY PUBLIC.
                                 Hartshorne Ind. Ter.

AFFIDAVIT OF ATTENDING PHYSICIAN OR MID-WIFE.

UNITED STATES OF AMERICA,
   INDIAN TERRITORY.
   Central   District.

I, Betsy Foster, a midwife, on oath state that I attended on Mrs. Sallie Harlin, wife of Logan Harlin on the 30th day of September, 1902; that there was born to her on said date a female child; that said child is now living and is said to have been named Cilliney Harlin

                                          her
                                    Betsy x Foster
WITNESSES TO MARK: mark
   { Alfred Seeley
     Lon Novick

Subscribed and sworn to before me this 10th *day of* April, *1903*

                                 Wm J. Hulsey, Mayor
                                    NOTARY PUBLIC.
                                 Hartshorne Ind. Ter.

Applications for Enrollment of Choctaw Newborn
Act of 1905   Volume VII

BIRTH AFFIDAVIT.

DEPARTMENT OF THE INTERIOR.
COMMISSION TO THE FIVE CIVILIZED TRIBES.

IN RE APPLICATION FOR ENROLLMENT, as a citizen of the   Choctaw   Nation, of Silaney[sic] Harlen   , born on the   30   day of   October[sic]   , 1902

Name of Father: Logan Harlen   a citizen of the   Choctaw   Nation.
Name of Mother: Sila Harlen   a citizen of the   Chickasaw   Nation.

Postoffice   Wilburton

AFFIDAVIT OF MOTHER.

UNITED STATES OF AMERICA, Indian Territory, }
      Central   DISTRICT.

I, Sila Harlen   , on oath state that I am   40   years of age and a citizen by blood   , of the   Chickasaw   Nation; that I am the lawful wife of   Logan Harlen , who is a citizen, by   blood   of the   Choctaw   Nation; that a   Female   child was born to me on   30   day of   October   , 1902, that said child has been named   Silaney Harlen   , and is ~~now~~ not living. Died on 8th March 1905

                                             her
                                     Sila x Harlen
Witnesses To Mark: mark
  { W.N. Nicholas
  { Sikey Jefferson

Subscribed and sworn to before me this   19   day of   April   , 1905.

My Com expires 1/11/1909   Chas H Hudson
                                      Notary Public.

AFFIDAVIT OF ATTENDING PHYSICIAN OR MID-WIFE.

UNITED STATES OF AMERICA, Indian Territory, }
      Central   DISTRICT.

I,   Mutsie Jones   , a   mid-wife   , on oath state that I attended on Mrs.   Sila Harlen   , wife of   Logan Harlen   on the   30   day of October , 1902; that there was born to her on said date a   Female   child; that said child is ~~now living~~ not living and is said to have been named   Silaney Harlen

                                             her
                                    Mutsie x Jones
                                        mark

184

Applications for Enrollment of Choctaw Newborn
Act of 1905   Volume VII

Witnesses To Mark:
{ W.N. Nicholas
{ Sikey Jefferson

Subscribed and sworn to before me this 19 day of April, 1905.

Chas H Hudson
Notary Public.

Com expires 1/11/1909

BIRTH AFFIDAVIT.
DEPARTMENT OF THE INTERIOR.
COMMISSION TO THE FIVE CIVILIZED TRIBES.

IN RE APPLICATION FOR ENROLLMENT, as a citizen of the Choctaw Nation, of Cilliney Harlen, born on the 30 day of Sept, 1902

Name of Father: Logan Harlan[sic]   a citizen of the Choctaw Nation.
Name of Mother: Sila Harlan   a citizen of the Choctaw Nation.

Postoffice   Wilburton, I.T.

AFFIDAVIT OF MOTHER.

UNITED STATES OF AMERICA, Indian Territory, }
    Central   DISTRICT.   }

I, Sila Harlen, on oath state that I am 40 years of age and a citizen by blood, of the ~~Choctaw~~ Chickasaw Nation; that I am the lawful wife of Logan Harlan, who is a citizen, by blood of the Choctaw Nation; that a female child was born to me on 30 day of September, 1902; that said child has been named Cilliney Harlen, and was living March 4, 1905.

                                    her
                              Sila x Harlan
Witnesses To Mark: mark
{ (Name Illegible) }
{ Clifford Perry   }   Wilburton I.T.

Subscribed and sworn to before me this 2nd day of June, 1905

Chas. H. Hudson
Notary Public.

Applications for Enrollment of Choctaw Newborn
Act of 1905 Volume VII

AFFIDAVIT OF ATTENDING PHYSICIAN OR MID-WIFE.

UNITED STATES OF AMERICA, Indian Territory,
Central DISTRICT.

I, Mulsie Jones, a Midwife, on oath state that I attended on Mrs. Sila Harlen, wife of Logan Harlan on the 30 day of September, 1902; that there was born to her on said date a female child; that said child was living March 4, 1905, and is said to have been named Cilliney Harlen

                                            her
Witnesses To Mark: Mulsie x Jones
  (Name Illegible)   mark
  Clifford Perry   Wilburton I.T.

Subscribed and sworn to before me this 2nd day of June, 1905

                              Chas. H. Hudson
                              Notary Public.

Choc New Born 408
    Dora Elizabeth Griggs b. 3-4-04

BIRTH AFFIDAVIT.

DEPARTMENT OF THE INTERIOR.
COMMISSION TO THE FIVE CIVILIZED TRIBES.

IN RE APPLICATION FOR ENROLLMENT, as a citizen of the Choctaw Nation, of Dora Elizabeth Griggs, born on the 4" day of March, 1904

Name of Father: Willy Griggs   a citizen of the Choctaw Nation.
Name of Mother: Mary Griggs   a citizen of the Choctaw Nation.

                    Postoffice   Nelson Ind. Ter

Applications for Enrollment of Choctaw Newborn
Act of 1905   Volume VII

AFFIDAVIT OF MOTHER.

UNITED STATES OF AMERICA, Indian Territory, }
Central   DISTRICT.

    I, Mary Griggs, on oath state that I am 31 years of age and a citizen by Blood, of the Choctaw Nation; that I am the lawful wife of Willy Griggs, who is a citizen, by Blood of the Choctaw Nation; that a Female child was born to me on 4" day of March, 1904; that said child has been named Dora Elizabeth Griggs, and was living March 4, 1905.

                                Mary Griggs

Witnesses To Mark:
{

    Subscribed and sworn to before me this 20th day of April, 1905

My Commission expires   W.E. Larecy
July 9th 1908   Notary Public.

AFFIDAVIT OF ATTENDING PHYSICIAN OR MID-WIFE.

UNITED STATES OF AMERICA, Indian Territory, }
Central   DISTRICT.

    I, Vinn Colbert, a Midwife, on oath state that I attended on Mrs. Mary Griggs, wife of Willy Griggs on the 4" day of March, 1904; that there was born to her on said date a Female child; that said child was living March 4, 1905, and is said to have been named Dora Elizabeth Griggs

                              her
                          Vinn x Colbert
Witnesses To Mark: mark
  { Ida Williams
    Henry Williams

    Subscribed and sworn to before me this 20th day of April, 1905

My Commission expires   W.E. Larecy
July 9th 1908   Notary Public.

Applications for Enrollment of Choctaw Newborn
Act of 1905   Volume VII

N. B. 408

Muskogee, Indian Territory, April 10, 1905.

Willy Griggs,
    Nelson, Indian Territory.

Dear Sir:

    There is inclosed you herewith for execution application for the enrollment of your infant child, Dora Elizabeth Griggs, born March 4, 1904.

    The affidavits heretofore filed with the Commission show the child was living on October 17, 1904. It is necessary, for the child to be enrolled, that she was living on March 4, 1905. You will please insert the mother's age in the place left blank for that purpose.

    In having these affidavits executed care should be exercised to see that all names are written in full, as they appear in the body of the affidavit, and in the event that either of the persons signing the affidavit are unable to write, signatures by mark must be attested by two witnesses. Each affidavit must be executed before a Notary Public and the notarial seal and signature of the officer must be attached to each separate affidavit.

Respectfully,

SEV 6-10.   Commissioner in Charge.

7-NB-408.

Muskogee, Indian Territory, April 25, 1905.

Willy Griggs,
    Nelson, Indian Territory.

Dear Sir:

    Receipt is hereby acknowledged of the affidavits of Mary Griggs and Vinn Colbert, to the birth of Dora Elizabeth Griggs, child of Willy and Mary Griggs, March 4, 1904, and the same have been filed with our records in the matter of the enrollment of said child.

Respectfully,

Chairman.

Applications for Enrollment of Choctaw Newborn
Act of 1905   Volume VII

7 NB 408

Muskogee, Indian Territory, June 19, 1905.

Willie[sic] Griggs,
    Nelson, Indian Territory.

Dear Sir:

    Receipt is hereby acknowledged of your letter of June 9, 1905, stating that your[sic] made application for the enrollment of your daughter Dora Elizabeth Griggs and you wish to know if you will be notified when she is approved or if you can file for her now.

    In reply to your letter you are advised that the name of your daughter Dora Elizabeth Griggs has been placed upon a schedule of citizens by blood of the Choctaw Nation prepared for forwarding to the Secretary of the Interior, but her enrollment has not yet been approved by him. You will be notified when her enrollment is approved, but until such time as the Secretary of the Interior approves her enrollment no selection of allotment can be made in her behalf.

                  Respectfully,

                                          Chairman.

BIRTH AFFIDAVIT.

DEPARTMENT OF THE INTERIOR.
COMMISSION TO THE FIVE CIVILIZED TRIBES.

    IN RE APPLICATION FOR ENROLLMENT, as a citizen of the   Choctaw   Nation, of Dora Elizabeth Griggs   , born on the   4   day of March , 1904

Name of Father: Willy Griggs   a citizen of the   Choctaw   Nation.
Name of Mother: Mary Griggs   a citizen of the   Choctaw   Nation.

                    Postoffice   Nelson IT

AFFIDAVIT OF MOTHER.

UNITED STATES OF AMERICA, Indian Territory, ⎫
    Central   **DISTRICT.** ⎭

    I,   Mary Griggs   , on oath state that I am   30   years of age and a citizen by Blood   , of the   Choctaw   Nation; that I am the lawful wife of   Willy Griggs ,

Applications for Enrollment of Choctaw Newborn
Act of 1905   Volume VII

who is a citizen, by   Blood   of the   Choctaw   Nation; that a   Girl   child was born to me on   4   day of   March   , 1904, that said child has been named   Dora Elizabeth Griggs   , and is now living.

                                          Mary Griggs

Witnesses To Mark:
{

Subscribed and sworn to before me this   17   day of   Oct   , 1904

                                          Thos E Oakes
                                          Notary Public.

AFFIDAVIT OF ATTENDING PHYSICIAN OR MID-WIFE.

UNITED STATES OF AMERICA, Indian Territory, }
    Central   DISTRICT. }

I,   Vinn Colbert   , a   Midwife   , on oath state that I attended on Mrs. Mary Griggs   , wife of   Willy Griggs   on the   4   day of   March , 1904; that there was born to her on said date a   girl   child; that said child is now living and is said to have been named Dora Elizabeth Griggs

                                         her
                                    Vinn x Colbert

Witnesses To Mark: mark
{ Henry Williams
  Ida Williams

Subscribed and sworn to before me this   17   day of   Oct   , 1904

                                     Thos E Oakes
                                       Notary Public.

Applications for Enrollment of Choctaw Newborn
Act of 1905 Volume VII

NEW-BORN AFFIDAVIT.

Number..................

Choctaw Enrolling Commission.

IN THE MATTER OF THE APPLICATION FOR ENROLLMENT, as a citizen of the Choctaw Nation, of Dora E Griggs

born on the 4 day of March 190 4

Name of father   Willy Griggs   a citizen of   Choctaw
Nation final enrollment No   14010
Name of mother   Mary Griggs   a citizen of   Choctaw
Nation final enrollment No   14011

Postoffice   Nelson

AFFIDAVIT OF MOTHER.

UNITED STATES OF AMERICA,
INDIAN TERRITORY,
Central   DISTRICT

I   Mary Griggs   on oath state that I am   31 years of age and a citizen by   Blood   of the   Choctaw   Nation, and as such have been placed upon the final roll of the   Choctaw   Nation, by the Honorable Secretary of the Interior my final enrollment number being   14011   ; that I am the lawful wife of Willy Griggs   , who is a citizen of the   Choctaw   Nation, and as such has been placed upon the final roll of said Nation by the Honorable Secretary of the Interior, his final enrollment number being   14010   and that a   Female   child was born to me on the 4   day of   March   190 4 ; that said child has been named   Dora E. Griggs   , and is now living.

WITNESSETH: Mary Griggs
Must be two ⎫ Henry Williams
Witnesses who ⎬
are Citizens. ⎭ John D McKee

Subscribed and sworn to before me this   23   day of   Jan   190 5

My commission expires
July 9th 1908   WE Larecy
                                   Notary Public.
My commission expires

Applications for Enrollment of Choctaw Newborn
Act of 1905   Volume VII

Affidavit of Attending Physician or Midwife

UNITED STATES OF AMERICA, }
INDIAN TERRITORY,
Central   DISTRICT

I, Vinn Colbert a mid-wife on oath state that I attended on Mrs. Mary Griggs wife of Willy Griggs on the 4 day of March , 190 4, that there was born to her on said date a Female child, that said child is now living, and is said to have been named Dora E. Griggs

                    her
                Vinn x Colbert   M. D.
                  mark

Subscribed and sworn to before me this the 23 day of Jan 1905

My commission expires
July 9th 1908

WE Larecy
    Notary Public.

WITNESSETH:

Must be two witnesses who are citizens and know the child. { Henry Williams
John D McKee

We hereby certify that we are well acquainted with Vinn Colbert a Mid-wife and know her to be reputable and of good standing in the community.

Must be two citizen witnesses. { Thomas Ashford
Mary A. McKee

Choc New Born 409
    Nora A. Renick b. 9-4-04

BIRTH AFFIDAVIT.

DEPARTMENT OF THE INTERIOR.
COMMISSION TO THE FIVE CIVILIZED TRIBES.

IN RE APPLICATION FOR ENROLLMENT, as a citizen of the Choctaw Nation, of Nora A Renick , born on the 4 day of Sep , 1904

Name of Father: M.A. Renick a citizen of the .... Nation.
Name of Mother: Ella Renick a citizen of the Choctaw Nation.

Applications for Enrollment of Choctaw Newborn
Act of 1905   Volume VII

Postoffice   Abner I.T.

AFFIDAVIT OF MOTHER.

UNITED STATES OF AMERICA, Indian Territory,
Southern   DISTRICT.

I, Ella Renick, on oath state that I am 26 years of age and a citizen by birth, of the Choctaw Nation; that I am the lawful wife of M.A. Renick, who is a citizen, by Marriage of the Choctaw Nation; that a Female child was born to me on 4 day of Sept, 1904; that said child has been named Nora A Renick, and was living March 4, 1905.

Ella Renick

Witnesses To Mark:
{ John CHowell
  Delia Hammond

Subscribed and sworn to before me this 24 day of March, 1905

E.S. Hammond
Notary Public.

AFFIDAVIT OF ATTENDING PHYSICIAN OR MID-WIFE.

UNITED STATES OF AMERICA, Indian Territory,
Southern   DISTRICT.

I, W.M. Kearney, a Physician, on oath state that I attended on Mrs. Ella Renick, wife of M.A. Renick on the 4 day of Sept, 1904; that there was born to her on said date a female child; that said child was living March 4, 1905, and is said to have been named Nora A Renick

W.M. Kearney M.D.

Witnesses To Mark:
{ John C Howell
  Delia Hammond

Subscribed and sworn to before me this 24 day of Sept, 1905

E.S. Hammond
Notary Public.

Applications for Enrollment of Choctaw Newborn
Act of 1905   Volume VII

BIRTH AFFIDAVIT.

DEPARTMENT OF THE INTERIOR.
COMMISSION TO THE FIVE CIVILIZED TRIBES.

IN RE APPLICATION FOR ENROLLMENT, as a citizen of the Choctaw Nation, of Nora A Renick, born on the 4th day of September, 1904

Name of Father: M.A. Renick   a citizen of the U.S. Nation.
Name of Mother: Ella Renick   a citizen of the Choctaw Nation.

Postoffice   Abner I.T.

AFFIDAVIT OF MOTHER.

UNITED STATES OF AMERICA, Indian Territory,
Southern DISTRICT.

I, Ella Renick, on oath state that I am 26 years of age and a citizen by Blood, of the Choctaw Nation; that I am the lawful wife of M.A. Renick, who is a citizen, by ——— of the United States Nation; that a Female child was born to me on 4th day of September, 1904; that said child has been named Nora A Renick, and was living March 4, 1905.

Ella Renick

Witnesses To Mark:
{ W~~m Kearney M.D.~~
  Delia Hammond
J.C. Luttrell
Subscribed and sworn to before me this 30 day of May, 1905.

E.S. Hammond
Notary Public.

AFFIDAVIT OF ATTENDING PHYSICIAN OR MID-WIFE.

UNITED STATES OF AMERICA, Indian Territory,
Southern DISTRICT.

I, W.M. Kearney, a Physician, on oath state that I attended on Mrs. Ella Renick, wife of M.A. Renick on the 4 day of Sept, 1904; that there was born to her on said date a female child; that said child was living March 4, 1905, and is said to have been named Nora A Renick

~~Ella Renick~~
W.M. Kearney M.D.

Applications for Enrollment of Choctaw Newborn
Act of 1905 Volume VII

Witnesses To Mark:
{ ~~Wm Kearney MD~~
{ Delia Hammond
J.C. Luttrell

Subscribed and sworn to before me this 30 day of May, 1905

E.S. Hammond
Notary Public.

CERTIFICATE OF RECORD OF MARRIAGE

UNITED STATES OF AMERICA,
  INDIAN TERRITORY, } sct.
    SOUTHERN DISTRICT.

I, C. M. CAMPBELL, Clerk of the United States Court, in the Territory and District aforesaid Do HEREBY CERTIFY, that the License for and Certificate of Marriage of

MR M.A. Renick   and

M Ella Shipman

were filed in my office in said Territory and District the 28 day of Jan A.D., 190 4 and duly recorded in Book G of Marriage Record, Page 516

WITNESS my hand and Seal of said Court, at Ardmore, this 28 day of Jan A.D. 190 4

C. M. Campbell
CLERK.

Return this License to the United States Clerk at Ardmore, that it may be recorded, when it will be mailed to the proper address.

Applications for Enrollment of Choctaw Newborn
Act of 1905   Volume VII

No person is authorized to perform the Marriage Ceremony in the Indian Territory unless the proper credentials have first been recorded in the Clerk's office.

MARRIAGE LICENSE.

No. _____

United States of America
Indian Territory, } ss   To Any Person Authorized by Law to
Southern District.   Solemnize Marriage, Greeting:

You are hereby Commanded to solemnize the Rite and publish the Banns of Matrimony between Mr. M. A. Renick of Abner in the Indian Territory, aged 22 years, and Miss Ella Shipman of Abner in the Indian Territory, aged 24 years, according to law; and do you officially sign and return this license to the parties therein named.

Witness my hand and official Seal, this 24 day of November A. D. 190 3

C. M. Campbell
Clerk of the United States Court.

Certificate of Marriage.

United States of America
Indian Territory, } ss
Southern District.   I,   J. T. Whitington

do hereby certify that on the 27 day of November A. D. 190 3, I did duly and according to law, as commanded in the foregoing License, solemnize the Rite and publish the Banns of Matrimony between the parties therein named.

Witness my hand this 27 day of November A. D. 190 3

My credentials are recorded in the office of the Clerk of the United States Court, Indian Territory, Southern District, at Ardmore, Book A , Page 196

Eld. J.T. Whitington

NOTE. (a)- This License and Certificate of Marriages must be returned to the office of the Clerk of the United States Court in the Indian Territory, at Ardmore, within sixty days from the date thereof, or the party to whom the License was issued will be liable in the amount of ONE HUNDRED DOLLARS ($100).

Applications for Enrollment of Choctaw Newborn
Act of 1905   Volume VII

7-NB-409.

Muskogee, Indian Territory, May 25, 1905.

M. A. Renick,
    Abner, Indian Territory.

Dear Sir:

    There is enclosed you herewith for execution application for the enrollment of your infant child, Nora A. Renick, born September 4, 1904.

    In the application heretofore filed in this office it appears that the physician's affidavit was executed on September 24, 1905. This is apparently an error, and it will be necessary that you have the enclosed application executed.

    In having these affidavits executed care should be exercised to see that all names are written in full, as they appear in the body of the affidavit, and in the event that either of the persons signing the affidavit are unable to write, signatures by mark must be attested by two witnesses. Each affidavit must be executed before a Notary Public and the notarial seal and signature of the officer must be attached to each separate affidavit.

    Respectfully,

VR 25-7.   Chairman.

7-N.B. 409.

Muskogee, Indian Territory, June 5, 1905.

M. A. Renick,
    Abner, Indian Territory.

Dear Sir:

    Receipt is hereby acknowledged of the affidavits of Ella Renick and W. M. Kearney to the birth of Nora A. Renick, daughter of M. A. and Ella Renick, September 4, 1904, and the same have been filed with our records in the matter of the enrollment of said child.

    Respectfully,

                                                      Commissioner in Charge.

Applications for Enrollment of Choctaw Newborn
Act of 1905   Volume VII

Choc New Born 410
    Margaret Chivers   b. 5-22-04

7-5559

Muskogee, Indian Territory, March 31, 1905.

Edgar J. Chivers,
    Daneville[sic], Indian Territory.

    Receipt is hereby acknowledged of the affidavits of Maud A. Chivers and S. A. Heflin to the birth of Margaret Chivers, daughter of Edgar Eynon and Maud A. Chivers, May 22, 1904, and the ssame have been filed with our records as an application for the enrollment of said child.

        Respectfully,

        Chairman.

BIRTH AFFIDAVIT.

DEPARTMENT OF THE INTERIOR.
COMMISSION TO THE FIVE CIVILIZED TRIBES.

    IN RE APPLICATION FOR ENROLLMENT, as a citizen of the   Choctaw   Nation, of Margaret Chivers   , born on the 22   day of   May , 1904

Name of Father: Edgar Eynon Chivers   a citizen of the   Choctaw   Nation.
Name of Mother: Maud A Chivers   a citizen of the   Choctaw   Nation.

        Postoffice   Mannsville, I.T.

AFFIDAVIT OF MOTHER.

UNITED STATES OF AMERICA, Indian Territory,
....DISTRICT.

    I,   Maud A Chivers   , on oath state that I am   28   years of age and a citizen by   Blood   , of the   Choctaw   Nation; that I am the lawful wife of   Edgar E. Chivers , who is a citizen, by marriage   of the   Choctaw   Nation; that a female   child was born to me on 22nd day of   May   , 1904; that said child has been named   Margaret Chivers   , and was living March 4, 1905.

        Maud A Chivers

Witnesses To Mark:

Applications for Enrollment of Choctaw Newborn
Act of 1905   Volume VII

Subscribed and sworn to before me this 25   day of   Mch   , 1905

Thos J White
Notary Public.

AFFIDAVIT OF ATTENDING PHYSICIAN OR MID-WIFE.

UNITED STATES OF AMERICA, Indian Territory, }
....DISTRICT. }

I,   S. A. Heflin   , a   Physician   , on oath state that I attended on Mrs. E. E. Chivers   , wife of   Edgar E Chivers   on the 22nd day of May , 1904; that there was born to her on said date a   female   child; that said child was living March 4, 1905, and is said to have been named Margaret Chivers

S.A. Heflin

Witnesses To Mark:
{

Subscribed and sworn to before me this 25th day of   Mch   , 1905

Thos J White
Notary Public.

Choc New Born 411
   Sampson Francis McCann   b. 4-20-04

Choctaw N.B. 412[sic]

Muskogee, Indian Territory, April 22, 1905.

Austin McCann,
   Cowlington, Indian Territory.

Dear Sir:

Receipt is hereby acknowledged of the affidavits of Alice McCann and Francis D. Bush to the birth of Samson[sic] Francis McCann, son of Austin and Alice McCann, April 20, 1904, and the same are returned you herewith for the reason that the Notary Public before whom the affidavit of the physician was executed has failed to affix his seal thereto.

Applications for Enrollment of Choctaw Newborn
Act of 1905   Volume VII

You are requested to have this seal affixed at once and the affidavits returned to the Commission.

Respectfully,

Chairman.

LM-8-24

$W^m O.B.$

COMMISSIONERS:
TAMS BIXBY,
THOMAS B. NEEDLES,
C.R. BRECKINBRIDGE.

DEPARTMENT OF THE INTERIOR,
COMMISSIONER TO THE FIVE CIVILIZED TRIBES.

REFER IN REPLY TO THE FOLLOWING:

Choctaw N.B. 412[sic]

WM. O. BEALL
Secretary

ADDRESS ONLY THE
COMMISSION TO THE FIVE CIVILIZED TRIBES.

Muskogee, Indian Territory, April 22, 1905.

Austin McCann,
    Cowlington, Indian Territory.

Dear Sir:

    Receipt is hereby acknowledged of the affidavits of Alice McCann and Francis D. Bush to the birth of Samson[sic] Francis McCann, son of Austin and Alice McCann, April 20, 1904, and the same are returned you herewith for the reason that the Notary Public before whom the affidavit of the physician was executed has failed to affix his seal thereto.

    You are requested to have this seal affixed at once and the affidavits returned to the Commission.

Respectfully,

Tams Bixby
Chairman.

LM-8-24

Applications for Enrollment of Choctaw Newborn
Act of 1905   Volume VII

7 N B 412[sic]

Muskogee, Indian Territory, April 17, 1905.

O. L. Johnson,
    Wister, Indian Territory.

Dear Sir:

    There is inclosed you herewith the application for the enrollment of Sampson Francis McCann, infant child of Austin and Alice McCann. You will notice that you failed to attach your seal to the mother's affidavit. After doing so you will please return same to this office at the earliest practicable date.

Respectfully,

LM 17-110   Chairman.

Choctaw 5585.

Muskogee, Indian Territory, April 12, 1905.

Austin McCann,
    Cowlington, Indian Territory.

Dear Sir:

    Receipt is hereby acknowledged of the affidavits of Alice McCann and F. D. Bush to the birth of Sampson Francis McCann, daughter of Austin and Alice McCann, April 20, 1904, and the same have been filed with our records as an application for the enrollment of said child.

Respectfully,

Commissioner in Charge.

Applications for Enrollment of Choctaw Newborn
Act of 1905   Volume VII

N. B. 412

Muskogee, Indian Territory, April 8, 1905.

Austin McCann,
    Cowlington, Indian Territory.

Dear Sir:

    There is inclosed you herewith for execution application for the enrollment of your infant child, Samson[sic] Francis McCann, born April 20, 1904.

    The affidavits heretofore filed with the Commission show the child was living on August 9, 1904. It is necessary, for the child to be enrolled, that he was living on March 4, 1905. Please insert mother's age in space provided for the purpose.

    In having these affidavits executed care should be exercised to see that all names are written in full, as they appear in the body of the affidavit, and in the event that either of the persons signing the affidavit are unable to write, signatures by mark must be attested by two witnesses. Each affidavit must be executed before a Notary Public and the notarial seal and signature of the officer must be attached to each separate affidavit.

Respectfully,

LM 8-24   Commissioner in Charge.

(The letter below does not belong with the current applicant.)

9-NB-412[sic]

Muskogee, Indian Territory, July 25, 1905.

Thomas M. Randolph,
    Marietta, Indian Territory.

Dear Sir:

    Receipt is hereby acknowledged of your affidavit and the affidavit of Nellie P. Randolph and Dr. W. V. Batson to the birth of Maude Elizabeth Randolph, daughter of Thomas M. and Nellie P. Randolph, February 21, 1905, and the same have been filed with the records of this office in the matter of the enrollment of said child.

Respectfully,

Commissioner.

Applications for Enrollment of Choctaw Newborn
Act of 1905 Volume VII

BIRTH AFFIDAVIT.

DEPARTMENT OF THE INTERIOR,
COMMISSION TO THE FIVE CIVILIZED TRIBES.

In Re Application for Enrollment, as a citizen of the Choctaw Nation, of Samson Francis McCann , born on the 20 day of April , 1904

Name of Father: Austin McCann   a citizen of the Choctaw Nation.
Name of Mother: Alice McCann   a citizen of the Choctaw Nation.

Post-office   Cowlington

AFFIDAVIT OF MOTHER.

UNITED STATES OF AMERICA, }
  INDIAN TERRITORY,
  Central   District.

    I, Alice McCann , on oath state that I am 27 years of age and a citizen by marriage , of the Choctaw Nation; that I am the lawful wife of Austin McCann , who is a citizen, by blood of the Choctaw Nation; that a male child was born to me on 20 day of April , 190 4, that said child has been named Samson Francis McCann , and is now living.

                                                  her
                                    Alice x McCann
WITNESSES TO MARK: mark
  { Ida Crouthamel
    Virtie Callicoatt

    Subscribed and sworn to before me this 9 day of August , 1904

                                  A.H. Crouthamel
                                      NOTARY PUBLIC.
My Commission expires Feb 3 1907

AFFIDAVIT OF ATTENDING PHYSICIAN OR MID-WIFE.

UNITED STATES OF AMERICA, }
  INDIAN TERRITORY,
  Central   District.

    I, Francis D Bush , a Physician , on oath state that I attended on Mrs. Alice McCann , wife of Austin McCann on the 20 day of April , 190 4; that

Applications for Enrollment of Choctaw Newborn
Act of 1905   Volume VII

there was born to her on said date a   male   child; that said child is now living and is said to have been named   Samson Francis McCann

Francis D. Bush, MD

WITNESSES TO MARK:
{

Subscribed and sworn to before me this   9 day of   August   , 1904

A.H. Crouthamel
NOTARY PUBLIC.

My Commission expires Feb 3 1907

BIRTH AFFIDAVIT.

DEPARTMENT OF THE INTERIOR.
COMMISSION TO THE FIVE CIVILIZED TRIBES.

IN RE APPLICATION FOR ENROLLMENT, as a citizen of the   Choctaw   Nation, of Samson Francis McCann   , born on the 20" day of April   , 1904

Name of Father: Austin McCann   a citizen of the Choctaw Nation.
Name of Mother: Alice McCann   a citizen of the Choctaw Nation.

Postoffice   Cowlington Ind Ter

AFFIDAVIT OF MOTHER.

UNITED STATES OF AMERICA, Indian Territory, }
    Central   DISTRICT.

(will be
I,   Alice McCann   , on oath state that I am   28 Aug 15 1905) years of age and a citizen by   Intermarriage   , of the   Choctaw   Nation; that I am the lawful wife of   Austin McCann   , who is a citizen, by Blood   of the   Choctaw Nation; that a   Male   child was born to me on   20" day of April   , 1904; that said child has been named   Samson Francis McCann   , and was living March 4, 1905.

her
Alice x McCann
mark

Witnesses To Mark:
{ L Piatt
  Mrs L. Piatt

Subscribed and sworn to before me this   13 day of   April   , 1905

Francis D Bush
My Commission expires Mar 13, 1906   Notary Public.

Applications for Enrollment of Choctaw Newborn
Act of 1905   Volume VII

AFFIDAVIT OF ATTENDING PHYSICIAN OR MID-WIFE.

UNITED STATES OF AMERICA, Indian Territory,
....DISTRICT.

I, Francis D Bush, MD , a Physician , on oath state that I attended on Mrs. Alice McCann , wife of Austin McCann on the 20" day of April , 1904; that there was born to her on said date a Male child; that said child was living March 4, 1905, and is said to have been named Samson Francis McCann

Francis D Bush M.D.

Witnesses To Mark:

Subscribed and sworn to before me this 14 day of April , 1905

Francis D Bush
My Commission expires Mar 13, 1906   Notary Public.

7-617 7.W.   7-14129
BIRTH AFFIDAVIT.

DEPARTMENT OF THE INTERIOR.
COMMISSION TO THE FIVE CIVILIZED TRIBES.

IN RE APPLICATION FOR ENROLLMENT, as a citizen of the Choctaw Nation, of Sampson Francis McCann , born on the 20 day of April , 1904

Name of Father: Austin McCann   a citizen of the Choctaw Nation.
Name of Mother: Alice McCann   a citizen of the Choctaw Nation.

Postoffice   Cowlington Ind Ter

AFFIDAVIT OF MOTHER.

UNITED STATES OF AMERICA, Indian Territory,
     Central   DISTRICT.

I, Alice McCann , on oath state that I am 27 years of age and a citizen by intermarriage , of the Choctaw Nation; that I am the lawful wife of Austin McCann , who is a citizen, by blood of the Choctaw Nation; that a male child was born to me on 20 day of April , 1904; that said child has been named Sampson Francis McCann , and was living March 4, 1905.

Applications for Enrollment of Choctaw Newborn
Act of 1905   Volume VII

Witnesses To Mark:
{ Chas T Difendafer
{ OL Johnson

                         her
                     Alice x McCann
                        mark

Subscribed and sworn to before me this   3   day of   April   , 1905

                        OL Johnson
                             Notary Public.

AFFIDAVIT OF ATTENDING PHYSICIAN OR MID-WIFE.

UNITED STATES OF AMERICA, Indian Territory,
       Central   **DISTRICT.**

     I,   F. D. Bush   , a   Physician   , on oath state that I attended on Mrs. Alice McCann   , wife of Austin McCann   on the 20 day of April , 1904; that there was born to her on said date a   male   child; that said child was living March 4, 1905, and is said to have been named Sampson Francis McCann

                     F D Bush M.D.

Witnesses To Mark:
{

Subscribed and sworn to before me this   3   day of   April   , 1905

                     A.H. Crouthamel
My Com Ex 2-3-1907   Notary Public.

Choc New Born 412
     Leona Conn   b. 11-3-02
     John R. Conn   b. 1-11-04

Applications for Enrollment of Choctaw Newborn
Act of 1905   Volume VII

BIRTH AFFIDAVIT.

DEPARTMENT OF THE INTERIOR.
COMMISSION TO THE FIVE CIVILIZED TRIBES.

IN RE APPLICATION FOR ENROLLMENT, as a citizen of the Choctaw Nation, of Leona Conn, born on the 3^d day of November, 1902

Name of Father: John A Conn   a citizen of the Choctaw Nation.
Name of Mother: Minnie J Conn   a citizen of the Choctaw Nation.

Postoffice   Roberta Ind Ter

AFFIDAVIT OF MOTHER.

UNITED STATES OF AMERICA, Indian Territory,
Central   DISTRICT.

I, Minnie J Conn, on oath state that I am 29 years of age and a citizen by Blood, of the Choctaw Nation; that I am the lawful wife of John A Conn, who is a citizen, by Intermarriage of the Choctaw Nation; that a Female child was born to me on Third day of November, 1902; that said child has been named Leona Conn, and was living March 4, 1905.

Minnie J Conn

Witnesses To Mark:
{

Subscribed and sworn to before me this 31st day of May, 1905

Charles A Phillips
Notary Public.

AFFIDAVIT OF ATTENDING PHYSICIAN OR MID-WIFE.

UNITED STATES OF AMERICA, Indian Territory,
Central   DISTRICT.

I, Robert A Lively, a Physician, on oath state that I attended on Mrs. Minnie J Conn, wife of John A Conn on the Third day of November, 1902; that there was born to her on said date a Female child; that said child was living March 4, 1905, and is said to have been named Leona Conn

Robt. A. Lively MD

Witnesses To Mark:
{

Applications for Enrollment of Choctaw Newborn
Act of 1905 Volume VII

Subscribed and sworn to before me this 31st day of   May   , 1905

Charles A Phillips
Notary Public.

BIRTH AFFIDAVIT.

DEPARTMENT OF THE INTERIOR.
COMMISSION TO THE FIVE CIVILIZED TRIBES.

IN RE APPLICATION FOR ENROLLMENT, as a citizen of the   Chocktaw[sic]   Nation, of   Leona Conn   , born on the 7th [sic] day of   November   , 1902

Name of Father: John A Conn   a citizen of the Intermarried Nation.
Name of Mother: Minnie J Conn   a citizen of the   Choctaw   Nation.

Postoffice   Roberta Indian Territory

AFFIDAVIT OF MOTHER.

UNITED STATES OF AMERICA, Indian Territory, }
Central   DISTRICT. }

I,   Minnie J Conn   , on oath state that I am   29   years of age and a citizen by   blood   , of the   Chocktaw   Nation; that I am the lawful wife of   John A Conn   , who is a citizen, by   Intermarried   of the ——— Nation; that a   female   child was born to me on   Seventh[sic]   day of   November   , 1902; that said child has been named   Leona Conn   , and was living March 4, 1905.

Minnie J Conn

Witnesses To Mark:
{

Subscribed and sworn to before me this 22^d day of   March   , 1905

Charles A Phillips
Notary Public.

AFFIDAVIT OF ATTENDING PHYSICIAN OR MID-WIFE.

UNITED STATES OF AMERICA, Indian Territory, }
Central   DISTRICT. }

I,   Robert A Lively   , a   Practicing Physician   , on oath state that I attended on Mrs.   Minnie J Conn   , wife of   John A Conn   on the   Seventh[sic]   day of

Applications for Enrollment of Choctaw Newborn
Act of 1905   Volume VII

November , 1902; that there was born to her on said date a female child; that said child was living March 4, 1905, and is said to have been named Leona Conn

                                     Robt. A. Lively MD

Witnesses To Mark:

{ Subscribed and sworn to before me this 24th day of   March   , 1905

                                  Charles A Phillips

Com Expires   Notary Public.
Feb 8th 1908

BIRTH AFFIDAVIT.

Department of the Interior,
COMMISSION TO THE FIVE CIVILIZED TRIBES.

                                                 CHOCTAW
    IN RE APPLICATION FOR ENROLLMENT, as a citizen of the Chickasaw Nation, of Leona Conn , born on the 3rd day of Nov , 190 2

Name of Father: John Conn   a citizen of the Chickasaw Nation.
Name of Mother: Minnie Jane Conn   a citizen of the Chickasaw Nation.

                    Post-Office: Durant Ind. Ter.

                  AFFIDAVIT OF MOTHER.

UNITED STATES OF AMERICA, ⎫
     INDIAN TERRITORY,   ⎬
  Central   District. ⎭

    I, Minnie Jane Conn , on oath state that I am 27 years of age and a citizen by blood , of the Chickasaw^{CHOCTAW} Nation; that I am the lawful wife of John Conn , who is a citizen, by Marriage of the Chickasaw Nation; that a female child was born to me on 3rd day of November , 190 2, that said child has been named Leona , and is now living.

                                     Minnie J Conn

WITNESSES TO MARK:
{

    Subscribed and sworn to before me this 15" day of December , 1902

                                     W.H. Richey
                                       Notary Public.

Applications for Enrollment of Choctaw Newborn
Act of 1905   Volume VII

AFFIDAVIT OF ATTENDING PHYSICIAN OR MID-WIFE.

UNITED STATES OF AMERICA,
INDIAN TERRITORY,
Central   District.

I, Robert A Lively , a Physician , on oath state that I attended on Mrs. Minnie Jane Conn , wife of John Conn on the 3rd day of November , 1902; that there was born to her on said date a female child; that said child is now living and is said to have been named Leona Conn

Robt A Lively MD

WITNESSES TO MARK:

Subscribed and sworn to before me this 15" day of December , 1902

W.H. Richey
Notary Public.

BIRTH AFFIDAVIT.

DEPARTMENT OF THE INTERIOR.
COMMISSION TO THE FIVE CIVILIZED TRIBES.

IN RE APPLICATION FOR ENROLLMENT, as a citizen of the Chocktaw[sic] Nation, of John R Conn , born on the 11th day of January , 1904

Name of Father: John A Conn   a citizen of the Intermarried Nation.
Name of Mother: Minnie J Conn   a citizen of the Chocktaw Nation.

Postoffice   Roberta Indian Territory

AFFIDAVIT OF MOTHER.

UNITED STATES OF AMERICA, Indian Territory,
Central   DISTRICT.

I, Minnie J Conn , on oath state that I am 29 years of age and a citizen by blood , of the Chocktaw Nation; that I am the lawful wife of John A Conn , who is a citizen, by Intermarried of the .... Nation; that a male child was born to me on Eleventh day of January , 1904; that said child has been named John R Conn , and was living March 4, 1905.

Minnie J Conn

Witnesses To Mark:

Applications for Enrollment of Choctaw Newborn
Act of 1905 Volume VII

Subscribed and sworn to before me this 22^d day of   March   , 1905

Charles A Phillips
Notary Public.

AFFIDAVIT OF ATTENDING PHYSICIAN OR MID-WIFE.

UNITED STATES OF AMERICA, Indian Territory,
Central   DISTRICT.

I, Robert A Lively , a Practicing Physician , on oath state that I attended on Mrs. Minnie J Conn , wife of John A Conn   on the Eleventh day of January , 1904; that there was born to her on said date a   male   child; that said child was living March 4, 1905, and is said to have been named John R. Conn

Robt. A. Lively MD

Witnesses To Mark:

Subscribed and sworn to before me this 24th day of   March   , 1905

Charles A Phillips
Com Expires   Notary Public.
Feb 8th 1908

NEW-BORN AFFIDAVIT.

Number............

Choctaw Enrolling Commission.

IN THE MATTER OF THE APPLICATION FOR ENROLLMENT, as a citizen of the Choctaw   Nation, of   John Conn Jr.

born on the   11 day of   January   190 4

Name of father   John Conn Sr   a citizen of   White
Nation final enrollment No ——
Name of mother   Minnie J Conn   a citizen of   Choctaw
Nation final enrollment No   14062

Postoffice   Roberta IT

Applications for Enrollment of Choctaw Newborn
Act of 1905 Volume VII

AFFIDAVIT OF MOTHER.

UNITED STATES OF AMERICA,
INDIAN TERRITORY,
Central   DISTRICT

I   Minnie J Conn   on oath state that I am   29   years of age and a citizen by   blood   of the   Choctaw   Nation, and as such have been placed upon the final roll of the   Choctaw   Nation, by the Honorable Secretary of the Interior my final enrollment number being   14062 ; that I am the lawful wife of   John Conn Sr , who is a citizen of the   White   Nation, and as such has been placed upon the final roll of said Nation by the Honorable Secretary of the Interior, his final enrollment number being ——   and that a   male   child was born to me on the   11   day of   January   190 4; that said child has been named   John Conn Jr , and is now living.

WITNESSETH: Minnie J Conn

Must be two Witnesses who are Citizens.   Jas Yorbrough   Cyrus Byington

Subscribed and sworn to before me this   11   day of   January   190 5

James Bower
Notary Public.

My commission expires   Sept 23-1907

AFFIDAVIT OF ATTENDING PHYSICIAN OR MIDWIFE

UNITED STATES OF AMERICA
INDIAN TERRITORY
Central   DISTRICT

I,   Robt A Lively   a   Practicing Physician on oath state that I attended on Mrs.   Minnie J Conn   wife of   John Conn Sr. on the   11   day of   January , 190 4, that there was born to her on said date a   Male   child, that said child is now living, and is said to have been named   John Conn Jr

Robt A Lively   M.D.

Subscribed and sworn to before me this, the   16   day of   January   190 5

James Bower
Notary Public.

WITNESSETH:

Must be two witnesses who are citizens and know the child.   Jas Yorbrough   Cyrus Byington

Applications for Enrollment of Choctaw Newborn
Act of 1905   Volume VII

We hereby certify that we are well acquainted with   Robt A Lively
a   Practicing Physician   and know   him   to be reputable and of good standing in the community.

$\left\{\begin{array}{l}\text{Jas Yorbrough} \\ \text{Cyrus Byington}\end{array}\right.$

7-5561

Muskogee, Indian Territory, March 30, 1905.

John A. Conn,
    Roberta, Indian Territory.

Dear Sir:

    Receipt is hereby acknowledged of the affidavits of Minnie J. Conn and Rob A. Liveley[sic] to the birth of Leona Conn, and John R. Conn, child[sic] of John A. and Minnie J. Conn, November 7, 1902, and January 11, 1904, respectively and the same have been filed with our records as an application for the enrollment of said children.

Respectfully,

Chairman.

7-NB-411[sic].

Muskogee, Indian Territory, May 25, 1905.

John A. Conn,
    Roberta, Indian Territory.

Dear Sir:

    There is enclosed you herewith for execution application for the enrollment of your infant child, Leona Conn.

    The affidavits of December 15, 1902, heretofore filed in this office, give the date of the applicant's birth as November 3, 1902, while in those of March 22, and 24, 1905, it is given as November 7, 1903. In the enclosed application the date of birth is left blank. You will please insert the correct date and when the affidavits are properly executed return the application to this office.

    In having these affidavits executed care should be exercised to see that all names are written in full, as they appear in the body of the affidavit, and in the event that either

Applications for Enrollment of Choctaw Newborn
Act of 1905   Volume VII

of the persons signing the affidavit are unable to write, signatures by mark must be attested by two witnesses. Each affidavit must be executed before a Notary Public and the notarial seal and signature of the officer must be attached to each separate affidavit.

Respectfully,

VT 25-6.   Chairman.

7-N.B. 411[sic].

Muskogee, Indian Territory, June 5, 1905.

John A. Conn,
    Roberta, Indian Territory.

Dear Sir:

    Receipt is hereby acknowledged of the affidavits of Minnie J. Conn and Robt. A. Lively to the birth of Leona Conn, daughter of John A. and Minnie J. Conn, November 3, 1902, and the same have been filed with our records in the matter of the enrollment of said child.

Respectfully,

Commissioner in Charge.

Choc New Born 413
    Coy Smith Wilkinson b. 9-23-03

    Died on Nov 15, 1904
    No.   Dismissed June 15, 1905

Applications for Enrollment of Choctaw Newborn
Act of 1905   Volume VII

DEPARTMENT OF THE INTERIOR,
COMMISSION TO THE FIVE CIVILIZED TRIBES.

Record in the matter of the application for enrollment as a citizen by blood of the Choctaw Nation of:

COY SMITH WILKINSON   7-NB-413.

BIRTH AFFIDAVIT.

DEPARTMENT OF THE INTERIOR,
COMMISSION TO THE FIVE CIVILIZED TRIBES.

IN RE Application for Enrollment, as a citizen of the   Choctaw   Nation, of   Coy Smith Wilkerson[sic]   , born on the   23   day of   September   , 1903

Name of Father: Henry Q Wilkerson[sic]   a citizen of the .... Nation.
Name of Mother: Mary Ada Wilkerson   a citizen of the   Choctaw   Nation.

Post-Office: Durant, Ind. Ter.

AFFIDAVIT OF MOTHER.

UNITED STATES OF AMERICA, ⎫
    INDIAN TERRITORY.   ⎬
    Central   District.   ⎭

I,   Mary Ada Wilkerson   , on oath state that I am .... years of age and a citizen by   blood   , of the Choctaw   Nation; that I am the lawful wife of   Henry Q Wilkerson , who is a citizen, by   blood   of the Choctaw   Nation; that a   male child was born to me on   23   day of   September   , 190 3, that said child has been named   Coy Smith Wilkerson   , and is now living.

                                              Mary Ada Wilkinson

WITNESSES TO MARK:

Subscribed and sworn to before me this   7   day of   April   , 1904

                                              W. L. Boner
                                                   NOTARY PUBLIC.

Applications for Enrollment of Choctaw Newborn
Act of 1905   Volume VII

AFFIDAVIT OF ATTENDING PHYSICIAN OR MID-WIFE.

UNITED STATES OF AMERICA,
   INDIAN TERRITORY.
Central   District.

I, Alice Nabors , a midwife , on oath state that I attended on Mrs. Mary Ada Wilkerson , wife of Henry Q Wilkerson on the 23 day of September , 190 3; that there was born to her on said date a male child; that said child is now living and is said to have been named Coy Smith Wilkerson

Alice Nabors

WITNESSES TO MARK:

Subscribed and sworn to before me this 7 day of April , 1904

W.L. Boner
NOTARY PUBLIC.

BIRTH AFFIDAVIT.

Department of the Interior,
COMMISSION TO THE FIVE CIVILIZED TRIBES.

IN RE APPLICATION FOR ENROLLMENT, as a citizen of the Choctaw Nation, of Coy Smith Wilkinson , born on the 23 day of Sept , 190 3

Name of Father: Henry Q. Wilkinson   a citizen of the non citizen Nation.
Name of Mother: Ada Wilkinson   a citizen of the Choctaw Nation.

Post-Office: Durant, Ind Ter

AFFIDAVIT OF MOTHER.

UNITED STATES OF AMERICA,
   INDIAN TERRITORY,
Central   District.

I, Ada Wilkinson , on oath state that I am 21 years of age and a citizen by blood , of the Choctaw Nation; that I am the lawful wife of Henry Q Wilkinson , who is a citizen, by .... of the non Indian Nation; that a male child was born to me on 23 day of September , 190 3, that said child has been named Coy Smith Wilkinson , and is now living.

Ada Wilkinson

216

Applications for Enrollment of Choctaw Newborn
Act of 1905 Volume VII

WITNESSES TO MARK:

{

Subscribed and sworn to before me this 18 day of March , 1905

W.L. Boner
Notary Public.

My commission expires 14 day of May 19 6[sic]

AFFIDAVIT OF ATTENDING PHYSICIAN OR MID-WIFE.

UNITED STATES OF AMERICA,
    INDIAN TERRITORY,
    Central   District.

    I,   G M Rushing , a Physician , on oath state that I attended on Mrs. Ada Wilkinson , wife of Henry Q Wilkinson on the 23 day of September, 190 3; that there was born to her on said date a male child; that said child is now living and is said to have been named Coy Smith Wilkinson

                      G M Rushing M.D.

WITNESSES TO MARK:

{

Subscribed and sworn to before me this 18 day of March , 1905

W.L. Boner
Notary Public.

My commission expires 14 day of May 19 6[sic]

DEPARTMENT OF THE INTERIOR.
COMMISSION TO THE FIVE CIVILIZED TRIBES.

    In the matter of the death of Coy Smith Wilkinson a citizen of the Choctaw Nation, who formerly resided at or near Durant , Ind. Ter., and died on the 15 day of November , 1904

AFFIDAVIT OF RELATIVE.

UNITED STATES OF AMERICA, Indian Territory,
    Central   DISTRICT.

    I,   Henry Q. Wilkinson , on oath state that I am 33 years of age and a citizen by ...., of the................Nation; that my postoffice address is Durant , Ind. Ter.; that I am Father of Coy Smith Wilkinson who was a citizen, by blood ,

Applications for Enrollment of Choctaw Newborn
Act of 1905   Volume VII

of the Choctaw Nation and that said Coy Smith Wilkinson died on the 15 day of November , 1904

H.Q. Wilkinson

Witnesses To Mark:
{

Subscribed and sworn to before me this 27 day of March , 1905.

My commission expires 14 *day of* May *1906*   W. L. Boner

Notary Public.

***

AFFIDAVIT OF ACQUAINTANCE.

UNITED STATES OF AMERICA, Indian Territory, }
Central   DISTRICT.

I, Dr. J. C. *(Illegible)*   , on oath state that I am .... years of age, and a citizen by .... of the .... Nation; that my postoffice address is Durant , Ind. Ter.; that I was personally acquainted with Coy Smith Wilkinson who was a citizen, by blood , of the Choctaw Nation; and that said Coy Smith Wilkinson died on the 15 day of November , 1904

J. C. *(Illegible)* M.D.

Witnesses To Mark:
{

Subscribed and sworn to before me this 27 day of March , 1905.

My commission expires 14 *day of* May *1906*   W. L. Boner

Notary Public.

***

N. B. 413

Muskogee, Indian Territory, April 8, 1905.

Henry Q. Wilkinson,
    Durant, Indian Territory.

Dear Sir:

Referring to the application for the enrollment of your infant child, Cay[sic] Smith Wilkinson, born September 23, 1903, as a citizen of the Choctaw Nation, it appears that the applicant was dead on March 18, 1905. In this event you will please have the inclosed blank death affidavits executed and returned to this office; paying particular attention that the exact date of the applicant's death be inserted in both affidavits.

Applications for Enrollment of Choctaw Newborn
Act of 1905 Volume VII

In having these affidavits executed care should be exercised to see that all names are written in full, as they appear in the body of the affidavit, and in the event that either of the persons signing the affidavit are unable to write, signatures by mark must be attested by two witnesses. Each affidavit must be executed before a Notary Public and the notarial seal and signature of the officer must be attached to each separate affidavit.

Respectfully,

SIGNED *T. B. Needles.*

LM 8-4. Commissioner in Charge.

DEPARTMENT OF THE INTERIOR.
COMMISSION TO THE FIVE CIVILIZED TRIBES.

In the matter of the death of Coy Smith Wilkinson a citizen of the Choctaw Nation, who formerly resided at or near Durant , Ind. Ter., and died on the 15 day of November , 1904

AFFIDAVIT OF RELATIVE.

UNITED STATES OF AMERICA, Indian Territory,
Central DISTRICT.

I, Mrs. Ada Wilkinson , on oath state that I am 21 years of age and a citizen by blood of the Choctaw Nation; that my postoffice address is Durant , Ind. Ter.; that I am Mother of Coy Smith Wilkinson who was a citizen, by blood, of the Choctaw Nation and that said Coy Smith Wilkinson died on the 15 day of November , 1904

Ada Wilkinson

Witnesses To Mark:
{

Subscribed and sworn to before me this 15 day of April , 1905.

My commission expires 14 *day of* May 1906   W. L. Boner
Notary Public.

AFFIDAVIT OF ACQUAINTANCE.

UNITED STATES OF AMERICA, Indian Territory,
Central DISTRICT.

I, Ollie Lindsey , on oath state that I am 21 years of age, and a citizen by .... of the .... Nation; that my postoffice address is Durant , Ind.

Applications for Enrollment of Choctaw Newborn
Act of 1905   Volume VII

Ter.; that I was personally acquainted with   Coy Smith Wilkinson   who was a citizen, by blood , of the Choctaw Nation; and that said   Coy Smith Wilkinson   died on the 15   day of   November , 1904

Ollie Lindsey

Witnesses To Mark:

{

Subscribed and sworn to before me this 15   day of   April   , 1905.

My commission expires 14 *day of* May   1906   W. L. Boner

Notary Public.

Choctaw N.B. 413.

Muskogee, Indian Territory, April 21, 1905.

W. L. Doner[sic],
    Attorney at Law,
        Durant, Indian Territory.

Dear Sir:

    Receipt is hereby acknowledged of your letter of April 15, transmitting the affidavits of Ada Wilkinson and Ollie Lindsey to the death of Coy Smith Wilkinson which occurred November 15, 1904, and the same have been filed with our records in the matter of the enrollment of said child.

Respectfully,

SIGNED   *Tams Bixby*
Chairman.

Applications for Enrollment of Choctaw Newborn
Act of 1905   Volume VII

W.F.
7-NB-413.

DEPARTMENT OF THE INTERIOR,
COMMISSION TO THE FIVE CIVILIZED TRIBES.

In the matter of the application for the enrollment of Coy Smith Wilkinson as a citizen by blood of the Choctaw Nation.

---oOo---

It appears from the record herein that on March 4, 1905, there was filed with the Commission application for the enrollment of Coy Smith Wilkinson as a citizen by blood of the Choctaw Nation.

It further appears from the record in this case and the records of the Commission that the applicant was born on September 23, 1903; that he is a son of Ada Wilkinson, a recognized and enrolled citizen by blood of the Choctaw nation whose name appears as number 14137 upon the final roll of citizens by blood of the Choctaw Nation, approved by the Secretary of the Interior March 19, 1903, and Henry Q. Wilkinson, a noncitizen; and that said applicant died on November 15, 1904.

The Act of Congress approved March 3, 1905 (Public No. 212) among other things provides:
> "That the Commission to the Five Civilized Tribes is authorized for sixty days after the date of the approval of this act to receive and consider applications for enrollment of children born subsequent to September twenty-fifth, nineteen hundred and two, and prior to March fourth, nineteen hundred and five, and who were living on said latter date, to citizens by blood of the Choctaw and Chickasaw tribes of Indians whose enrollment has been approved by the Secretary of the Interior prior to the date of the approval of this act; and to enroll and make allotments to such children."

It is, therefore, hereby ordered that the application for the enrollment of Coy Smith Wilkinson as a citizen by blood of the Choctaw Nation be dismissed in accordance with the order of the Commission of March 31, 1905.

COMMISSION TO THE FIVE CIVILIZED TRIBES.

Tams Bixby   Commissioner.

Muskogee, Indian Territory.
JUN 15 1905

Applications for Enrollment of Choctaw Newborn
Act of 1905   Volume VII

7-NB-413

Muskogee, Indian Territory, June 15, 1905.

Henry Q. Wilkinson, **COPY.**
Durant, Indian Territory.

Dear Sir:

Inclosed herewith you will find a copy of the order of this Commission, dated June 15, 1905, dismissing the application for the enrollment of your infant child, Coy Smith Wilkinson, as a citizen by blood of the Choctaw Nation.

Respectfully,

SIGNED

Tams Bixby

Registered. Chairman.
Incl. 7-NB-413

7-NB-413

Muskogee, Indian Territory, June 15, 1905.

Mansfield, McMurray & Cornish, **COPY.**
Attorneys for Choctaw and Chickasaw Nations,
South McAlester, Indian Territory.

Gentlemen:

Inclosed herewith you will find a copy of the order of this Commission, dated June 15, 1905, dismissing the application for the enrollment of your infant child, Coy Smith Wilkinson, as a citizen by blood of the Choctaw Nation.

Respectfully,

SIGNED

Tams Bixby
Chairman.

Incl. 7-NB-413

Applications for Enrollment of Choctaw Newborn
Act of 1905 Volume VII

7-5588

Muskogee, Indian Territory, March 22, 1905.

Ada Wilkinson,
    Durant, Indian Territory.

Dear Madam:

    Receipt is hereby acknowledged of the affidavits of Ada Wilkinson and G. M. Rushing to the birth of Coy Smith Wilkinson, son of Henry L[sic]. and Ada Wilkinson, September 23, 1903.

    It appears from the affidavits that this child was not living on March 8, 1905, and for the purpose of making its death a matter of record you are requested to have the enclosed blank filled out and returned to this office at the earliest practicable date showing the correct date of the death of said child.

                  Respectfully,

B. C.   Chairman.

<u>Choc New Born 414</u>
        Mary Watson b. 8-22-03

(The handwritten letter below typed as given.)

Ind. Ter.   }
Central Judicial District }

I C D Moore on oath state that I am 38 yrs of age and a citizen by blood of the Choctaw Nation That within 5 days after the birth of Mary Watson born Aug. 22nd 1903 who is the child of Edna Watson and Julian J. Watson I was at their house and saw the infant and know that she Mary Watson now living is the same child I saw at Watsons house soon after Mrs Edna Watson gave birth to a child.
                                                CD Moore
Subscribed and sworn to before me this 28th Mch 1905
                                              D S Kennedy
                                                      Notary Public

Applications for Enrollment of Choctaw Newborn
Act of 1905   Volume VII

Central Judicial Dist Ind Ter

Personally came before me a Notary Public within and for the Central Dist Ind Ter Sally Bond aged 18 years whose Post office is Stringtown, I.T. who being by me duly sworn declares as follows:
    That she was at Watson house on the morning of Aug 23 1902 and saw the child born to Edna Watson the night of Aug 22 1902 and child was living *(illegible...)* and is said to have been named Mary Watson

Sallie Bond

Subscribed and sworn to before me this *(illegible...)* of June 1905

Lark Sadler
Notary Public

D. S. KENNEDY	KENNEDY BROTHERS,	J. W. KENNEDY
DRY GOODS	DEALERS IN	HATS CAPS
&	**GENERAL**	&
GROCERIES	**MERCHANDISE**	BOOTS
&	MANUFACTURERS OF AND WHOLESALE DEALERS IN	&
AND NOTIONS	**YELLOW PINE**	AND SHOES
	LUMBER	

STRINGTOWN, I. T. _____ 190__

Ind. Ter. }
Central Judicial District

Personally came before me a Notary Public in and for the Central Judicial District, Ind Ter, Edna Watson aged 22 years whose post office is Stringtown I.T. and who being by me duly sworn declares as follows
    My maiden name was Bond. My parents names are Jessie Bond, and Mary Bond I was married to Juilus[sic] J. Watson in 1897 and I think Julius J. Watson first listed my self and children for enrollment at ~~Durant~~, Colbert, I.T. but can not recall the year. My husband Julius J. Watson died Jan 13th 1905.

Edna Watson

Subscribed and sworn to before me this 11th day April 1905.

D.S. Kennedy
Notary Public.

Applications for Enrollment of Choctaw Newborn
Act of 1905   Volume VII

Ind. Ter.
Central Judicial District

I Edna Watson on oath state that I am 22 yrs of age that a female child was born to me on Aug 22nd 1903 and my husband Julius J Watson deceased was the only one in attendance when the child was born

Edna Watson

Subscribed and sworn to before me on this 28th day Mch. 1905.

D.S. Kennedy
Notary Public.

BIRTH AFFIDAVIT.

DEPARTMENT OF THE INTERIOR.
COMMISSION TO THE FIVE CIVILIZED TRIBES.

IN RE APPLICATION FOR ENROLLMENT, as a citizen of the Choctaw Nation, of Mary Watson   , born on the .... day of ...., 1........

Name of Father: Julius J Watson, died   a citizen of the   Choctaw   Nation.
Name of Mother: Edna Watson   a citizen of the   Choctaw   Nation.

Postoffice   Stringtown Ind Ter

AFFIDAVIT OF MOTHER.

UNITED STATES OF AMERICA, Indian Territory,
   Southern   DISTRICT.

I, ..., on oath state that I am ..... years of age and a citizen by ...., of the .... Nation; that I am the lawful wife of ...., who is a citizen, by .... of the .... Nation; that a .... child was born to me on ..... day of ...., 1......, that said child has been named ...., and was living March 4, 1905.

Witnesses To Mark:

Subscribed and sworn to before me this ..... day of ...., 1905.

Notary Public.

Applications for Enrollment of Choctaw Newborn
Act of 1905   Volume VII

AFFIDAVIT OF ATTENDING PHYSICIAN OR MID-WIFE.

UNITED STATES OF AMERICA, Indian Territory, }
~~Southern~~   Central   DISTRICT.

  I, Sallie Bond, a ————, on oath state that I ~~attended on~~ am personally acquainted with Mrs. Edna Watson, wife of Julius J Watson and that on or about the 22 day of August, 1903; that there was born to her on said date a female child; that said child was living March 4, 1905, and is said to have been named Mary Watson

            Salle Bond

Witnesses To Mark:
{

  Subscribed and sworn to before me this 15th day of Aug, 1905

         D.S. Kennedy
           Notary Public.

BIRTH AFFIDAVIT.

DEPARTMENT OF THE INTERIOR,
COMMISSION TO THE FIVE CIVILIZED TRIBES.

  In Re Application for Enrollment, as a citizen of the Choctaw Nation, of Mary Watson, born on the 22nd day of August, 1903

Name of Father: J. J. Watson   a citizen of the Choctaw Nation.
Name of Mother: Edna Watson   a citizen of the Choctaw Nation.

      Post-office   Stringtown, I.T.

AFFIDAVIT OF MOTHER.

UNITED STATES OF AMERICA, }
INDIAN TERRITORY,
 Central Judicial   District.

  I, Edna Watson, on oath state that I am 21 years of age and a citizen by blood, of the Choctaw Nation; that I am the lawful wife of J. J. Watson, who is a citizen, by blood of the Choctaw Nation; that a female child was born to me on 22nd day of August, 1903, that said child has been named Mary Watson, and is now living.

          Edna Watson

WITNESSES TO MARK:
{

Applications for Enrollment of Choctaw Newborn
Act of 1905   Volume VII

Subscribed and sworn to before me this 7th   day of   Sept , 1903

D. S. Kennedy
NOTARY PUBLIC.

AFFIDAVIT OF ATTENDING PHYSICIAN OR MID-WIFE.

UNITED STATES OF AMERICA,
INDIAN TERRITORY,
Central Judicial   District.

I,   J. J. Watson   , ~~a~~   , on oath state that I ~~attended on~~ was the only person and attended Edna Watson my wife on the 22nd   day of August , 1903 ; that there was born to her on said date a   female   child; that said child is now living and ~~is said to have~~ been named Mary Watson
                  has

WITNESSES TO MARK: Julius J Watson

Subscribed and sworn to before me this 7th   day of   Sept , 1903

D. S. Kennedy
NOTARY PUBLIC.

BIRTH AFFIDAVIT.
DEPARTMENT OF THE INTERIOR.
COMMISSION TO THE FIVE CIVILIZED TRIBES.

IN RE APPLICATION FOR ENROLLMENT, as a citizen of the   Choctaw   Nation, of Mary Watson   , born on the   22nd   day of Aug   1903

Name of Father: Julius J Watson   a citizen of the   Choctaw   Nation.
Name of Mother: Edna Watson   a citizen of the   Choctaw   Nation.

Postoffice   Stringtown Ind Ter

AFFIDAVIT OF MOTHER.

UNITED STATES OF AMERICA, Indian Territory,
Central Judicial   DISTRICT.

I,   Edna Watson   , on oath state that I am 22   years of age and a citizen by blood   , of the   Choctaw   Nation; that I am the lawful wife of   Julius J Watson , who is a citizen, by blood   of the   Choctaw   Nation; that a   female   child

Applications for Enrollment of Choctaw Newborn
Act of 1905   Volume VII

was born to me on 22nd day of Aug , 1903; that said child has been named Mary Watson , and was living March 4, 1905.

                                      Edna Watson

Witnesses To Mark:
{

    Subscribed and sworn to before me this 28th day of Mch , 1905

                                      D.S. Kennedy
                                        Notary Public.

NEW-BORN AFFIDAVIT.

                Number............

...Choctaw Enrolling Commission...

IN THE MATTER OF THE APPLICATION FOR ENROLLMENT, as a citizen of the Choctaw Nation, of Mary Watson

born on the 22nd day of Aug 190 3

Name of father   J J Watson   a citizen of   Choctaw
Nation final enrollment No. 5419
Name of mother   Edna Watson   a citizen of   Choctaw
Nation final enrollment No. 13717

                            Postoffice   Stringtown, I.T.

AFFIDAVIT OF MOTHER.

UNITED STATES OF AMERICA
INDIAN TERRITORY
Central Judicial DISTRICT

        I   Edna Watson , on oath state that I am 22 years of age and a citizen by blood of the Choctaw Nation, and as such have been placed upon the final roll of the Choctaw Nation, by the Honorable Secretary of the Interior my final enrollment number being 13717 ; that I am the lawful wife of   J. J. Watson , who is a citizen of the Choctaw Nation, and as such has been placed upon the final roll of said Nation by the Honorable Secretary of the Interior, his final enrollment number being   5419   and that a   female   child was born to me on the 22 day of Aug 190 3; that said child has been named Mary Watson , and is now living.

                                      Edna Watson

Applications for Enrollment of Choctaw Newborn
Act of 1905 Volume VII

Witnesseth.

Must be two Witnesses who are Citizens. } Cornelius Bond

Bensie Bond

Subscribed and sworn to before me this 16th day of Jan 1905

D.S. Kennedy
Notary Public.

My commission expires:
Nov 1st 1905

AFFIDAVIT OF ATTENDING PHYSICIAN OR MIDWIFE

UNITED STATES OF AMERICA
INDIAN TERRITORY
Central Judicial DISTRICT

I, Mary Bond a Midwife on oath state that I attended on Mrs. Edna Watson wife of J J Watson on the 22nd day of Aug., 1903, that there was born to her on said date a female child, that said child is now living, and is said to have been named Mary Watson

her
Mary x Bond *M.D.*
mark

Subscribed and sworn to before me this, the 16th day of Jan 1905

D.S. Kennedy Notary Public.

WITNESSETH:

Must be two witnesses who are citizens { Cornelius Bond

Bensie Bond

We hereby certify that we are well acquainted with Mary Bond a midwife and know her to be reputable and of good standing in the community.

Cornelius Bond

Bensie Bond

Applications for Enrollment of Choctaw Newborn
Act of 1905   Volume VII

Muskogee, Indian Territory, March 31, 1905.

Julius J. Watson,
    Stringtown, Indian Territory.

Dear Sir:

    Receipt is hereby acknowledged of the affidavits of Edna Watson and C. D. Moore to the birth of Mary Watson, daughter of Julius J. and Edna Watson, August 22, 1903. It is stated in the affidavit of the mother that she is a citizen by blood of the ~~Chickasaw~~ Choctaw Nation. If this is correct, you are requested to state her maiden name, the names of her parents, and the name under which she was listed for enrollment, together with such other information as you may possess which would enable us to identify her upon our records.

                          Respectfully,

                                            Chairman.

Choctaw N.B. 414.

Muskogee, Indian Territory, April 18, 1905.

Edna Watson,
    Stringtown, Indian Territory.

Dear Sir[sic]:

    Receipt is hereby acknowledged of your affidavit relative to the names of your parents and your application as a citizen by blood of the Choctaw Nation, and the same have been filed with our records in the matter of the enrollment of your child, Mary Watson.

                          Respectfully,

                                            Chairman.

Applications for Enrollment of Choctaw Newborn
Act of 1905   Volume VII

7-NB-414.

Muskogee, Indian Territory, May 25, 1905.

Edna Watson,
    Stringtown, Indian Territory.

Dear Madam:

    Referring to the application for the enrollment of your infant child, Mary Watson, born August 22, 1902, it is noted from the affidavits heretofore filed in this office that there was no physician or midwife in attendance upon you at the time of birth of the applicant.

    If this is correct the affidavits of two disinterested persons are required. You have filed the affidavit of one only, C. D. Moore. It will, therefore, be necessary that you secure the affidavit of another disinterested person who has actual knowledge of the facts that the child was born, the date of her birth; that she was living on March 4, 1905, and that you are her mother.

                      Respectfully,

                                            Chairman.

7-NB-414

Muskogee, Indian Territory, July 1, 1905.

Julius J. Watson,
    Stringtown, Indian Territory.

Dear Sir:

    Receipt is hereby acknowledged of the affidavit of Sallie Bond to the birth of Mary Watson, child of Edna Watson, August 22, 1902, and the same has been filed with our records in the matter of the enrollment of said child.

                      Respectfully,

                                            Chairman.

Applications for Enrollment of Choctaw Newborn
Act of 1905   Volume VII

7-NB-414

Muskogee, Indian Territory, July 29, 1905.

Edna Watson,
Stringtown, Indian Territory.

Dear Madam:

There is inclosed herewith an affidavit to be executed by Sallie Bond, in the matter of the enrollment of your infant child, Mary Watson.

In the affidavit of Sallie Bond, executed June 26, 1905, heretofore filed in this office, the date of birth of the child, is given as August 23, 1902, while in your affidavit and the affidavit of C. B[sic]. Moore, executed March 28, 1905, the date of birth is given as August 22, 1903.

The letter date is apparently correct, so please have the inclosed affidavit executed by Sallie Bond and return to this office immediately, as no further action can be taken relative to the enrollment of your said child, until this evidence is supplied.

Respectfully,

LM 3/29

Commissioner.

7-NB-414

Muskogee, Indian Territory, July 3, 1905.

Julius J. Watson,
Stringtown, Indian Territory.

Dear Sir:

Receipt is hereby acknowledged of the affidavit of Sallie Bond to the birth of Mary Watson, August 22, 1902, and the same has been filed with the records of this office in the matter of the enrollment of said child.

Respectfully,

Commissioner.

Applications for Enrollment of Choctaw Newborn
Act of 1905   Volume VII

7-NB-414

Muskogee, Indian Territory, August 17, 1905.

Edna Watson,
    Stringtown, Indian Territory.

Dear Madam:

    Receipt is hereby acknowledged of the affidavit of Sallie Bond to the birt of Mary Watson, daughter of yourself and Julius J. Watson, deceased, August 22, 1903, and the same has been filed with the record in this case.

                  Respectfully,

                                Acting Commissioner.

Choc New Born 415
    Minnie Turnbull   b. 10-11-02

BIRTH AFFIDAVIT.

DEPARTMENT OF THE INTERIOR.
COMMISSION TO THE FIVE CIVILIZED TRIBES.

IN RE APPLICATION FOR ENROLLMENT, as a citizen of the   Choctaw   Nation, of Minnie Turnbull   , born on the 11th day of October , 1902

Name of Father: George W. Turnbull   a citizen of the Choctaw   Nation.
Name of Mother: Etta Turnbull   applicant as   a citizen of the Choctaw   Nation.

                  Postoffice   Emil, Indian Territory

AFFIDAVIT OF MOTHER.

UNITED STATES OF AMERICA, Indian Territory,
    Central   DISTRICT.

                                      applicant as
    I,   Etta Turnbull   , on oath state that I am 24   years of age and^a citizen by Marriage   , of the   Choctaw   Nation; that I am the lawful wife of   George W Turnbull   , who is a citizen, by blood   of the   Choctaw   Nation; that a

Applications for Enrollment of Choctaw Newborn
Act of 1905   Volume VII

female   child was born to me on   11th   day of   October   , 1902; that said child has been named   Minnie Turnbull   , and was living March 4, 1905.

Etta Turnbull

Witnesses To Mark:
{

Subscribed and sworn to before me this 25th day of   March   , 1905

W.H. Angell
Notary Public.

AFFIDAVIT OF ATTENDING PHYSICIAN OR MID-WIFE.

UNITED STATES OF AMERICA, Indian Territory, }
.... DISTRICT.

I,   Roza York   , a   mid wife   , on oath state that I attended on Mrs.   Etta Turnbull   , wife of   George W Turnbull   on the   11th day of October   , 1902; that there was born to her on said date a   female   child; that said child was living March 4, 1905, and is said to have been named   Minnie Turnbull

her
Roza x York
mark

Witnesses To Mark:
{ Arthur O. Archer
  Lewis T Martin

Subscribed and sworn to before me this 25th day of   March   , 1905

W.H. Angell
Notary Public.

Choc New Born 416
    Viola Glodis Anderson   b. 3-13-03

Applications for Enrollment of Choctaw Newborn
Act of 1905   Volume VII

DEPARTMENT OF THE INTERIOR,
COMMISSIONER TO THE FIVE CIVILIZED TRIBES.

- - - - -

In the matter of the application for the enrollment as a citizen by blood of the Choctaw Nation of . . . .

VIOLA GLODIS ANDERSON....7-NB-416.

BIRTH AFFIDAVIT.

DEPARTMENT OF THE INTERIOR,
COMMISSION TO THE FIVE CIVILIZED TRIBES.

IN RE APPLICATION FOR ENROLLMENT, as a citizen of the   Choctaw   Nation, of   Vola[sic] Glodis Anderson   , born on the   13   day of   Mch   , 1903

Name of Father: Tandy Anderson   a citizen of the   Choctaw   Nation.
Name of Mother: Lallia Anderson   a citizen of the   Choctaw   Nation.

Post-Office :   Antlers

AFFIDAVIT OF MOTHER.

UNITED STATES OF AMERICA,
INDIAN TERRITORY,
Central   District.

I,   Lallis Anderson   , on oath state that I am   20   years of age and a citizen by *(illegible)*   , of the   Choctaw   Nation; that I am the lawful wife of   Tandy Anderson   , who is a citizen, by   Blood   of the   Choctaw   Nation; that a   Girl   child was born to me on the   13   day of   Mch   , 190 3, that said child has been named   Viola Glodis Anderson   , and is now living.

Lallis Anderson

WITNESSES TO MARK:

Subscribed and sworn to before me this   14   day of   April   , 1903

C.E. Wassar
NOTARY PUBLIC.

Applications for Enrollment of Choctaw Newborn
Act of 1905 Volume VII

AFFIDAVIT OF ATTENDING PHYSICIAN OR MID-WIFE.

UNITED STATES OF AMERICA, }
INDIAN TERRITORY,
Central District.

I, Melvina Impson, a Midwife, on oath state that I attended on Mrs. Lallis Anderson, wife of Tandy Anderson on the 13 day of Mch, 1903; that there was born to her on said date a female child; that said child is now living and is said to have been named Viola Glodis Anderson

Melvina Impson

WITNESSES TO MARK:

Subscribed and sworn to before me this 14 day of April, 1903

C.E. Wassar
NOTARY PUBLIC.

DEPARTMENT OF THE INTERIOR,
COMMISSIONER TO THE FIVE CIVILIZED TRIBES.
CHOCTAW-CHICKASAW DIVISION.
Antlers, Indian Territory, February 24, 1905.

In the matter of the enrollment of Viola Gladis[sic] Anderson, Choctaw by blood, Card No. 416.

Testimony taken at Tuskahoma, Indian Territory, on the 23rd day of February, 1905.

TANDY ANDERSON, being first duly sworn, testified as follows:

BY THE COMMISSIONER:

Q What is your name? A Tandy Anderson.
Q What is your post office address? A Antlers, I. T.
Q How old are you, Mr. Anderson? A Going on 30.
Q In what official capacity do you at present serve the Choctaw Nation?
A I am a representative from Jackfork County.
Q Who was your wife?
A Lyles[sic] Anderson.
Q How many children have you living? A Just one.
Q What's his name? A Bedford Anderson.
Q How old is Bedford Anderson?

Applications for Enrollment of Choctaw Newborn
Act of 1905 Volume VII

A Three years old past;-now I may be mistaken about these ages; but when I come to the Land Office I will fix it all right. I am going up there soon.
Q Where did you apply and have Bedford Anderson enrolled as a citizen by blood of the Choctaw Nation?
A I appeared at Tuskahoma.
Q What was your wife's maiden name?
A Lyles Hotubbee.
Q Did you have a child named Viola Gladis[sic] Anderson? A Yes, sir.
Q The records of the Five Tribes Commission show that Lallis Anderson, as mother, made affidavit on the 14th of April, 1903, that Viola Gladis Anderson was born on the 13th of March 1903: Do you affirm that this child was born March 13, 1903?
A Yes, sir, I do.
Q Did Viola Gladis Anderson die in the same year in which she was born? A Yes, sir.
Q In what month? A In November.
Q How much difference was there between the birth of Bedford Anderson and Viola Gladis Anderson?
Q Just about 9 months difference.
Q Who attended your wife in the capacity of mid-wife or Physician when Viola Gladis Anderson was born?
A Why I got a neighbor who was living close by--Mrs. Alpha Johnson
Q Who made the coffin in which Viola Gladis Anderson was buried?
A A fellow by the name of Bostock, I do not remember his given name.
Q Is he now living?
A I think he is living some where in Texas now--I believe his given name is George.
Q You state upon oath and positively that your child, Viola Gladis Anderson, died in November after her birth the 13th of March, 1903?
A It died the same year, I can remember that.

Witness Excused.

    W. P. Covington, being first duly sworn, states that the above and foregoing is a full, true and correct transcript of his stenographic notes taken in said case on said date.

W.P. Covington

Subscribed and sworn to before me this 24 day of Feby ; 1906.

Lacey P Bobo
Notary Public.

Applications for Enrollment of Choctaw Newborn
Act of 1905 Volume VII

7-NB-416.	O.L.J.

DEPARTMENT OF THE INTERIOR,
COMMISSIONER TO THE FIVE CIVILIZED TRIBES.

- - - - -

In the matter of the application for the enrollment of Viola Glodis Anderson as a citizen by blood of the Choctaw Nation.

DECISION.

It appears from the record herein that on March 4, 1905, application was made to the Commission to the Five Civilized Tribes for the enrollment of Viola Glodis Anderson (born March 13, 1903) as a citizen by blood of the Choctaw Nation under the provisions of the Act of Congress approved March 3, 1905 (33 Stats., 1060).

It further appears from the record herein that said applicant died in November, 1903.

I am, therefore, of the opinion that the application for the enrollment of Viola Glodis Anderson as a citizen by blood of the Choctaw Nation should be dismissed, and it is so ordered.

Tams Bixby   Commissioner.

Muskogee, Indian Territory.
FEB 16 1907

N. B. 416

Muskogee, Indian Territory, April 8, 1905.

Tandy Anderson,
	Antlers, Indian Territory.

Dear Sir:

There is inclosed you herewith for execution application for the enrollment of your infant child, Viola Glodis Anderson, born March 13, 1903.

The affidavits heretofore filed with the Commission show the child was living on April 14, 1903. It is necessary, for the child to be enrolled, that she was living on March 4, 1905. You will please insert mother's age in the space provided for the purpose.

Referring to the affidavits heretofore forwarded, it is stated in the affidavit of the mother, Lallis Anderson, that she is a citizen by blood of the Choctaw Nation.

If this is correct you are requested to state when, where and under what name she was listed for enrollment, the names of her parents and other members of her family for

Applications for Enrollment of Choctaw Newborn
Act of 1905   Volume VII

whom application was made at the same time, and if she has selected her allotment, give her roll number as the same appears upon her allotment certificate.

In having these affidavits executed care should be exercised to see that all names are written in full, as they appear in the body of the affidavit, and in the event that either of the persons signing the affidavit are unable to write, signatures by mark must be attested by two witnesses. Each affidavit must be executed before a Notary Public and the notarial seal and signature of the officer must be attached to each separate affidavit.

Respectfully,

LM 8-25.   Commissioner in Charge.

7-NB-416.

Muskogee, Indian Territory, May 24, 1905.

Tandy Anderson,
    Antlers, Indian Territory.

Dear Sir:

There is inclosed you herewith for execution application for the enrollment of your infant child, Viola Glodis Anderson, born March 13, 1903.

Your attention is called to the Commissions[sic] letter of the 8th ultimo, which contained affidavits similar to the ones above mentioned, an in which you were requested to furnish information by which your wife might be identified.

The affidavits heretofore filed with the Commission show the child was living on April 14, 1903. It is necessary, for the child to be enrolled, that she was living on March 4, 1905. If your wife is a Choctaw by blood you will please state when, where and under what name she was listed for enrollment, the names of her parents and other members of her family for whom application was made at the same time, and if she has selected an allotment, give her roll number as the same appears on her allotment certificate. Before this matter can be finally disposed of it will be necessary that you supply this information, and return the enclosed application, when properly executed, to this office.

In having these affidavits executed care should be exercised to see that all names are written in full, as they appear in the body of the affidavit, and in the event that either of the persons signing the affidavit are unable to write, signatures by mark must be attested by two witnesses. Each affidavit must be executed before a Notary Public and the notarial seal and signature of the officer must be attached to each separate affidavit.

Respectfully,

VR 24-8.   Chairman.

Applications for Enrollment of Choctaw Newborn
Act of 1905   Volume VII

7-NB-416

Muskogee, Indian Territory, July 29, 1905.

Tandy Anderson,
    Antlers, Indian Territory.

Dear Sir:

    Your attention is called to communications addressed to you by the Commission to the Five Civilized Tribes under dates of April 8, and May 24, 1905, in which there was inclosed application for the enrollment of your infant child, Viola Glodis Anderson, born March 13, 1903.

    In said communications you were advised that the affidavits heretofore filed in this office, show that the child was living on April 14, 1903, and that if[sic] was necessary for her enrollment that she was living March 4, 1905. No reply to these letters has been received.

    In the event that your said child has died since application was made for her enrollment, you are requested to erase the words "was living March 4, 1905" and insert instead, the date of her death. If your said child was living March 4, 1905, it is necessary that you have the application heretofore forwarded you properly executed and return to this office immediately as no further action can be taken relative to the enrollment of your said child until the evidence heretofore requested has been supplied.

    Respectfully,

    Commissioner.

7-NB-416

Muskogee, Indian Territory, August 24, 1905.

Tandy Anderson,
    Zoraya, Indian Territory.

Dear Sir:

    Receipt is hereby acknowledged of your letter of August 19, 1905, stating that your child Viola Glodis Anderson was born March 14[sic], 1903, and died in November of the same year; you therefore ask to be informed if this child is entitled to an allotment.

Applications for Enrollment of Choctaw Newborn
Act of 1905 Volume VII

In reply to your letter you are advised that the Commission to the Five Civilized Tribes was authorized by the act of Congress approved March 3, 1905, to enroll only such children of enrolled citizens by blood of the Choctaw Nation who were born subsequent to September 25, 1902, and were living on March 4, 1905; you are therefore requested to have the inclosed blank executed showing the correct date of the death of your child Viola Glodis Anderson.

Respectfully,

D C   Commissioner.

D C   7836-1906.

A C 416

(correct date of letter if Feb. 27, <u>1906</u>)
Antlers, Indian Territory, February 27, 1905.

Commissioner to the Five Civilized Tribes,
    Choctaw-Chickasaw Enrolling Division,
        Miss Anna Bell, in Charge,
            Muskogee, Indian Territory.

Dear Sir[sic]:

There is enclosed herewith the original and two carbon copies of the testimony of Tandy Anderson, of Antlers, Indian Territory, regarding the death of Viola Gladis[sic] Anderson, Choctaw by blood, Card Number 416. Said testimony shows conclusively that Viola Gladis Anderson died in November 1903. The mother, Lyles[sic] Anderson, is now deceased, and I have so far been unable to ascertain of any one else the date of the child's death.

Please advise me if you consider the evidence of Tandy Anderson sufficient in this case. If so, upon receipt of your advice, I will forward the duplicate papers entrusted me in the matter of the application for the enrollment of said child. It the testimony of mid-wife or acquaintance is needed, please advise me at once.

Very respectfully,
(signed) Lacey P. Bobo.

Applications for Enrollment of Choctaw Newborn
Act of 1905   Volume VII

416
7-NB-~~614~~

Muskogee, Indian Territory, March 7, 1906.

Lacey P. Bobo,
    Hugo, Indian Territory.

Dear Sir:

    Receipt is hereby acknowledged of your letter of February 27, 1906, relative to the death of Viola Gladys[sic] Anderson, November 19, 1903; you also inclose the testimony of Tandy Anderson, father of said child, and state you have so far been unable to ascertain of any one else the date of the child's death, but if the testimony of an acquaintance is needed you will endeavor to obtain the same.

    In reply to your letter you are advised that is possible you should secure testimony of an acquaintance to the death of Viola Gladys Anderson and it is desirable to have the evidence of two witnesses to the death of citizens before dismissing their applications for enrollment.

                                     Respectfully,

                                     Acting Commissioner.

<u>Choc New Born 417</u>
    Ula H. Griffith   b. 5-22-03

Choctaw 5615.

Muskogee, Indian Territory, April 4, 1905.

C. G. Griffith,
    Sallisaw, Indian Territory.

Dear Sir:

    Receipt is hereby acknowledged of the affidavits of Emma J. Griffith (Fargo) and V. W. Hudson to the birth of Ula Griffith, daughter of C. G. and Emma J. Griffith, may 22, 1903, and the same have been filed with our records as an application for the enrollment of said child.

                                     Respectfully,

                                     Commissioner in Charge.

Applications for Enrollment of Choctaw Newborn
Act of 1905   Volume VII

COPY

7 NB 417

Muskogee, Indian Territory, April 26, 1905.

Credo G. Griffith,
    Salisaw[sic], Indian Territory.

Dear Sir:

    Receipt is hereby acknowledged of the affidavits of Emily[sic] Griffith (Fargo) and V. W. Hudson to the birth of Ula H. Griffith, daughter of Credo G. and Emily Griffith (Fargo), May 22, 1903, and the same have been filed with our records in the matter of the enrollment of said child.

                  Respectfully,
                  SIGNED

                  Tams Bixby
                  Chairman.

N. B. 417

Muskogee, Indian Territory, April 8, 1905.

Credo G. Griffith,
    Salisaw[sic], Indian Territory.

Dear Sir:

    There is inclosed you herewith for execution application for the enrollment of your infant child, --- Griffith, born May 22, 1903.

    In the affidavits heretofore filed with the Commission the name of the applicant appears in one place as "Ula H. Griffith" and as "Ula Griffith" in another. You will please insert the correct name in the inclosed application. You will note that the name of the mother appears in this application as Emily Griffith (Fargo), for the purpose of identification.

    In having these affidavits executed care should be exercised to see that all names are written in full, as they appear in the body of the affidavit, and in the event that either of the persons signing the affidavit are unable to write, signatures by mark must be attested by two witnesses. Each affidavit must be executed before a Notary Public and the notarial seal and signature of the officer must be attached to each separate affidavit.

Applications for Enrollment of Choctaw Newborn
Act of 1905   Volume VII

Respectfully,
SIGNED

T. B. Needles.

LM 8-15.   Commissioner in Charge.

BIRTH AFFIDAVIT.

DEPARTMENT OF THE INTERIOR,
COMMISSION TO THE FIVE CIVILIZED TRIBES.

IN RE Application for Enrollment, as a citizen of the Choctaw Nation, of Ula H Griffith , born on the 22 day of May , 1903

Name of Father: Crado[sic] G. Griffith   a citizen of the   U.S.   Nation.
(nee Fargo)
Name of Mother: Emily Jane Griffith   a citizen of the   Choctaw   Nation.

Post-Office: Sallisaw Ind Ter

AFFIDAVIT OF MOTHER.

UNITED STATES OF AMERICA, }
INDIAN TERRITORY.   }
Northern   District.   }

I, Emily Jane Griffith (nee Fargo) , on oath state that I am 24 years of age and a citizen by blood , of the Choctaw Nation; that I am the lawful wife of Credo G Griffith , who is a citizen, ~~by~~ U.S. of the .... Nation; that a female child was born to me on 22 day of May , 1903 , that said child has been named Ula H. Griffith , and is now living.

nee Fargo
Emily Jane Griffith

WITNESSES TO MARK:
{

Subscribed and sworn to before me this 20 day of Jan , 1904

My Commission Expires Sep't 24, 1905.   John Hannah
                                                                NOTARY PUBLIC.

Applications for Enrollment of Choctaw Newborn
Act of 1905   Volume VII

AFFIDAVIT OF ATTENDING PHYSICIAN OR MID-WIFE.

UNITED STATES OF AMERICA,
   INDIAN TERRITORY.
Northern   District.

I, V.W. Hudson   , a physician   , on oath state that I attended on Mrs. Emily Jane Griffith   , wife of Credo G. Griffith   on the   22   day of May , 1903; that there was born to her on said date a   female   child; that said child is now living and is said to have been named   Ula H. Griffith

                                      V.W. Hudson

WITNESSES TO MARK:
{

Subscribed and sworn to before me this   21   day of   Jan   , 1904

My Commission Expires Sep't 24, 1905.   John Hannah
                                                      NOTARY PUBLIC.

BIRTH AFFIDAVIT.

DEPARTMENT OF THE INTERIOR.
COMMISSION TO THE FIVE CIVILIZED TRIBES.

IN RE APPLICATION FOR ENROLLMENT, as a citizen of the   Choctaw   Nation, of Ula Griffith   , born on the 22" day of May , 1903

Name of Father: C.G. Griffith   a ######### white man   Nation.
Name of Mother: Emma J. Griffith (nee Fargo)   a citizen of the   Choctaw   Nation.

                            Postoffice   Sallisaw, I.T.

AFFIDAVIT OF MOTHER.

UNITED STATES OF AMERICA, Indian Territory,
   Northern   DISTRICT.

I, Emma J. Griffith   , on oath state that I am 26#[sic]   years of age and a citizen by   Blood   , of the   Choctaw   Nation; that I am the lawful wife of C.G. Griffith a white man   , who is a citizen, by .... of the ....Nation; that a   female   child was born to me on 22" day of May   , 1903; that said child has been named   Ula Griffith   , and was living March 4, 1905.

                                        Emma J. Griffith

Applications for Enrollment of Choctaw Newborn
Act of 1905   Volume VII

Witnesses To Mark:
{

    Subscribed and sworn to before me this 25" day of   March   , 1905

                            W.L. Curtis Mayor.
                            & Exofficio Commission Notary Public.
                            Sallisaw, I.T.

AFFIDAVIT OF ATTENDING PHYSICIAN OR MID-WIFE.

UNITED STATES OF AMERICA, Indian Territory, }
  Northern   DISTRICT. }

    I,   Dr. V.W. Hudson   , a   Physician   , on oath state that I attended on Mrs. Emma J. Griffith   , wife of   C.G. Griffith   on the 22" day of May , 1903; that there was born to her on said date a   female   child; that said child was living March 4, 1905, and is said to have been named   Ula Griffith

                            V.W. Hudson M.D.

Witnesses To Mark:
{

    Subscribed and sworn to before me this 25" day of   March   , 1905

                            W.L. Curtis Mayor.
                            & Exofficio Commission Notary Public.
                            Sallisaw, I.T.

BIRTH AFFIDAVIT.
                        DEPARTMENT OF THE INTERIOR.
                COMMISSION TO THE FIVE CIVILIZED TRIBES.

    IN RE APPLICATION FOR ENROLLMENT, as a citizen of the   Choctaw   Nation, of Ula H. Griffith   , born on the 22 day of May   , 1903

Name of Father: Credo G. Griffith   a citizen of the   U.S.   Nation.
Name of Mother: Emily Griffith (Fargo)   a citizen of the   Choctaw   Nation.

                      Postoffice   Sallisaw, I.T.

Applications for Enrollment of Choctaw Newborn
Act of 1905   Volume VII

AFFIDAVIT OF MOTHER.

UNITED STATES OF AMERICA, Indian Territory, }
Northern   DISTRICT.

I, Emily Griffith (Fargo), on oath state that I am 26 years of age and a citizen by blood, of the Choctaw Nation; that I am the lawful wife of Credo G. Griffith, who is a citizen, ~~by~~ .... of the U.S. Nation; that a female child was born to me on 22" day of May, 1903; that said child has been named Ula H. Griffith, and was living March 4, 1905.

                                      Emily Griffith (Fargo)

Witnesses To Mark:
{

Subscribed and sworn to before me this 21st day of April, 1905

My Com ex. 3/28/09
                                        W.L. Curtis
                                        Notary Public.

AFFIDAVIT OF ATTENDING PHYSICIAN OR MID-WIFE.

UNITED STATES OF AMERICA, Indian Territory, }
Northern   DISTRICT.

I, V.W. Hudson, a Physician, on oath state that I attended on Mrs. Emily Griffith (Fargo), wife of Credo G. Griffith on the 22 day of May, 1903; that there was born to her on said date a female child; that said child was living March 4, 1905, and is said to have been named Ula H. Griffith

                                        V.W. Hudson M.D.

Witnesses To Mark:
{

Subscribed and sworn to before me this 21st day of April, 1905

                                        W.L. Curtis
                                        Notary Public.

My Com ex. 3/28/09

Applications for Enrollment of Choctaw Newborn
Act of 1905   Volume VII

Choc New Born 418
   Laclara A. Seago   b. 1-16-03

7-5654
7-3525
7-5359
7-3606

Muskogee, Indian Territory, March 31, 1905.

J. L. Rappolee,
   Attorney at Law,
      Caddo, Indian Territory.

Dear Sir:

   Receipt is hereby acknowledged of the affidavits of Addie A. Seago and H. E. Rappolee to the birth of LaClara A. Seago, daughter of Charles W. and Addie A. Seago, January 16, 1903; also the affidavits of Katie Owens and W. J. Melton to the birth of Estella Owens, daughter of John and Katie Owens October 28, 1902.

   Receipt is also acknowledged of your affidavit and the affidavit of Ellon Airington to the birth of Alvin Airington, son of Noah and Ellen Airington, February 9, 1905; also the affidavits of Amanda Damron and W. J. Melton to the birth of Ethel Damron, daughter of W. R. and Amanda Damron, January 19, 1905, and the same have been filed with our records as applications for the enrollment of said children.

Respectfully,

Chairman.

7-NB-418.

Muskogee, Indian Territory, May 24, 1905.

Charles W. Seago,
   Caddo, Indian Territory.

Dear Sir:

   There is enclosed you herewith for execution application for the enrollment of your infant child, LaClara A. Seago.

   In the affidavits filed in this office on March 27, 1905, the date of the applicants birth is given as January 16, 1903, while in those filed on the 26th ultimo, the date of

Applications for Enrollment of Choctaw Newborn
Act of 1905   Volume VII

birth is given as January 16, 1902. In the enclosed application the date of birth is left blank, in which you will please insert the correct date of birth and, when the affidavits are properly executed, return them to this office.

In having these affidavits executed care should be exercised to see that all names are written in full, as they appear in the body of the affidavit, and in the event that either of the persons signing the affidavit are unable to write, signatures by mark must be attested by two witnesses. Each affidavit must be executed before a Notary Public and the notarial seal and signature of the officer must be attached to each separate affidavit.

Respectfully,

Chairman.

VR 24-7.

7-N.B. 418.

Muskogee, Indian Territory, June 2, 1905.

Charles W. Seago,
Caddo, Indian Territory.

Dear Sir:

Receipt is hereby acknowledged of the affidavits of Addie A. Seago and H. E. Rappolee to the birth of LaClara A. Seago, daughter of Charles W. and Addie A. Seago, January 16, 1903, and the same have been filed with our records in the matter of the enrollment of said child.

Respectfully,

(End of letter)

NEW-BORN AFFIDAVIT.

Number

Choctaw Enrolling Commission.

IN THE MATTER OF THE APPLICATION FOR ENROLLMENT, as a citizen of the Choctaw   Nation, of   LaClara A Seago

born on the   16   day of   January   1903

Name of father   Charles W. Seago   a citizen of   Choctaw Nation final enrollment No   533

Applications for Enrollment of Choctaw Newborn
Act of 1905   Volume VII

Name of mother   Addie A. Seago   a citizen of   Choctaw Nation final enrollment No 14957

Postoffice   Caddo, I.T.

AFFIDAVIT OF MOTHER.

UNITED STATES OF AMERICA,
INDIAN TERRITORY,
Central   DISTRICT

I   Addie A. Seago   on oath state that I am   35   years of age and a citizen by   blood   of the   Choctaw   Nation, and as such have been placed upon the final roll of the   Choctaw   Nation, by the Honorable Secretary of the Interior my final enrollment number being   14957 ; that I am the lawful wife of   Charles W. Seago   , who is a citizen of the   Choctaw   intermarriage   Nation, and as such has been placed upon the final roll of said Nation by the Honorable Secretary of the Interior, his final enrollment number being   533   and that a   Female   child was born to me on the   16   day of   January   190 2 ; that said child has been named   Leclara[sic] A. Seago   , and is now living.

Addie A Seago

WITNESSETH:
Must be two Witnesses who are Citizens.   C.D. Robinson
John Owens

Subscribed and sworn to before me this   16   day of   January   190 5

James Bower
Notary Public.

My commission expires   Sept 23-1907

AFFIDAVIT OF ATTENDING PHYSICIAN OR MIDWIFE

UNITED STATES OF AMERICA
INDIAN TERRITORY
Central   DISTRICT

I,   HE Rappolee   a   Practicing Physician on oath state that I attended on Mrs.   Addie A Seago   wife of   Charles W Seago on the   16   day of   January   , 190 2, that there was born to her on said date a   Female   child, that said child is now living, and is said to have been named   Leclara A Seago

HE Rappolee   M.D.
Subscribed and sworn to before me this, the   17th   day of   January   190 5

J L Rappolee
Notary Public.

250

Applications for Enrollment of Choctaw Newborn
Act of 1905   Volume VII

WITNESSETH:

Must be two witnesses who are citizens and know the child.
{ C.D. Robinson
  John Owens

We hereby certify that we are well acquainted with   H E Rappolee a   Physician   and know   him   to be reputable and of good standing in the community.

{ C D Robinson
  John Owens

BIRTH AFFIDAVIT.

DEPARTMENT OF THE INTERIOR.
COMMISSION TO THE FIVE CIVILIZED TRIBES.

IN RE APPLICATION FOR ENROLLMENT, as a citizen of the   Choctaw   Nation, of LaClara A Seago   , born on the   16th day of   January   , 1903

Name of Father: Charles W Seago   a citizen of the   Choctaw   Nation.
Name of Mother: Addie A Seago   a citizen of the   Choctaw   Nation.

Postoffice   Caddo Ind Ter

AFFIDAVIT OF MOTHER.

UNITED STATES OF AMERICA, Indian Territory,
Central   DISTRICT.

I,   Addie A Seago   , on oath state that I am   35   years of age and a citizen by   Blood   , of the   Choctaw   Nation; that I am the lawful wife of   Charles W Seago   , who is a citizen, by Intermarriage   of the   Choctaw   Nation; that a   Female   child was born to me on   16th day of   January   , 1903; that said child has been named   LaClara A Seago   , and was living March 4, 1905.

Addie A Seago

Witnesses To Mark:
{

Subscribed and sworn to before me this   29   day of   May   , 1905

J L Rappolee
Notary Public.

251

Applications for Enrollment of Choctaw Newborn
Act of 1905   Volume VII

AFFIDAVIT OF ATTENDING PHYSICIAN OR MID-WIFE.

UNITED STATES OF AMERICA, Indian Territory, }
Central   DISTRICT. }

I,   H E Rappolee   , a   Physician   , on oath state that I attended on Mrs.   Addie A Seago   , wife of   Charles W Seago   on the   16th day of   January   , 1903; that there was born to her on said date a   Female   child; that said child was living March 4, 1905, and is said to have been named   LaClara A Seago

                                H.E. Rappolee
Witnesses To Mark:
{

   Subscribed and sworn to before me this 29   day of   May   , 1905

                                J L Rappolee
                                   Notary Public.

Choc New Born 419
       Jewel Floyd   b. 11-7-04

                                          7-5685

                     Muskogee, Indian Territory, March 29, 1905.

J. F. Mckeel[sic],
       Ada, Indian Territory.

Dear Sir:

   Receipt is hereby acknowledged of your letter of March 22, 1905, enclosing affidavits of Eliza Floyd and W. T. Nolen to the birth of Jewel Floyd, daughter of Charles W. and Eliza Floyd, November 7, 1904, and the same have been filed with our records as an application for the enrollment of said child.

                     Respectfully,

                                Chairman.

Applications for Enrollment of Choctaw Newborn
Act of 1905   Volume VII

BIRTH AFFIDAVIT.

DEPARTMENT OF THE INTERIOR.
COMMISSION TO THE FIVE CIVILIZED TRIBES.

IN RE APPLICATION FOR ENROLLMENT, as a citizen of the   Choctaw   Nation, of Jewel Floyd   , born on the 7th   day of   Nov   , 1904

Name of Father: Charles W. Floyd   a citizen of the   Choctaw   Nation.
Name of Mother: Eliza Floyd   a citizen of the   Choctaw   Nation.

Postoffice   Ada, I.T.

AFFIDAVIT OF MOTHER.

UNITED STATES OF AMERICA, Indian Territory,
Southern   DISTRICT.

I,   Eliza Floyd   , on oath state that I am 23   years of age and a citizen by Blood   , of the   Choctaw   Nation; that I am the lawful wife of   Charles W Floyd , who is a citizen, by Marriage   of the   Choctaw   Nation; that a   Female   child was born to me on   7th   day of   Nov   , 1904; that said child has been named Jewel Floyd , and was living March 4, 1905.

Eliza Floyd

Witnesses To Mark:
{

Subscribed and sworn to before me this 21st   day of   Mch   , 1905

J.F. McKeel
Notary Public.

AFFIDAVIT OF ATTENDING PHYSICIAN OR MID-WIFE.

UNITED STATES OF AMERICA, Indian Territory,
Southern   DISTRICT.

I,   W.T. Nolen   , a   Physician   , on oath state that I attended on Mrs. Eliza Floyd   , wife of   Charles W. Floyd   on the 7th day of   Nov , 1904; that there was born to her on said date a   Female   child; that said child was living March 4, 1905, and is said to have been named Jewel Foyd

W. T. Nolen

Witnesses To Mark:
{

253

Applications for Enrollment of Choctaw Newborn
Act of 1905 Volume VII

Subscribed and sworn to before me this 21st day of Mch, 1905

J.F. McKeel
Notary Public.

Choc New Born 420
    Frank Huddleston, Jr b. 8-9-03
    Nora Huddleston b. 12-18-04

Allen, I. T.
Mar. 21 1905.

To The Commission To The Five Civilized Tribes:-

I, W.C. Threlkeld a practicing physician do solemnly swear that on December 18, 1904, there was born to Mrs. May Huddleston, wife of Frank Huddleston, a female child. Said child is now living and is said to be named Nora Huddleston.

W.C. Threlkeld M.D.

Subscribed and sworn to before me Mar 21 1905.

WW Jones
Notary Public
My Commission expires Jan. 8 1907

BIRTH AFFIDAVIT.

DEPARTMENT OF THE INTERIOR.
COMMISSION TO THE FIVE CIVILIZED TRIBES.

IN RE APPLICATION FOR ENROLLMENT, as a citizen of the Choctaw Nation, of Nora Huddleston, born on the 18th day of December, 1904

Name of Father: Frank Huddleston   a citizen of the Choctaw Nation.
Name of Mother: May Huddleston   a citizen of the United States Nation.

Postoffice   Allen, Ind. Ter.

Applications for Enrollment of Choctaw Newborn
Act of 1905 Volume VII

AFFIDAVIT OF MOTHER.

UNITED STATES OF AMERICA, Indian Territory,
Central   DISTRICT.

    I, May Huddleston , on oath state that I am 21 years of age and a citizen by ———, of the United States ~~Nation~~; that I am the lawful wife of Frank Huddleston , who is a citizen, by blood of the Choctaw Nation; that a female child was born to me on 18th day of December , 1904; that said child has been named Nora Huddleston , and was living March 4, 1905.

                              May Huddleston

Witnesses To Mark:
{

    Subscribed and sworn to before me this 23rd day of March , 1905

                              Wirt Franklin
                              Notary Public.

BIRTH AFFIDAVIT.

DEPARTMENT OF THE INTERIOR,
COMMISSION TO THE FIVE CIVILIZED TRIBES.

    In Re Application for Enrollment, as a citizen of the Choctaw Nation, of Frank Huddleston Jr , born on the 9 day of August , 1903

Name of Father: Frank Huddleston   a citizen of the Choctaw Nation.
Name of Mother: May Huddleston   a citizen of the .... Nation.

                        Post-office   Allen, I.T.

AFFIDAVIT OF MOTHER.

UNITED STATES OF AMERICA,
    INDIAN TERRITORY,
    Central   District.

    I, May Huddleston , on oath state that I am nineteen years of age and a citizen by marriage , of the Choctaw Nation; that I am the lawful wife of Frank Huddleston , who is a citizen, by blood of the Choctaw Nation; that a male child was born to me on ninth day of August , 190 3, that said child has been named Frank Huddleston Jr , and is now living.

                              May Huddleston

Applications for Enrollment of Choctaw Newborn
Act of 1905   Volume VII

WITNESSES TO MARK:

{

Subscribed and sworn to before me this   24   day of   Sept   , 1903

W.B. Soney

NOTARY PUBLIC.

AFFIDAVIT OF ATTENDING PHYSICIAN OR MID-WIFE.

UNITED STATES OF AMERICA, }
INDIAN TERRITORY,
Central   District.

I,   W.C. Threlkeld   , a   physician   , on oath state that I attended on Mrs.   May Huddleston , wife of   Frank Huddleston   on the   ninth   day of August , 1903 ; that there was born to her on said date a   male   child; that said child is now living and is said to have been named   Frank Huddleston Jr

W.C. Threlkeld M.D.

WITNESSES TO MARK:

{

Subscribed and sworn to before me this   24   day of   Sept   , 1903

W.B. Soney

My Com Exp May 12, 1906.   **NOTARY PUBLIC.**

7-NB-420

Muskogee, Indian Territory, July 21, 1905.

Frank Huddleston,
    Allen, Indian Territory.

Dear Sir:

Receipt is hereby acknowledged of the marriage license and certificate between yourself and May Smith which you offer in support of the application for the enrollment of your minor children, Frank Huddleston Jr., and May[sic] Huddleston, and the same has been filed with the records in this case.

Respectfully,

Commissioner.

Applications for Enrollment of Choctaw Newborn
Act of 1905   Volume VII

7-NB-420

Muskogee, Indian Territory, July 15, 1905.

Frank Huddleston,
    Allen, Indian Territory.

Dear Sir:

    Referring to the applications for the enrollment of your infant children, Frank and Nora Huddleston, it is noted that the applicants claim through you.

    In this event it will be necessary that you file in this office either the original or a certified copy of the license and certificate of marriage between yourself and your wife, May Huddleston, the mother of the children.

    This matter should receive your immediate attention as no further action can be taken realtive[sic] to the enrollment of said applicants until the evidence requested is supplied.

                              Respectfully,

                                         Commissioner.

Muskogee, Indian Territory, August 3, 1905.

Chief Clerk,
    Chickasaw Land Office,
        Atoka, Indian Territory.

Dear Sir:

    You are advised that the following notation has this day been entered on Choctaw New Born Roll Card No. 420:

    "Evidence of marriage, of parents of Nos. 1 and 2, filed July 21, 1905."

    You are instructed to enter said notation upon the duplicate Card in the possession of your office.

                              Respectfully,

                                         Commissioner.

Applications for Enrollment of Choctaw Newborn
Act of 1905   Volume VII

Muskogee, Indian Territory, August 3, 1905.

Chief Clerk,
    Choctaw Land Office,
        Atoka, Indian Territory.

Dear Sir:

You are advised that the following notation has this day been entered on Choctaw New Born Roll Card No. 420:

"Evidence of marriage, of parents of Nos. 1 and 2, filed July 21, 1905."

You are instructed to enter said notation upon the duplicate Card in the possession of your office.

    Respectfully,

        Commissioner.

7-NB-420

Muskogee, Indian Territory, August 8, 1905.

Frank Huddleston, Sr.,
    Allen, Indian Territory.

Dear Sir:

Receipt is hereby acknowledged of your letter of August 3, 1905, asking if your son Frank Huddleston, Jr., has been approved.

In reply to your letter you are advised that the name of Frank Huddleston, Jr., has been placed upon a schedule of citizens by blood of the Choctaw Nation which has been forwarded the Secretary of the Interior and you will be notified when his enrollment is approved by the Department.

    Respectfully,

        Commissioner.

Applications for Enrollment of Choctaw Newborn
Act of 1905   Volume VII

Marriage License.

THE CHOCTAW NATION.
Indian Territory, } SS.
TOBUCKSY COUNTY.

To any Minister of the Gospel, Judge or any person in the Choctaw Nation authorized to solemnize the rites of matrimony,
   GREETING:-

Whereas,   Frank Huddleston   a citizen of the ~~United States~~ Choctaw Nation, has duly made application to the undersigned, Clerk of the County and Probate Court, within and for the County of Tobucksy, Choctaw Nation, for a license to enter into the Bonds of Matrimony with Miss May Smith a citizen of the ~~Choctaw Nation~~ United States And the undersigned being satisfied that the said Frank Huddleston   is a suitable person to be granted license to enter into the Bonds of Matrimony with the said   Miss May Smith

Now, I therefore grant unto the   said Frank Huddleston   a license to marry the said Miss May Smith   And any Minister of the Gospel, Judge or any person authorized to solemnize the rites of Matrimony, is hereby authorized to join in Matrimony the said   Frank Huddleston and the said   Miss May Smith

In testimony whereof I,   Will T. Walker   County and Probate Clerk, in and for the County of Tobucksy, Choctaw Nation, have hereunto set my hand and seal of said Court, this   23" day of   September   A. D. ~~189....~~ 1902

Will T. Walker   Clerk.

By .... D. C.
of Tobucksy County, C. N.

CERTIFICATE OF MARRIAGE.

CHOCTAW NATION,   I,   D.J. Austin
                   } ss.   A   Minister
Tobucksy   County.

do hereby certify that on the   24th   day of   September   A. D.   1902   I did duly and according to law, as commanded in the foregoing License, solemnize the Rite and publish the Banns of Matrimony between the parties therein named.

Witness my hand this   24th   day of   September   A. D. 1902

Applications for Enrollment of Choctaw Newborn
Act of 1905 Volume VII

My credentials are recorded in the office of the Clerk of the   U. S.
Court   at So. McAlester I.T.   , Book .... Page

	D J Austin
A	Minister

Allen, I. T.
Mar. 21 1905.

To The Commission To The Five Civilized Tribes:-

I, W.C. Threlkeld a practicing physician do solemnly swear that on August 9", 1903, there was born to Mrs. May Huddleston, wife of Frank Huddleston, a male child. Said child is now living and is said to be named Frank Huddleston Jr.

W.C. Threlkeld M.D.

Subscribed and sworn to before me this twenty first day of Mar. 1905.

WW Jones
Notary Public
My Commission expires Jan. 8 1907

BIRTH AFFIDAVIT.
DEPARTMENT OF THE INTERIOR.
COMMISSION TO THE FIVE CIVILIZED TRIBES.

IN RE APPLICATION FOR ENROLLMENT, as a citizen of the Choctaw Nation, of Frank Huddleston Jr, born on the 9th day of August, 1903

Name of Father: Frank Huddleston   a citizen of the Choctaw Nation.
Name of Mother: May Huddleston   a citizen of the United States Nation.

Postoffice   Allen, I.T.

AFFIDAVIT OF MOTHER.

UNITED STATES OF AMERICA, Indian Territory,
Central   **DISTRICT.**

I, May Huddleston, on oath state that I am 21 years of age and a citizen by ———, of the United States ~~Nation~~; that I am the lawful wife of Frank Huddleston, who is a citizen, by blood of the Choctaw Nation; that a

Applications for Enrollment of Choctaw Newborn
Act of 1905   Volume VII

male   child was born to me on   9th   day of   August   , 1903; that said child has been named   Frank Huddleston Jr   , and was living March 4, 1905.

May Huddleston

Witnesses To Mark:
{

Subscribed and sworn to before me this   23rd   day of   March   , 1905

Wirt Franklin
Notary Public.

Choc New Born 421
    James Harvey Ashford   b. 12-5-02

BIRTH AFFIDAVIT.

DEPARTMENT OF THE INTERIOR.
COMMISSION TO THE FIVE CIVILIZED TRIBES.

IN RE APPLICATION FOR ENROLLMENT, as a citizen of the   Choctaw   Nation, of   James Harvey Ashford   , born on the   5   day of   Dec   , 1905

Name of Father: James D Ashford   a citizen of the   Choctaw   Nation.
Name of Mother: Lizzie Ashford   a citizen of the   Choctaw   Nation.

Postoffice   Coalgate Ind Ter

AFFIDAVIT OF MOTHER.

UNITED STATES OF AMERICA, Indian Territory, }
   Central   DISTRICT. }

    I,   Lizzie Ashford   , on oath state that I am   28   years of age and a citizen by   Intermarriage   , of the   Choctaw   Nation; that I am the lawful wife of   James D Ashford   , who is a citizen, by Blood   of the   Choctaw   Nation; that a   male   child was born to me on   5th   day of   Dec   , 1902; that said child has been named   James Harvey Ashford   , and was living March 4, 1905.

Lizzie Ashford

Witnesses To Mark:
{

Applications for Enrollment of Choctaw Newborn
Act of 1905   Volume VII

Subscribed and sworn to before me this   27 day of   May   , 1905

                         PE Wilhelm
                         Notary Public.

AFFIDAVIT OF ATTENDING PHYSICIAN OR MID-WIFE.

UNITED STATES OF AMERICA, Indian Territory, }
     Central   DISTRICT.

     I, Martha James , a midwife , on oath state that I attended on Mrs. Lizzie Ashford , wife of James D Ashford on the 5th day of Dec , 1905; that there was born to her on said date a   male   child; that said child was living March 4, 1905, and is said to have been named James Harvey Ashford

                        Mrs Martha James
Witnesses To Mark: mid-wife
{

Subscribed and sworn to before me this   27 day of   May   , 1905

                         PE Wilhelm
                         Notary Public.

BIRTH AFFIDAVIT.
                 DEPARTMENT OF THE INTERIOR.
          COMMISSION TO THE FIVE CIVILIZED TRIBES.

     IN RE APPLICATION FOR ENROLLMENT, as a citizen of the   *Choctaw*   Nation, of *James Harvey Ashford* , born on the *5th* day of *Dec 1902* , 1........

Name of Father: *James D Ashford*   a citizen of the *Choctaw* Nation.
Name of Mother: *Lizzie Ashford*   a citizen of the *Choctaw* Nation.

                 Postoffice   *Coalgate Ind Ter*

                 AFFIDAVIT OF MOTHER.

UNITED STATES OF AMERICA, Indian Territory, }
     Central   DISTRICT.

     I, *Lizzie Ashford* , on oath state that I am 28 years of age and a citizen by *intermarriage* , of the *Choctaw* Nation; that I am the lawful wife of *James D Ashford* , who is a citizen, by *blood* of the *Choctaw* Nation; that a

Applications for Enrollment of Choctaw Newborn
Act of 1905   Volume VII

male   child was born to me on   *5th*   day of   *Dec 1902*   , 1........; that said child has been named   *James Harvey Ashford*   , and is now living.

Lizzie Ashford

Witnesses To Mark:
{ Robt Shaw
{ M O Niles

Subscribed and sworn to before me this   *15th*   day of   *December 1904*, 190.....

P E Wilhelm
Notary Public.

AFFIDAVIT OF ATTENDING PHYSICIAN OR MID-WIFE.

UNITED STATES OF AMERICA, Indian Territory, }
   Central   DISTRICT. }

I,   *Martha James*   , a   *mid-wife*   , on oath state that I attended on Mrs.   *Lizzie Ashford*   , wife of   *James D Ashford*   on the 2nd[sic]   day of *December, 1902*; that there was born to her on said date a   *Male*   child; that said child is now living and is said to have been named *James Harvey Ashford*

Martha James

Witnesses To Mark:
{ Robt Shaw
{ M O Niles

Subscribed and sworn to before me this   *15th*   day of   *Dec 1904*   , 190.....

P E Wilhelm
Notary Public.

NEW-BORN AFFIDAVIT.

    Number............

...Choctaw Enrolling Commission...

IN THE MATTER OF THE APPLICATION FOR ENROLLMENT, as a citizen of the Choctaw   Nation, of   *James Harvey Ashford*

born on the   *5th*   day of __December 1902__   190........

Applications for Enrollment of Choctaw Newborn
Act of 1905 Volume VII

Name of father *James D Ashford* a citizen of Choctaw
Nation final enrollment No. *15066*
Name of mother *Lizzie Ashford* a citizen of Chcotaw[sic]
Nation final enrollment No. *7-5700*

Postoffice *Coalgate, Ind Ter*

AFFIDAVIT OF MOTHER.

UNITED STATES OF AMERICA
INDIAN TERRITORY
Central   DISTRICT

I   *Lizzie Ashford*   , on oath state that I am *28* years of age and a citizen by *intermarriage* of the *Choctaw* Nation, and as such have been placed upon the final roll of the *Choctaw* Nation, by the Honorable Secretary of the Interior my final enrollment number being *7-7500* ; that I am the lawful wife of *James D Ashford* , who is a citizen of the *Choctaw* Nation, and as such has been placed upon the final roll of said Nation by the Honorable Secretary of the Interior, his final enrollment number being *15066* and that a *Male* child was born to me on the *5th* day of *December 1902* 190...... ; that said child has been named *James Harvey Ashford* , and is now living.

Witnesseth.   Lizzie Ashford

Must be two Witnesses who are Citizens.   Geo W Sorrells
                                           Osborne D Lawrence

Subscribed and sworn to before me this *22nd* day of *Jan 1902*   190......

PE Wilhelm
Notary Public.

My commission expires:..................................

AFFIDAVIT OF ATTENDING PHYSICIAN OR MIDWIFE

UNITED STATES OF AMERICA
INDIAN TERRITORY
Central   DISTRICT

I, *Martha James* a *Mid-wife* on oath state that I attended on Mrs. *Lizzie Ashford* wife of *James D Ashford* on the *5th* day of *December* , 190 *2*, that there was born to her on said date a *Male* child, that said child is now living, and is said to have been named *James Harvey Ashford*

Martha James Mid-wife   ~~M.D.~~

Applications for Enrollment of Choctaw Newborn
Act of 1905   Volume VII

Subscribed and sworn to before me this, the 22nd day of Jan 1905 190......

P E Wilhelm
Notary Public.

WITNESSETH:
Must be two witnesses who are citizens and know the child.
{ Geo W Sorrells
  Osborne D Lawrence

We hereby certify that we are well acquainted with   Martha James a *mid-wife*   and know her   to be reputable and of good standing in the community.

{ Geo W Sorrells
  Osborne D Lawrence

BIRTH AFFIDAVIT.

DEPARTMENT OF THE INTERIOR.
COMMISSION TO THE FIVE CIVILIZED TRIBES.

IN RE APPLICATION FOR ENROLLMENT, as a citizen of the   Choctaw   Nation, of   James Harvey Ashford , born on the 5th day of December , 1902

Name of Father: James D Ashford   a citizen of the   Choctaw   Nation.
Name of Mother: Lizzie Ashford   a citizen of the   Choctaw   Nation.

Postoffice   Coalgate Ind Ter

AFFIDAVIT OF MOTHER.

UNITED STATES OF AMERICA, Indian Territory, }
Central **DISTRICT.** }

I, Lizzie Ashford , on oath state that I am 28 years of age and a citizen by   Intermarriage , of the   Choctaw   Nation; that I am the lawful wife of   James D Ashford , who is a citizen, by Blood of the   Choctaw   Nation; that a   Male   child was born to me on 5th day of December , 1902; that said child has been named James Harvey Ashford , and was living March 4, 1905.

Lizzie Ashford

Witnesses To Mark:
{ Geo England
  R J Parker

Applications for Enrollment of Choctaw Newborn
Act of 1905   Volume VII

Subscribed and sworn to before me this *12th* day of   *April 1905*   , 190......

P E Wilhelm
Notary Public.

AFFIDAVIT OF ATTENDING PHYSICIAN OR MID-WIFE.

UNITED STATES OF AMERICA, Indian Territory, }
  Central   DISTRICT.

I,   *Martha James*   , a ...., on oath state that I attended on Mrs. Lizzie Ashford , wife of   James D Ashford   on the 5th day of December , 1902; that there was born to her on said date a   Male   child; that said child was living March 4, 1905, and is said to have been named James Harvey Ashford

Mrs Martha James
Witnesses To Mark: Mid-wife
 { Geo England
   R J Parker

Subscribed and sworn to before me this *12th* day of   *April 1905*   , 190......

P E Wilhelm
Notary Public.

---

7 N.B. 421.

Muskogee, Indian Territory, June 2, 1905.

James D. Ashford,
  Coalgate, Indian Territory.

Dear Sir:

Receipt is hereby acknowledged of the affidavits of Lizzie Ashford and Mrs. Martha James to the birth of James Harvey Ashford, son of James D. and Lizzie Ashford, December 5, 1902, and the same have been filed with our records in the matter of the enrollment of said child.

Respectfully,

(End of letter.)

Applications for Enrollment of Choctaw Newborn
Act of 1905   Volume VII

Choctaw N.B. 421.

COPY

Muskogee, Indian Territory, April 18, 1905.

Lizzie Ashford,
    Coalgate, Indian Territory.

Dear Madam:

    Receipt is hereby acknowledged of your letter of April 12, transmitting the affidavits of yourself and Martha James to the birth of James Harvey Ashford, son of James D. and Lizzie Ashford, December 5, 1902, and the same have been filed with our records in the matter of the enrollment of said child.

Respectfully,

SIGNED *Tams Bixby*
Chairman.

COPY

Choctaw N.B. 421.

Muskogee, Indian Territory, April 14, 1905.

James D. Ashford,
    Coalgate, Indian Territory.

Dear Sir:

    Receipt is hereby acknowledged of your letter of April 7, asking if you need another blank for the enrollment of your child, James Harvey Ashford.

    In reply to your letter you are advised that on April 10, 1905, there was forwarded a blank for the enrollment of your child, James Harvey Ashford, and you should execute same in accordance with the instructions contained therein.

Respectfully,

SIGNED

T. B. Needles.
Commissioner in Charge.

Applications for Enrollment of Choctaw Newborn
Act of 1905   Volume VII

7-NB-421.

Muskogee, Indian Territory, May 24, 1905.

James D. Ashford,
Coalgate, Indian Territory.

Dear Sir:

There is enclosed you herewith for execution application for the enrollment of your infant child, James Harvey Ashford.

In the applications filed in this office on the 18th and 25th ultimo, the date of the applicants[sic] birth is given as December 5, 1902, while in the one filed March 4, 1905, the mother gives the date of birth as December 5, 1902, and the physician gives it as December 2, 1902. In the enclosed application the date of the applicants[sic] birth is left blank, in which you will please insert the correct date of birth, and, when properly executed, return to this office.

In having these affidavits executed care should be exercised to see that all names are written in full, as they appear in the body of the affidavit, and in the event that either of the persons signing the affidavit are unable to write, signatures by mark must be attested by two witnesses. Each affidavit must be executed before a Notary Public and the notarial seal and signature of the officer must be attached to each separate affidavit.

Respectfully,

Vr 24-6.   Chairman.

Choc New Born 422
    Stephen Brown   b. 8-1-04

Applications for Enrollment of Choctaw Newborn
Act of 1905 Volume VII

7-NB-422

Muskogee, Indian Territory, July 28, 1905.

F. M. Brown,
    Indianola, Indian Territory.

Dear Sir:

    Receipt is hereby acknowledged of your letter without date in regard to the enrollment of your child Steve Brown.

    In reply to your letter you are advised that the name of your child Stephen Brown has been placed upon a schedule of citizens by blood of the Choctaw Nation which has been forwarded the Secretary of the Interior and you will be notified when his enrollment is approved by the Department.

                  Respectfully,

                                  Commissioner.

BIRTH AFFIDAVIT.

DEPARTMENT OF THE INTERIOR.
COMMISSION TO THE FIVE CIVILIZED TRIBES.

IN RE APPLICATION FOR ENROLLMENT, as a citizen of the Choctaw Nation, of Steve Brown, born on the 1st day of Aug, 1904

Name of Father: Foster M. Brown   a citizen of the United States Nation.
Name of Mother: Hettie A Brown   a citizen of the Choctaw Nation.

                  Postoffice   Indianola I.T.

AFFIDAVIT OF MOTHER.

UNITED STATES OF AMERICA, Indian Territory,
    Western   DISTRICT.

    I, Hettie A Brown, on oath state that I am 23 years of age and a citizen by Blood, of the Choctaw Nation; that I am the lawful wife of Foster M Brown, who is a citizen, ~~by~~ of United States ~~of the~~ ~~Nation~~; that a male child was born to me on 1st day of Aug, 1904, that said child has been named Steve Brown, and is now living.

                                  Hettie A Brown

Applications for Enrollment of Choctaw Newborn
Act of 1905 Volume VII

Witnesses To Mark:
- R.B. Moore
- H.L. Oliver

Subscribed and sworn to before me this 7 day of Dec , 1904

T.J. Rice
Notary Public.

AFFIDAVIT OF ATTENDING PHYSICIAN OR MID-WIFE.

UNITED STATES OF AMERICA, Indian Territory,
Western DISTRICT.

I, Phebe C. Staton , a mid wife , on oath state that I attended on Mrs. Hettie A Brown , wife of Foster M Brown on the 1st day of Aug , 1904; that there was born to her on said date a male child; that said child is now living and is said to have been named Steve Brown

Phebe C Staton

Witnesses To Mark:
- R.B. Moore
- HL Oliver

Subscribed and sworn to before me this 7 day of Dec , 1904

T.J. Rice
Notary Public.

NEW-BORN AFFIDAVIT.

Number................

...Choctaw Enrolling Commission...

IN THE MATTER OF THE APPLICATION FOR ENROLLMENT, as a citizen of the Choctaw Nation, of Steve Brown

born on the 1st day of August 1904

Name of father Foster M Brown a non citizen of Choctaw Nation final enrollment No. ———
Name of mother Hettie A Brown a citizen of Choctaw Nation final enrollment No. 15514

Applications for Enrollment of Choctaw Newborn
Act of 1905   Volume VII

Postoffice   Indianola IT

AFFIDAVIT OF MOTHER.

UNITED STATES OF AMERICA
INDIAN TERRITORY
Western   DISTRICT

I   Hettie A Brown   , on oath state that I am 22 years of age and a citizen by Blood of the Choctaw Nation, and as such have been placed upon the final roll of the Choctaw Nation, by the Honorable Secretary of the Interior my final enrollment number being 15514 ; that I am the lawful wife of Foster M Brown , who is a non citizen of the Choctaw Nation, and as such has been placed upon the final roll of said Nation by the Honorable Secretary of the Interior, his final enrollment number being .... and that a Male child was born to me on the 1st day of August 190 4; that said child has been named Steve Brown , and is now living.

Witnesseth.   Hettie A Brown

Must be two Witnesses who are Citizens.
Will T Walker
John J Beams

Subscribed and sworn to before me this 25 day of Feb 190 5

S.M. Gold
Notary Public.

My commission expires: 2/19 - 1908

AFFIDAVIT OF ATTENDING PHYSICIAN OR MIDWIFE

UNITED STATES OF AMERICA
INDIAN TERRITORY
Western   DISTRICT

I, Phoeby C Staton a Midwife on oath state that I attended on Mrs. Hettie A Brown wife of Foster M Brown on the 1st day of August , 190 4, that there was born to her on said date a Male child, that said child is now living, and is said to have been named Steve Brown

Phoeby C x Staton   M.D.
her   mark

WITNESSETH:
Must be two witnesses who are citizens and know the child.
Will T. Walker
John J Beams

Applications for Enrollment of Choctaw Newborn
Act of 1905   Volume VII

Subscribed and sworn to before me this, the 25th day of February 1905

S M Gold
Notary Public.

We hereby certify that we are well acquainted with Phoeby C Staton a Midwife and know her to be reputable and of good standing in the community.

{ Will T Walker

{ John J Beams

BIRTH AFFIDAVIT.

DEPARTMENT OF THE INTERIOR.
COMMISSION TO THE FIVE CIVILIZED TRIBES.

IN RE APPLICATION FOR ENROLLMENT, as a citizen of the Choctaw Nation, of Stephen Brown, born on the 1st day of August, 1904

Name of Father: Foster M Brown   a citizen of the .... Nation.
Name of Mother: Hettie A Brown   a citizen of the Choctaw Nation.

Postoffice   Indianola, I.T.

AFFIDAVIT OF MOTHER.

UNITED STATES OF AMERICA, Indian Territory, }
Central   DISTRICT. }

I, Hettie A Brown, on oath state that I am 23 years of age and a citizen by blood, of the Choctaw Nation; that I am the lawful wife of Foster M Brown, who is a citizen, ~~by~~ .... of the United States ~~Nation~~; that a male child was born to me on 1st day of August, 1904; that said child has been named Stephen Brown, and was living March 4, 1905.

Hettie A Brown

Witnesses To Mark:
{

Subscribed and sworn to before me this 20th day of March, 1905

Wirt Franklin
Notary Public.

Applications for Enrollment of Choctaw Newborn
Act of 1905   Volume VII

AFFIDAVIT OF ATTENDING PHYSICIAN OR MID-WIFE.

UNITED STATES OF AMERICA, Indian Territory, }
Central   DISTRICT.

I, Phoebe C Staton, a mid-wife, on oath state that I attended on Mrs. Hettie A Brown, wife of Foster M Brown on the 1st day of August, 1904; that there was born to her on said date a male child; that said child was living March 4, 1905, and is said to have been named Stephen Brown

         her
       Phoebe x C. Staton
Witnesses To Mark: mark
 { Harriet Farrill
  G.W. Choate

Subscribed and sworn to before me this 20th day of March, 1905

       Wirt Franklin
       Notary Public.

Choc New Born 423
 Edna Irene Hallmark b. 12-12-02

AFFIDAVIT OF ATTENDING PHYSICIAN OR MID-WIFE.

Territory of Oklahoma
~~UNITED STATES OF AMERICA, Indian Territory,~~ }
Cleveland Co ~~DISTRICT.~~

I, Dr. C.P. Kelley, a Physician, on oath state that I attended on Mrs. Lula[sic] Edna Hallmark, wife of James Hallmark on the 12th day of December, 1902; that there was born to her on said date a female child; that said child was living March 4, 1905, and is said to have been named Edna Irene Hallmark

       Dr C P Kelley
Witnesses To Mark:
 { Henry Applegate
  B.W. Williams

Subscribed and sworn to before me this 1st day of May, 1905

       E.H. Brand
MY COMMISSION EXP. MARCH 16th. 1908. Notary Public.

Applications for Enrollment of Choctaw Newborn
Act of 1905   Volume VII

BIRTH AFFIDAVIT.

DEPARTMENT OF THE INTERIOR.
COMMISSION TO THE FIVE CIVILIZED TRIBES.

IN RE APPLICATION FOR ENROLLMENT, as a citizen of the Choctaw Nation, of Edna Irene Hallmark, born on the 12th day of December, 1902

Name of Father: James W. Hallmark   a citizen of the United States Nation.
Name of Mother: Lulu Edna Hallmark   a citizen of the Choctaw Nation.

Postoffice   New Castle I.T.

AFFIDAVIT OF MOTHER.

UNITED STATES OF AMERICA, ~~Indian~~ Territory, *Oklahoma* }
Cleveland County   ~~DISTRICT~~.

I, Lulu Edna, on oath state that I am 20 years of age and a citizen by Birth, of the Choctaw Nation; that I am the lawful wife of James W Hallmark, who is a citizen, by Birth of the United States ~~Nation~~; that a female child was born to me on 12th day of December, 1902; that said child has been named Edna Irene Hallmark, and was living March 4, 1905.

Lulu Edna Hallmark

Witnesses To Mark:
{ Andrew Kingkade[sic]
  E.F. Nesbitt

Subscribed and sworn to before me this 22nd day of March, 1905

Andrew Kingkade
Notary Public.

AFFIDAVIT OF ATTENDING PHYSICIAN OR MID-WIFE.

UNITED STATES OF AMERICA, ~~Indian~~ Territory, *Oklahoma* }
Cleveland County   ~~DISTRICT~~.

I, Minnie F Foster, a Mid-wife, on oath state that I attended on Mrs. Lulu Edna Hallmark, wife of James W Hallmark on the 12th day of December, 1902; that there was born to her on said date a female child; that

Applications for Enrollment of Choctaw Newborn
Act of 1905   Volume VII

said child was living March 4, 1905, and is said to have been named   Edna Irene Hallmark

Minnie B Foster

Witnesses To Mark:
{ S.A. Brewer
{ E.F. Nesbitt

Subscribed and sworn to before me this 22 day of   March   , 1905

S.A. Brewer
Notary Public.

My Com Expires Dec 15 1908

BIRTH AFFIDAVIT.

DEPARTMENT OF THE INTERIOR.
COMMISSION TO THE FIVE CIVILIZED TRIBES.

IN RE APPLICATION FOR ENROLLMENT, as a citizen of the   Choctaw   Nation, of   Edna Irene Hallmark   , born on the   12   day of   December   , 1902

Name of Father: James W. Hallmark   a citizen of the United States Nation.
Name of Mother: Lula Edna Hallmark   a citizen of the   Choctaw   Nation.

Postoffice   New Castle Ind Ter

AFFIDAVIT OF MOTHER.

UNITED STATES OF AMERICA, Indian Territory, }
Southern   DISTRICT. }

I,   Lula Hallmark   , on oath state that I am   20   years of age and a citizen by   blood   , of the   Choctaw   Nation; that I am the lawful wife of   James W Hallmark   , who is a citizen, by ——— of the   United States   ~~Nation~~; that a female   child was born to me on   12th   day of   December   , 1902; that said child has been named   Edna Irene Hallmark   , and was living March 4, 1905.

Lula Hallmark

Witnesses To Mark:
{

Subscribed and sworn to before me this 29th day of   April   , 1905

H.C. Miller
Notary Public.

Applications for Enrollment of Choctaw Newborn
Act of 1905   Volume VII

BIRTH AFFIDAVIT.

DEPARTMENT OF THE INTERIOR,
COMMISSION TO THE FIVE CIVILIZED TRIBES.

IN RE APPLICATION FOR ENROLLMENT, as a citizen of the Choctaw Nation, of Edna Hallmark, born on the 12th day of December, 190 2

Name of Father: J W Hallmark   a citizen of the .... Nation.
Name of Mother: Lula Hallmark   a citizen of the Chickasaw Nation.

Post-Office : New Castle I.T.

AFFIDAVIT OF MOTHER.

UNITED STATES OF AMERICA,
INDIAN TERRITORY,
.... District.

I, Lula Hallmark, on oath state that I am Eighteen years of age and a citizen by Blood, of the Choctaw Nation; that I am the lawful wife of J.W. Hallmark, who is a citizen, by Marriage of the U S Nation; that a female child was born to me on the 12th day of December, 190 2, that said child has been named Edna Hallmark, and is now living.

Lula Hallmark

WITNESSES TO MARK:

Subscribed and sworn to before me this 29th day of Dec, 1902

My Commission expires Apr. 23rd 1904   *(Name Illegible)*
NOTARY PUBLIC.

AFFIDAVIT OF ATTENDING PHYSICIAN OR MID-WIFE.

UNITED STATES OF AMERICA,
INDIAN TERRITORY,
.... District.

I, CP Kelley, a Physician, on oath state that I attended on Mrs. Lula Hallmark, wife of J W Hallmark on the 12th day of Dec, 190 2; that there was born to her on said date a female child; that said child is now living and is said to have been named Edna

D^r C P Kelley

WITNESSES TO MARK:

Applications for Enrollment of Choctaw Newborn
Act of 1905   Volume VII

Subscribed and sworn to before me this   3rd day of   Jan   , 1903

My Commission expires Apr. 23rd 1904   *(Name Illegible)*
                                                          NOTARY PUBLIC.

7-D-93.

Muskogee, Indian Territory, January 21, 1903.

J.W. Hallmark,
     Newcastle, Indian Territory.

Dear Sir:

Receipt is hereby acknowledged of the application for enrollment as a citizen of the Choctaw Nation of Edna Hallmark, infant daughter of J.W. and Lula Hallmark, born December 12, 1902.

Your attention is invited to the following provisions in the act of Congress approved July 1, 1902, which was ratified by the citizens of the Choctaw and Chickasaw Nations September 25, 1902:

"The names of all persons living on the date of the final ratification of this agreement entitled to be enrolled as provided in section 27 hereof shall be placed upon the rolls made by said Commission; and no child born thereafter to a citizen or freedman and no person intermarried thereafter to a citizen shall be entitled to enrollment or to participate in the distribution of the tribal property of the Choctaws and Chickasaws."

And,

"During the ninety days first following the date of the final ratification of this agreement, the Commission to the Five Civilized Tribes may receive applications for enrollment only of persons whose names are on the tribal rolls, but who have not heretofore been enrolled by said Commission, commonly known as "delinquents," and such intermarried white persons as may have married recognized citizens of the Choctaw and Chickasaw Nations in accordance with the tribal laws, customs and usages on or before the date of the passage of this Act by Congress, and such infant children as may have been born to recognized and enrolled citizens on or before the date of the final ratification of this agreement; but the application of no person whomsoever for enrollment shall be received after the expiration of the said ninety days."

Under the above legislation, the Commission is without authority to enroll this child.

Applications for Enrollment of Choctaw Newborn
Act of 1905   Volume VII

Respectfully,

Commissioner in Charge.

7-D-93.

Muskogee, Indian Territory, January 21, 1903.

J.W. Hallmark,
    Newcastle, Indian Territory.

Dear Sir:

    Receipt is hereby acknowledged of the application for enrollment as a citizen of the Choctaw Nation of Edna Hallmark, infant daughter of J.W. and Lula Hallmark, born December 12, 1902.

    Your attention is invited to section thirty-four of the act of Congress approved July 1, 1902, which was ratified by the citizens of the Choctaw and Chickasaw Nations September 25, 1902, as follows:

    "During the ninety days first following the date of the final ratification of this agreement, the Commission to the Five Civilized Tribes may receive applications for enrollment only of persons whose names are on the tribal rolls, but who have not heretofore been enrolled by said Commission, commonly known as "delinquents," and such intermarried white persons as may have married recognized citizens of the Choctaw and Chickasaw Nations in accordance with the tribal laws, customs and usages on or before the date of the passage of this Act by Congress, and such infant children as may have been born to recognized and enrolled citizens on or before the date of the final ratification of this agreement; but the application of no person whomsoever for enrollment shall be received after the expiration of the said ninety days."

    Under the above legislation, the Commission is without authority to enroll this child.

Respectfully,

Commissioner in Charge.

Applications for Enrollment of Choctaw Newborn
Act of 1905   Volume VII

Choc New Born 424
    Raymond Booth Foster   b. 4-24-03

7-5717

Muskogee, Indian Territory, March 20, 1905.

William T. Foster,
    Ardmore, Indian Territory.

Dear Sir:

    Receipt is hereby acknowledged of the affidavits of Mattie Bell Foster and T. M. Booth M. D., to the birth of Raymond Booth Foster, infant son of Mattie Belle and William T. Foster, April 24, 1904, and the same have been filed with our records as an application for the enrollment of said child.

Respectfully,

Chairman.

BIRTH AFFIDAVIT.

DEPARTMENT OF THE INTERIOR.
COMMISSION TO THE FIVE CIVILIZED TRIBES.

IN RE APPLICATION FOR ENROLLMENT, as a citizen of the   Choctaw   Nation, of Raymond Booth Foster   , born on the 24   day of   April   , 1903

Name of Father: William T. Foster   a citizen of the   Choctaw   Nation.
Name of Mother: Mattie Belle Foster   a citizen of the   Choctaw   Nation.

Postoffice   Ardmore, I.T.

AFFIDAVIT OF MOTHER.

UNITED STATES OF AMERICA, Indian Territory,
    Southern   DISTRICT.

    I,   Mattie Belle Foster   , on oath state that I am   26   years of age and a citizen by   Intermarriage   , of the   Choctaw   Nation; that I am the lawful wife of   William T Foster   , who is a citizen, by   blood   of the   Choctaw   Nation; that a   male   child was born to me on 24th day of   April   , 1903; that said child has been named   Raymond Booth Foster   , and was living March 4, 1905.

Applications for Enrollment of Choctaw Newborn
Act of 1905   Volume VII

Mattie Belle Foster

Witnesses To Mark:
{

Subscribed and sworn to before me this 14 day of March   , 1905

JE Williams
Notary Public.

AFFIDAVIT OF ATTENDING PHYSICIAN OR MID-WIFE.

UNITED STATES OF AMERICA, Indian Territory, }
Southern   DISTRICT.

I,   T S Booth   , a*n*   M.D.   , on oath state that I attended on Mrs.   Mattie Belle Foster   , wife of   William F Foster   on the   24 day of April   , 1903; that there was born to her on said date a   male   child; that said child was living March 4, 1905, and is said to have been named Raymond Booth Foster

T S Booth MD

Witnesses To Mark:
{

Subscribed and sworn to before me this 14th day of March   , 1905

JE Williams
Notary Public.

Choc New Born 425
　　　　Frank Hazel Campbell   b. 2-2-04

Applications for Enrollment of Choctaw Newborn
Act of 1905   Volume VII

BIRTH AFFIDAVIT.
DEPARTMENT OF THE INTERIOR.
COMMISSION TO THE FIVE CIVILIZED TRIBES.

IN RE APPLICATION FOR ENROLLMENT, as a citizen of the   Choctaw   Nation, of Frank Hazel Campbell   , born on the 2nd day of   February   , 1904

Name of Father: James Lee Campbell   a citizen of the   Choctaw   Nation.
Name of Mother: Katie Campbell   a citizen of the   Choctaw   Nation.

Postoffice   Tuttle Ind Terr

AFFIDAVIT OF MOTHER.

UNITED STATES OF AMERICA, Indian Territory,
Southern   DISTRICT.

I,   Katie Campbell   , on oath state that I am   36   years of age and a citizen by   intermarriage   , of the   Choctaw   Nation; that I am the lawful wife of James Lee Campbell   , who is a citizen, by blood   of the   Choctaw Nation; that a   male   child was born to me on   2nd day of   February   , 1904; that said child has been named   Frank Hazel Campbell   , and was living March 4, 1905.

Mrs Katie Campbell

Witnesses To Mark:

Subscribed and sworn to before me this   13th   day of   April   , 1905

Com Expires 10-14-1908   *(Name Illegible)*
Notary Public.

AFFIDAVIT OF ATTENDING PHYSICIAN OR MID-WIFE.

UNITED STATES OF AMERICA, Indian Territory,
CENTRAL   ~~Southern~~   DISTRICT.

I,   W.E. Brown   , a   Physician   , on oath state that I attended on Mrs.   Katie Campbell   , wife of   James Lee Campbell   on the 2nd   day of February   , 1904; that there was born to her on said date a   male   child; that said child was living March 4, 1905, and is said to have been named   Frank Hazel Campbell

W E Brown

Applications for Enrollment of Choctaw Newborn
Act of 1905 Volume VII

Witnesses To Mark:

{

Subscribed and sworn to before me this 15th day of April , 1905

(Name Illegible)

My Commission expires Feb. 17th, 1907   Notary Public.

BIRTH AFFIDAVIT.

DEPARTMENT OF THE INTERIOR,
COMMISSION TO THE FIVE CIVILIZED TRIBES.

In Re Application for Enrollment, as a citizen of the Choctaw Nation, of Frank Hazel Campbell , born on the 2nd day of February , 1904

Name of Father: James Lee Campbell   a citizen of the Choctaw Nation.
Name of Mother: Katie Campbell   a citizen of the Choctaw Nation.

Post-office   Tuttle Ind. Ter.

AFFIDAVIT OF MOTHER.

UNITED STATES OF AMERICA, }
   INDIAN TERRITORY,
Southern   District.

I, Mrs. Katie Campbell , on oath state that I am Thirty-four years of age and a citizen by mariage[sic] , of the Choctaw Nation; that I am the lawful wife of James Lee Campbell , who is a citizen, by Blood of the Choctaw Nation; that a male child was born to me on 2nd day of Feb , 1904 , that said child has been named Frank Hazel Campbell , and is now living.

   Mrs. Katie Campbell

WITNESSES TO MARK:

{

Subscribed and sworn to before me this 17th day of Aug , 1904

My Com Ex Jan 26th 1907   J.H. Carlisle
   NOTARY PUBLIC.

Applications for Enrollment of Choctaw Newborn
Act of 1905 Volume VII

AFFIDAVIT OF ATTENDING PHYSICIAN OR MID-WIFE.

UNITED STATES OF AMERICA, }
   INDIAN TERRITORY,
Southern   District.

I, W E Brown , a Physician , on oath state that I attended on Mrs. Katie Campbell , wife of James Lee Campbell on the 2nd day of Feb. , 1904; that there was born to her on said date a Male child; that said child is now living and is said to have been named Frank Hazel Campbell

                             W.E. Brown

WITNESSES TO MARK:
{

Subscribed and sworn to before me this 17th day of Aug , 1904

                             J.H. Carlisle
                             NOTARY PUBLIC.

My Com Ex 26th of Jan 1907

7-5731

Muskogee, Indian Territory, August 22, 1904.

Mrs. Katie Campbell,
    Tuttle, Indian Territory.

Dear Madam :-

    Receipt is hereby acknowledged of your affidavit and that of W. E. Brown, relative to the birth of your son, Frank Hazell[sic] Campbell, February 2, 1904, which it is presumed has been forwarded to this Commission as an application for the enrollment of said child as a citizen by blood of the Choctaw Nation.

    You are advised that the Act of Congress approved July 1, 1902, which was ratified by the citizens of the Choctaw and Chickasaw Nations, September 25, 1902, among other things provides that no child born to a citizen of either of said Nations subsequent to the date of said ratification shall be entitled to enrollment or to participate in the distribution of the tribal property of the Choctaw and Chickasaws.

                             Respectfully,

                                                Chairman.

Applications for Enrollment of Choctaw Newborn
Act of 1905 Volume VII

7-5731

Muskogee, Indian Territory, March 17, 1905.

J. L. Campbell,
    Tuttle, Indian Territory.

Dear Sir:

    Receipt is hereby acknowledged of your letter of March 12, 1905, in which you ask if the affidavits heretofore forwarded as to the birth of your infant son Frank Hazel Campbell are sufficient.

    In reply to your letter you are advised that the affidavits heretofore forwarded to the birth of your son Frank Hazel Campbell have been filed with our records as an application for the enrollment of said child.

    In event further evidence is necessary to determine his right to enrollment you will be duly notified.

    Respectfully,

    Chairman.

COPY. N. B. 425

Muskogee, Indian Territory, April 7, 1905.

James Lee Campbell,
    Tuttle, Indian Territory.

Dear Sir:

    There is inclosed you herewith for execution application for the enrollment of your infant child, Frank Hazel Campbell, born February 2, 1904.

    The affidavits heretofore filed with the Commission show the child was living on August 17, 1904. It is necessary, for the child to be enrolled, that he was living on March 4, 1905. You will please insert the mother's age in space provided for the purpose.

    In having these affidavits executed care should be exercised to see that all names are written in full, as they appear in the body of the affidavit, and in the event that either of the persons signing the affidavit are unable to write, signatures by mark must be attested by two witnesses. Each affidavit must be executed before a Notary Public and the notarial seal and signature of the officer must be attached to each separate affidavit.

Applications for Enrollment of Choctaw Newborn
Act of 1905 Volume VII

LM 7-8

Respectfully,
SIGNED
T. B. Needles.
Commissioner in Charge.

Choctaw N.B. 425.

Muskogee, Indian Territory, April 21, 1905.

COPY.

James Lee Campbell,
    Tuttle, Indian Territory.

Dear Sir:

    Receipt is hereby acknowledged of the affidavits of Mrs. Kate Campbell and W. E. Brown, to the birth of Frank Hazel Campbell, son of James Lee and Katie Campbell, February 2, 1904, and the same have been filed with our records in the matter of the enrollment of said child.

Respectfully,
SIGNED
Tams Bixby
Chairman.

Choc New Born 426
    Ella Angelina Campbell b. 10-18-02
    Marshall A. Campbell b. 9-18-04

BIRTH AFFIDAVIT.

DEPARTMENT OF THE INTERIOR,
COMMISSION TO THE FIVE CIVILIZED TRIBES.

    IN RE Application for Enrollment, as a citizen of the Choctaw Nation, of Ella Angelina Campbell, born on the 18th day of October, 1902

Name of Father: Charles R. Campbell   a citizen of the Choctaw Nation.
Name of Mother: Susan J. Campbell   a citizen of the United States Nation.

Post-Office: Tuttle, Ind. Ter.

Applications for Enrollment of Choctaw Newborn
Act of 1905   Volume VII

AFFIDAVIT OF MOTHER.

UNITED STATES OF AMERICA,
    INDIAN TERRITORY.
Souhern District.

    I, Susan J Campbell, on oath state that I am Twenty-six years of age and a citizen by ...., of the United States Nation; that I am the lawful wife of Charles R. Campbell, who is a citizen, by blood of the Choctaw Nation; that a female child was born to me on 18th day of October, 1902, that said child has been named Ella Angilina[sic] Campbell, and is now living.

                                      Susan J. Campbell

WITNESSES TO MARK:

    Subscribed and sworn to before me this 24th *day of* February, 1904

My Commission expires 2/18/1905   J A Stewart
                                                NOTARY PUBLIC.

AFFIDAVIT OF ATTENDING PHYSICIAN OR MID-WIFE.

UNITED STATES OF AMERICA,
    INDIAN TERRITORY.
Southern District.

    I, P K Connaway, a Physician, on oath state that I attended on Mrs. Susan J Campbell, wife of Charles R Campbell on the 18th day of October, 1902 ; that there was born to her on said date a female child; that said child is now living and is said to have been named Ella Angelina Campbell

                                        P K Connaway

WITNESSES TO MARK:

    Subscribed and sworn to before me this 24th *day of* February, 1904

My Commission expires 2/18/1905   J A Stewart
                                                NOTARY PUBLIC.

Applications for Enrollment of Choctaw Newborn
Act of 1905 Volume VII

BIRTH AFFIDAVIT.

DEPARTMENT OF THE INTERIOR.
COMMISSION TO THE FIVE CIVILIZED TRIBES.

IN RE APPLICATION FOR ENROLLMENT, as a citizen of the Choctaw Nation, of Ella Angelina Campbell, born on the 18th day of Oct, 1902

Name of Father: Charles R. Campbell   a citizen of the Choctaw Nation.
Name of Mother: Susan J Campbell   a citizen of the ————Nation.

Postoffice   Tuttle, Ind. Ter

AFFIDAVIT OF MOTHER.

UNITED STATES OF AMERICA, Indian Territory,
Southern   DISTRICT.

I, Susan J Campbell, on oath state that I am Twenty-nine years of age and a citizen by ———, of the ——— Nation; that I am the lawful wife of Charles R. Campbell, who is a citizen, by birth of the Choctaw Nation; that a female child was born to me on 18th day of October, 1902; that said child has been named Ella Angelina Campbell, and was living March 4, 1905.

                           Susan J Campbell

Witnesses To Mark:

Subscribed and sworn to before me this 27th day of March, 1905

                           J A Stewart
My Commission expires Feb 25 1909   Notary Public.

AFFIDAVIT OF ATTENDING PHYSICIAN OR MID-WIFE.

UNITED STATES OF AMERICA, Indian Territory,
.... DISTRICT.

I, PK Connoway, a Physician, on oath state that I attended on Mrs. Susan J Campbell, wife of Chas R Campbell on the 18th day of October, 1902; that there was born to her on said date a Female child; that said child was living March 4, 1905, and is said to have been named Ella Angelina Campbell

                           PK Connoway MD

Applications for Enrollment of Choctaw Newborn
Act of 1905   Volume VII

Witnesses To Mark:
{ Indian Territory
{ Southern District

Subscribed and sworn to before me this 27th day of   March   , 1905

My Com expires Feb 25 1909

J A Stewart
Notary Public.

BIRTH AFFIDAVIT.

DEPARTMENT OF THE INTERIOR.
COMMISSION TO THE FIVE CIVILIZED TRIBES.

IN RE APPLICATION FOR ENROLLMENT, as a citizen of the   Choctaw   Nation, of Marshall A. Campbell   , born on the 18th day of September , 1904

Name of Father: Charles R. Campbell   a citizen of the   Choctaw   Nation.
Name of Mother: Susan J Campbell   a citizen of the   ————Nation.

Postoffice   Tuttle, I.T.

AFFIDAVIT OF MOTHER.

UNITED STATES OF AMERICA, Indian Territory,
   Southern   DISTRICT.

I,   Susan J Campbell   , on oath state that I am   29   years of age and a citizen by ——— , of the   ———   Nation; that I am the lawful wife of   Charles R. Campbell   , who is a citizen, by Blood   of the   Choctaw   Nation; that a male   child was born to me on 18th   day of September   , 1904; that said child has been named   Marshall A Campbell   , and was living March 4, 1905.

Susan J Campbell

Witnesses To Mark:
{

Subscribed and sworn to before me this 25th day of   March   , 1905

(Name Illegible)
Notary Public.

Applications for Enrollment of Choctaw Newborn
Act of 1905   Volume VII

AFFIDAVIT OF ATTENDING PHYSICIAN OR MID-WIFE.

UNITED STATES OF AMERICA, Indian Territory, }
Southern   DISTRICT.

   I,   W.A. Ewing   , a   Physician   , on oath state that I attended on Mrs.   Susan J Campbell   , wife of   Charles R Campbell   on the   18th day of September   , 1904; that there was born to her on said date a   male   child; that said child was living March 4, 1905, and is said to have been named   Marshall A Campbell

W.A. Ewing MD

Witnesses To Mark:
{

   Subscribed and sworn to before me this   17th day of   March   , 1905

(Name Illegible)
Notary Public.

BIRTH AFFIDAVIT.

DEPARTMENT OF THE INTERIOR.
COMMISSION TO THE FIVE CIVILIZED TRIBES.

   IN RE APPLICATION FOR ENROLLMENT, as a citizen of the   Choctaw   Nation, of   Ella Angelina Campbell   , born on the   18th day of   October   , 1902

Name of Father: Charles R. Campbell   a citizen of the   Choctaw   Nation.
Name of Mother: Susan J Campbell   a citizen of the United States Nation.

Postoffice   Tuttle, I.T.

AFFIDAVIT OF MOTHER.

UNITED STATES OF AMERICA, Indian Territory, }
Southern   DISTRICT.

   I,   Susan J Campbell   , on oath state that I am   Twenty-nine   years of age and a citizen by ———— , of the   United States   ~~Nation~~; that I am the lawful wife of   Charles R. Campbell   , who is a citizen, by blood   of the   Choctaw   Nation; that a   female   child was born to me on 18th day of   October   , 1902; that said child has been named   Ella Angelina Campbell   , and was living March 4, 1905.

Susan J Campbell

Applications for Enrollment of Choctaw Newborn
Act of 1905   Volume VII

Witnesses To Mark:
{ ~~J A Stewart~~

      Subscribed and sworn to before me this 19th day of   April   , 1905

                                J A Stewart

My Commission expires Feb. 25th, 1909   Notary Public.

AFFIDAVIT OF ATTENDING PHYSICIAN OR MID-WIFE.

UNITED STATES OF AMERICA, Indian Territory, }
.... DISTRICT. }

    I,   PK Connoway   , a   Physician   , on oath state that I attended on Mrs.   Susan J Campbell   , wife of   Chas R Campbell   on the 18th day of October   , 1902; that there was born to her on said date a   Female   child; that said child was living March 4, 1905, and is said to have been named   Ella Angelina Campbell

                                PK Connoway MD

Witnesses To Mark:
{

      Subscribed and sworn to before me this 19th day of   April   , 1905

                                J A Stewart
                                Notary Public.

                                  N. B. 426

COPY.

                      Muskogee, Indian Territory, April 7, 1905.

Charles R. Campbell,
    Tuttle, Indian Territory.

Dear Sir:

    There is inclosed you herewith for execution application for the enrollment of your infant child, Ella Angelina Campbell, born October 18, 1902.

    The affidavits heretofore filed with the Commission show the child was living on February 24, 1903. It is necessary, for the child to be enrolled, that she was living on March 4, 1905. You will please insert the age of the mother in space left blank for that purpose.

Applications for Enrollment of Choctaw Newborn
Act of 1905   Volume VII

In having these affidavits executed care should be exercised to see that all names are written in full, as they appear in the body of the affidavit, and in the event that either of the persons signing the affidavit are unable to write, signatures by mark must be attested by two witnesses. Each affidavit must be executed before a Notary Public and the notarial seal and signature of the officer must be attached to each separate affidavit.

Respectfully,
SIGNED
T. B. Needles.

LM 7-9   Commissioner in Charge.

Choctaw 5732.

Muskogee, Indian Territory, April 18, 1905.

Bond & Melton,
    Attorneys at Law,
        Chickasha, Indian Territory.

Gentlemen:

Receipt is hereby acknowledged of the affidavits of Susan J. Campbell and P. K. Connoway to the birth of Ella Angelina Campbell; also the affidavits of Susan J. Campbell and W. A. Ewing to the birth of Marshall A. Campbell, children of Charles R. and Susan J. Campbell, October 18, 1902, and September 18, 1904, respectively, and the same have been filed with our records as applications for the enrollment of said children.

The other applications mentioned in your letter have been made the subject of a separate communication.

Respectfully,

Chairman.

Choctaw N.B. 426.

Muskogee, Indian Territory, April 26, 1905.

COPY
Charles R. Campbell,
    Tuttle, Indian Territory.

Dear Sir:

Receipt is hereby acknowledged of the affidavits of Susan J. Campbell and P. K. Cannaway[sic] to the birth of Ella Angeline[sic] Campbell, daughter of Charles R. and

Applications for Enrollment of Choctaw Newborn
Act of 1905   Volume VII

Susan J. Cannaway[sic], October 18, 1902, and the same have been filed with our records in the matter of the enrollment of said child.

>Respectfully,
>SIGNED
>
>*Tams Bixby*
>Chairman.

7-D-103.

Muskogee, Indian Territory, March 3, 1903.

Charles R. Campbell,
    Tuttle, Indian Territory.

Dear Sir:

    Referring to the application for enrollment as a citizen of the Choctaw Nation of Ella Angelina Campbell, infant daughter of Charles R. and Susan J. Campbell, born October 18, 1902, your attention is invited to the following provision of section 34 of the act of Congress approved July 1, 1902, which was ratified by the citizens of the Choctaw and Chickasaw Nations September 25, 1902:

>"During the ninety days first following the date of the final ratification of this agreement, the Commission to the Five Civilized Tribes may receive applications for enrollment only of persons whose names are on the tribal rolls, but who have not heretofore been enrolled by said Commission, commonly known as "delinquents," and such intermarried white persons as may have married recognized citizens of the Choctaw and Chickasaw Nations in accordance with the tribal laws, customs and usages on or before the date of the passage of this Act by Congress, and such infant children as may have been born to recognized and enrolled citizens on or before the date of the final ratification of this agreement; but the application of no person whomsoever for enrollment shall be received after the expiration of the said ninety days."

    Under the above legislation, the Commission is without authority to enroll this child.

>Respectfully,
>
>Chairman.

Applications for Enrollment of Choctaw Newborn
Act of 1905 Volume VII

Choc New Born 427
    John Simmons b. 9-25-04

7-5740

Muskogee, Indian Territory, March 23, 1905.

Nathaniel Simmons,
    Aylesworth, Indian Territory.

Dear Sir:

    Receipt is hereby acknowledged of the affidavits of Matilda Elizabeth Simmons and W. N. Dean to the birth of John Simmons son of Nathaniel H. and Matilda Elizabeth Simmons, September 25, 1904, and the same have been filed with our records as an application for the enrollment of said child.

Respectfully,

Chairman.

BIRTH AFFIDAVIT.

DEPARTMENT OF THE INTERIOR.
COMMISSION TO THE FIVE CIVILIZED TRIBES.

    IN RE APPLICATION FOR ENROLLMENT, as a citizen of the Choctaw Nation, of John Simmons , born on the .... day of ...., 1 ....

Name of Father: Nathaniel H Simmons a citizen of the Choctaw Nation.
Name of Mother: Matilda Elizabeth Simmons a citizen of the Choctaw Nation.

Postoffice Aylesworth I.T.

AFFIDAVIT OF MOTHER.

UNITED STATES OF AMERICA, Indian Territory, }
    Southern DISTRICT.

    I, Matilda Elizabeth Simmons , on oath state that I am Thirty Six years of age and a citizen by blood , of the Choctaw Nation; that I am the lawful wife of Nathaniel H Simmons , who is a citizen, by intermarriage of the Choctaw Nation; that a male child was born to me on 25" day of

Applications for Enrollment of Choctaw Newborn
Act of 1905   Volume VII

September   , 1904, that said child has been named John Simmons   , and is now living".

                                          Matilda Elizabeth Simmons

Witnesses To Mark:
{ W T Young
  N. H. Simmons

    Subscribed and sworn to before me this Seventeenth   day of   March , 1905.

                                       J. Frank Adams
                                       Notary Public.

AFFIDAVIT OF ATTENDING PHYSICIAN OR MID-WIFE.

UNITED STATES OF AMERICA, Indian Territory, }
   Southern   DISTRICT.

    I,   W. N. Dean   , a   physician   , on oath state that I attended on Mrs.   Matilda Elizabeth Simmons   , wife of   Nathaniel H Simmons   on the 25" day of September , 1904; that there was born to her on said date a   male   child; that said child is now living and is said to have been named John Simmons

                                  W.N. Dean MD

Witnesses To Mark:
{

    Subscribed and sworn to before me this 17" day of March   , 1905.

                                     J. Frank Adams
                                     Notary Public.

Choc New Born 428
    Ruby Watson Davis b. 6-2-04

Applications for Enrollment of Choctaw Newborn
Act of 1905   Volume VII

7-5780

Muskogee, Indian Territory, February 27, 1905.

Burk Davis,
    Page, Indian Territory.

Dear Sir:

    Receipt is hereby acknowledged of the affidavits of Sarah Ann Davis and Adeline Davis to the birth of Ruby Watson Davis, infant daughter of Burk and Sarah Ann Davis June 2, 1904, which it is presumed have been forwarded as an application for the enrollment of said child.

    You are advised that under the provisions of the act of Congress approved July 1, 1902, no children born to citizens of the Choctaw and Chickasaw Nations subsequent to September 25, 1902, the date of the ratification of said act, are entitled to enrollment and allotment in the Choctaw and Chickasaw Nations.

                    Respectfully,

                                  Chairman.

Choctaw 5780.

Muskogee, Indian Territory, April 6, 1905.

Bert[sic] Davis,
    Page, Indian Territory.

Dear Sir:

    Receipt is hereby acknowledged of your letter of March 27, asking if a blank heretofore forwarded for the enrollment of your new born child is sufficient, or if it will be necessary for you to go before a Notary Public and have the same executed again because it was made out before March 4, 1905.

    In reply to your letter you are advised that the affidavits heretofore forwarded to the birth of your child, Rubie[sic] Watson Davis, have been filed as an application for the enrollment of your child and in the event further evidence is necessary for the Commission to determine the right of enrollment of your child, you will be duly advised.

                    Respectfully,

                                Commissioner in Charge.

Applications for Enrollment of Choctaw Newborn
Act of 1905   Volume VII

7 NB-428

COPY Muskogee, Indian Territory, April 26, 1905.

Burk Davis,
   Page, Indian Territory.

Dear Sir:

   Receipt is hereby acknowledged of the affidavits of Sarah Ann Dais and Adline Davis to the birth of Ruby Watson Davis, daughter of Burk and Sarah Ann Davis, June 2, 1904, and the same have been filed with our records in the matter of the enrollment of said child.

         Respectfully,
         SIGNED
         Tams Bixby
         Chairman.

COPY. N. B. 428

Muskogee, Indian Territory, April 10, 1905.

Burk Davis,
   Page, Indian Territory.

Dear Sir:

   There is inclosed you herewith for execution application for the enrollment of your infant child, Ruby Watson Davis, born June 2, 1904.

   The affidavits heretofore filed with the Commission show the child was living on February 20, 1905. It is necessary, for the child to be enrolled, that she was living on March 4, 1905.

   In having these affidavits executed care should be exercised to see that all names are written in full, as they appear in the body of the affidavit, and in the event that either of the persons signing the affidavit are unable to write, signatures by mark must be attested by two witnesses. Each affidavit must be executed before a Notary Public and the notarial seal and signature of the officer must be attached to each separate affidavit.

         Respectfully,
         SIGNED
         T. B. Needles.
LM 10-49   Commissioner in Charge.

Applications for Enrollment of Choctaw Newborn
Act of 1905   Volume VII

BIRTH AFFIDAVIT.

DEPARTMENT OF THE INTERIOR.
COMMISSION TO THE FIVE CIVILIZED TRIBES.

IN RE APPLICATION FOR ENROLLMENT, as a citizen of the   Choctaw   Nation, of Ruby Watson Davis , born on the 2" day of June , 1904

Name of Father: Burk Davis   a citizen of the Choctaw Nation.
Name of Mother: Sarah Ann Davis   a citizen of the U. S.   Nation.

Postoffice   Page, I.T.

AFFIDAVIT OF MOTHER.

UNITED STATES OF AMERICA, Indian Territory, }
        Central   DISTRICT.   }

I, Sarah Ann Davis , on oath state that I am 30 years of age and a citizen by Intermarriage , of the Choctaw Nation; that I am the lawful wife of Burk Davis , who is a citizen, by blood of the Choctaw Nation; that a Female child was born to me on 2nd day of June , 1904, that said child has been named Ruby Watson Davis , and is now living.

                                    her
                          Sarah Ann x Davis
Witnesses To Mark: mark
  { Carnolie Runton
  { Jefferson Quincy

Subscribed and sworn to before me this 20th day of Feby , 1905.

My Com Expires March 6, 1905   J. M. Young
                                       Notary Public.

AFFIDAVIT OF ATTENDING PHYSICIAN OR MID-WIFE.

UNITED STATES OF AMERICA, Indian Territory, }
        Central   DISTRICT.   }

I, Adline Davis , a midwife , on oath state that I attended on Mrs. Sarah Ann Davis , wife of Burk Davis on the 2nd day of June , 1904; that there was born to her on said date a Female child; that said child is now living and is said to have been named Ruby Watson Davis

                                    her
                           Adline x Davis
                                   mark

Applications for Enrollment of Choctaw Newborn
Act of 1905 Volume VII

Witnesses To Mark:
  { Carnolie Runton
  { Jefferson Quincy

Subscribed and sworn to before me this 20th day of Feby, 1905.

My Com Expires March 6, 1905   J. M. Young
                                        Notary Public.

BIRTH AFFIDAVIT.

DEPARTMENT OF THE INTERIOR.
COMMISSION TO THE FIVE CIVILIZED TRIBES.

IN RE APPLICATION FOR ENROLLMENT, as a citizen of the Choctaw Nation, of Ruby Watson Davis, born on the 2" day of June, 1904

Name of Father: Burk Davis   a citizen of the Choctaw Nation.
Name of Mother: Sarah Ann Davis   a citizen of the Choctaw Nation.

Postoffice   Page, Ind. Ter.

AFFIDAVIT OF MOTHER.

UNITED STATES OF AMERICA, Indian Territory, }
  Central   DISTRICT.   }

I, Sarah Ann Davis, on oath state that I am 30 years of age and a citizen by Intermarriage, of the Choctaw Nation; that I am the lawful wife of Burk Davis, who is a citizen, by Blood of the Choctaw Nation; that a Female child was born to me on 2" day of June, 1904; that said child has been named Ruby Watson Davis, and was living March 4, 1905.

                                        her
                               Sarah Ann x Davis
Witnesses To Mark: mark
  { Carnolie Runton
  { Jefferson Quincy

Subscribed and sworn to before me this 23rd day of April, 1905

My Com Exp Mch 9, 1909   J. M. Young
                                Notary Public.

Applications for Enrollment of Choctaw Newborn
Act of 1905   Volume VII

AFFIDAVIT OF ATTENDING PHYSICIAN OR MID-WIFE.

UNITED STATES OF AMERICA, Indian Territory,
Central   DISTRICT.

   I,   Adline Davis   , a   midwife   , on oath state that I attended on Mrs. Sarah Ann Davis , wife of Burk Davis   on the 2" day of   June , 1904; that there was born to her on said date a   Female   child; that said child was living March 4, 1905, and is said to have been named Ruby Watson Davis

                      her
               Adline x Davis
Witnesses To Mark: mark
  { Carnolie Runton
   Jefferson Quincy

   Subscribed and sworn to before me this 23rd day of   April   , 1905

My Com Exp Mch 9, 1909   J. M. Young
                               Notary Public.

Choc New Born 429
    David Oscar Nail, Jr. b. 8-2-04

                                      Choctaw 5589

               Muskogee, Indian Territory, March 30, 1905.

David Oscar Nail,
    Caddo, Indian Territory.

Dear Sir:

    Receipt is hereby acknowledged of the affidavits of Pearl E. Nail and R. P. Dickey to the birth of David Oscar Nail, Jr., son of David Oscar and Pearl E. Nail, August 2, 1904, and the same have been filed with our records as an application for the enrollment of said child.

                    Respectfully,

                          Chairman.

Applications for Enrollment of Choctaw Newborn
Act of 1905 Volume VII

NEW BORN AFFIDAVIT

No ....

CHOCTAW ENROLLING COMMISSION

IN THE MATTER OF THE APPLICATION FOR ENROLLMENT as a citizen of the Choctaw Nation, of   David O. Nail, Jr   born on the 2^d day of   August   190 4

Name of father   David O. Nail   a citizen of   Choctaw   Nation, final enrollment No. 13458
Name of mother   Pearl E Nail   a citizen of   Choctaw   Nation, final enrollment No. 618

Caddo I.T.   Postoffice.

AFFIDAVIT OF MOTHER

UNITED STATES OF AMERICA
INDIAN TERRITORY
DISTRICT   Central

I   Pearl E Nail   , on oath state that I am   25   years of age and a citizen by   Intermarriage   of the   Choctaw   Nation, and as such have been placed upon the final roll of the   Choctaw   Nation, by the Honorable Secretary of the Interior my final enrollment number being   618   ; that I am the lawful wife of   David Oscar Nail   , who is a citizen of the   Choctaw   Nation, and as such has been placed upon the final roll of said Nation by the Honorable Secretary of the Interior, his final enrollment number being   13458   and that a   male   child was born to me on the   day of   190 ; that said child has been named   David O. Nail, Jr   , and is now living.

WITNESSETH: Pearl E Nail
Must be two witnesses ⎰ S. J. Homer
who are citizens   ⎱ C.A. Bilbo

Subscribed and sworn to before me this, the   6"   day of   February   , 190 5

A. E. Folsom
Notary Public.

My Commission Expires:
Jan 9 1909

Applications for Enrollment of Choctaw Newborn
Act of 1905 Volume VII

Affidavit of Attending Physician or Midwife

UNITED STATES OF AMERICA,
   INDIAN TERRITORY,
Central DISTRICT

I, R.P. Dickey a Practicing Physician on oath state that I attended on Mrs. Pearl E Nail wife of David O Nail on the 2" day of August, 1904, that there was born to her on said date a male child, that said child is now living, and is said to have been named David O Nail, Jr

R.P. Dickey M. D.

Subscribed and sworn to before me this the 9 day of February 1905

J. G. Reeder
Notary Public.

WITNESSETH:
Must be two witnesses who are citizens and know the child. { S.J. Homer
C.A. Reeder

We hereby certify that we are well acquainted with Dickey a Physician and know him to be reputable and of good standing in the community.

Must be two citizen witnesses. { S. J. Homer
C.A. Bilbo

BIRTH AFFIDAVIT.

DEPARTMENT OF THE INTERIOR.
COMMISSION TO THE FIVE CIVILIZED TRIBES.

IN RE APPLICATION FOR ENROLLMENT, as a citizen of the Choctaw Nation, of David Oscar Nail, Jr, born on the 2nd day of August, 1904

Name of Father: David Oscar Nail   a citizen of the Choctaw Nation.
Name of Mother: Pearl E Nail   a citizen of the Choctaw Nation.

Postoffice Caddo, Ind. Ter.

Applications for Enrollment of Choctaw Newborn
Act of 1905   Volume VII

AFFIDAVIT OF MOTHER.

UNITED STATES OF AMERICA, Indian Territory, }
Central   DISTRICT.

    I,   Pearl E. Nail   , on oath state that I am   26   years of age and a citizen by intermarriage   , of the   Choctaw   Nation; that I am the lawful wife of   David Oscar Nail   , who is a citizen, by   blood   of the   Choctaw   Nation; that a male   child was born to me on   2nd day of   August 1904   , 1............; that said child has been named   David Oscar Nail, Jr.   , and was living March 4, 1905.

                                               Pearl E. Nail

Witnesses To Mark:
{

    Subscribed and sworn to before me this   25   day of   March   , 1905

                                       Sol. J. Homer
                                          Notary Public.

AFFIDAVIT OF ATTENDING PHYSICIAN OR MID-WIFE.

UNITED STATES OF AMERICA, Indian Territory, }
Central   DISTRICT.

    I,   R. P. Dickey   , a   Physician   , on oath state that I attended on Mrs.   Pearl E. Nail   , wife of   David Oscar Nail   on the   2nd day of   August 1904   , 1............; that there was born to her on said date a   male   child; that said child was living March 4, 1905, and is said to have been named David Oscar Nail, Jr.

                                           R. P. Dickey

Witnesses To Mark:
{

    Subscribed and sworn to before me this   20   day of   March   , 1905

                                       J. G. Reeder
                                       Notary Public.
                                   My Commission expires June 1908

Applications for Enrollment of Choctaw Newborn
Act of 1905   Volume VII

Choc New Born 430
    Aldon Freddie Robinson   b. 11-1-03

---

7 N.B. 430.

Muskogee, Indian Territory, June 2, 1905.

Jesse Robinson,
    Durant, Indian Territory.

Dear Sir:

    Receipt is hereby acknowledged of the affidavits of Sarah Robinson and Robert A. Lively, M. D., to the birth of Aldon Freddie Robinson, son of Jesse and Sarah Robinson, November 1, 1903, and the same have been filed with our records in the matter of the enrollment of said child.

                  Respectfully,

(End of letter.)

7-NB-430

Muskogee, Indian Territory, May 24, 1905.

Jessie Robinson,
    Durant, Indian Territory.

Dear Sir:

    There is enclosed you herewith for execution application for the enrollment of your infant child, Aldon Freddie Robinson.

    In the application field in this office on March 15, 1905, the date of the applicants[sic] birth is given as November 1, 1904, while in the one filed April 26, 1905, the date of birth is given as November 1, 1903. In the enclosed application the date of birth is left blank, in which you will please insert the correct date, and, when the affidavits are properly executed, return them to this office.

    In having these affidavits executed care should be exercised to see that all names are written in full, as they appear in the body of the affidavit, and in the event that either of the persons signing the affidavit are unable to write, signatures by mark must be attested by two witnesses. Each affidavit must be executed before a Notary Public and the notarial seal and signature of the officer must be attached to each separate affidavit.

Applications for Enrollment of Choctaw Newborn
Act of 1905   Volume VII

Respectfully,

VR 24-5.   Chairman.

NEW-BORN AFFIDAVIT.

Number

Choctaw Enrolling Commission.

IN THE MATTER OF THE APPLICATION FOR ENROLLMENT, as a citizen of the Choctaw   Nation, of   Aldon Fredie[sic] Robinson

born on the 1   day of   November   190 3

Name of father   Jesse Robinson   a citizen of   Choctaw   Nation final enrollment No 13445
Name of mother   Sarah Robinson   a citizen of   Choctaw   Nation final enrollment No 532

Postoffice   Durant I.T.

AFFIDAVIT OF MOTHER.

UNITED STATES OF AMERICA,
   INDIAN TERRITORY,
   Central   DISTRICT

I   Sarah Robinson   on oath state that I am 26 years of age and a citizen by   marriage   of the Choctaw   Nation, and as such have been placed upon the final roll of the   Choctaw   Nation, by the Honorable Secretary of the Interior my final enrollment number being   532   ; that I am the lawful wife of Jesse Robinson   , who is a citizen of the   Choctaw   Nation, and as such has been placed upon the final roll of said Nation by the Honorable Secretary of the Interior, his final enrollment number being 13445   and that a   male   child was born to me on the 1   day of   November   190 3; that said child has been named   Aldon Fredie[sic] Robinson   , and is now living.

WITNESSETH: Sarah Robinson
  Must be two   Renn Beal
  Witnesses who
  are Citizens.   Thos J Sexton

Subscribed and sworn to before me this   16   day of   January   190 5

James Bower
                                                                                    Notary Public.

My commission expires   Sept 23 1907

Applications for Enrollment of Choctaw Newborn
Act of 1905 Volume VII

AFFIDAVIT OF ATTENDING PHYSICIAN OR MIDWIFE

UNITED STATES OF AMERICA
INDIAN TERRITORY
Central DISTRICT

I, Robt A Lively a Practicing Physician on oath state that I attended on Mrs. Sarah Robinson wife of Jesse Robinson on the 1 day of November , 190 3 , that there was born to her on said date a Male child, that said child is now living, and is said to have been named Aldon Fredie Robinson

Robt A Lively M.D.

Subscribed and sworn to before me this, the 16 day of January 190 5

James Bower
Notary Public.

WITNESSETH:
Must be two witnesses who are citizens and know the child.
Renn Beal
Thos J Sexton

We hereby certify that we are well acquainted with Robt A Lively a Practicing Physician and know him to be reputable and of good standing in the community.

Renn Beal
Thos J Sexton

BIRTH AFFIDAVIT.   Roll No. 13445.

DEPARTMENT OF THE INTERIOR.
COMMISSION TO THE FIVE CIVILIZED TRIBES.

IN RE APPLICATION FOR ENROLLMENT, as a citizen of the Choctaw Nation, of Aldon Freddie Robinson , born on the 1st day of November , 1904[sic]

Name of Father: Jesse Robinson a citizen of the Choctaw Nation.
Name of Mother: Sarah Robinson a citizen of the Choctaw Nation.

Postoffice Durant Indian Ter

Applications for Enrollment of Choctaw Newborn
Act of 1905 Volume VII

AFFIDAVIT OF MOTHER.

UNITED STATES OF AMERICA, Indian Territory, ⎱
Central Judicial   DISTRICT. ⎰

I, Sarah Robinson, on oath state that I am 26 years of age and a citizen by Intermarriage, of the Choctaw Nation; that I am the lawful wife of Jesse Robinson, who is a citizen, by blood of the Choctaw Nation; that a male child was born to me on 1st day of November, 1904; that said child has been named Aldon Freddie Robinson, and was living March 4, 1905.

Sarah Robinson

Witnesses To Mark:
{

Subscribed and sworn to before me this 14 day of March, 1905

R.P. Bowles
Notary Public.

AFFIDAVIT OF ATTENDING PHYSICIAN OR MID-WIFE.

UNITED STATES OF AMERICA, Indian Territory, ⎱
Central Judicial   DISTRICT. ⎰

I, Robt A Lively, a Physician, on oath state that I attended on Mrs. Sarah Robinson, wife of Jesse Robinson on the 1st day of November, 1904; that there was born to her on said date a male child; that said child was living March 4, 1905, and is said to have been named Alden[sic] Freddie Robinson

Robt A Lively

Witnesses To Mark:
{

Subscribed and sworn to before me this 14 day of March, 1905

R.P. Bowles
Notary Public.

Applications for Enrollment of Choctaw Newborn
Act of 1905   Volume VII

BIRTH AFFIDAVIT.

DEPARTMENT OF THE INTERIOR.
COMMISSION TO THE FIVE CIVILIZED TRIBES.

IN RE APPLICATION FOR ENROLLMENT, as a citizen of the   Choctaw   Nation, of Aldon Freddie Robinson   , born on the 1st day of November , 1903

Name of Father: Jessie[sic] Robinson   a citizen of the   Choctaw   Nation.
Name of Mother: Sarah Robinson   a citizen of the   Choctaw   Nation.

Postoffice   Durant Ind Ter

AFFIDAVIT OF MOTHER.

UNITED STATES OF AMERICA, Indian Territory, }
   Central   DISTRICT.

I,   Sarah Robinson   , on oath state that I am 26   years of age and a citizen by   Intermarriage   , of the   Choctaw   Nation; that I am the lawful wife of Jessie Robinson   , who is a citizen, by Blood   of the   Choctaw   Nation; that a   male   child was born to me on   first   day of   November   , 1903; that said child has been named   Aldon Freddie Robinson   , and was living March 4, 1905.

Sarah Robinson

Witnesses To Mark:
{

Subscribed and sworn to before me this 29th day of   May   , 1905

Charles A Phillips
Notary Public.

AFFIDAVIT OF ATTENDING PHYSICIAN OR MID-WIFE.

UNITED STATES OF AMERICA, Indian Territory, }
   Central   DISTRICT.

I,   Robert A Lively   , a   Physician   , on oath state that I attended on Mrs. Sarah Robinson   , wife of   Jessie Robinson   on the first   day of November   , 1903; that there was born to her on said date a   Male   child; that said child was living March 4, 1905, and is said to have been named Aldon Freddie Robinson

Robt A Lively

Applications for Enrollment of Choctaw Newborn
Act of 1905 Volume VII

Witnesses To Mark:
{

Subscribed and sworn to before me this 29th day of May , 1905

Charles A Phillips
Notary Public.

Choc New Born 431
  Caroline Potts b. 8-29-03

N. B. 431

Muskogee, Indian Territory, April 10, 1905.

Sarah Potts,
  Talihina, Indian Territory.

Dear Madam:

There is inclosed you herewith for execution application for the enrollment of your infant child, Caroline Potts, born August 29, 1903.

The affidavits heretofore filed with the Commission show the child was living on May 17, 1904. It is necessary, for the child to be enrolled, that she was living on March 4, 1905.

In having these affidavits executed care should be exercised to see that all names are written in full, as they appear in the body of the affidavit, and in the event that either of the persons signing the affidavit are unable to write, signatures by mark must be attested by two witnesses. Each affidavit must be executed before a Notary Public and the notarial seal and signature of the officer must be attached to each separate affidavit.

Respectfully,

SEV 7-10.   Commissioner in Charge.

Applications for Enrollment of Choctaw Newborn
Act of 1905 Volume VII

7 NB 431

Muskogee, Indian Territory, June 12, 1905.

Sarah Potts,
    Talihina, Indian Territory.

Dear Madam:

    Receipt is hereby acknowledged of your affidavit and the affidavit of Sarly Battist[sic] to the birth of Caroline Potts, daughter of Dave Johnson and Sarah Potts, August 2, 1903, and the same have been filed in the matter of the enrollment of said child.

Respectfully,

Chairman.

BIRTH AFFIDAVIT.

DEPARTMENT OF THE INTERIOR.
COMMISSION TO THE FIVE CIVILIZED TRIBES.

    IN RE APPLICATION FOR ENROLLMENT, as a citizen of the   Choctaw   Nation, of Caroline Potts   , born on the 29 day of August, 1903

Name of Father: Dave Johnson   a citizen of the Choctaw Nation.
Name of Mother: Sarah Potts   a citizen of the Choctaw Nation.

Postoffice   Talihina, I.T.

AFFIDAVIT OF MOTHER.

UNITED STATES OF AMERICA, Indian Territory,
    Central   DISTRICT.

    I, Sarah Potts, on oath state that I am 25 years of age and a citizen by blood, of the Choctaw Nation; ~~that I am the lawful wife of~~ , ~~who is a citizen, by~~ .... ~~of the~~ .... ~~Nation;~~ that a female child was born to me on 29 day of August, 1903; that said child has been named Caroline Potts, and was living March 4, 1905.

                                                 her
                                       Sarah x Potts
Witnesses To Mark: mark
   { Emiziah Bohanan
     Ellen Jones

Applications for Enrollment of Choctaw Newborn
Act of 1905 Volume VII

Subscribed and sworn to before me this 6 day of June , 1905

F. M. Fuller
Notary Public.

AFFIDAVIT OF ATTENDING PHYSICIAN OR MID-WIFE.

UNITED STATES OF AMERICA, Indian Territory, }
  Central   DISTRICT.

I, Sarly Battiest , a Nurse , on oath state that I attended on Mrs. Sarah Potts , ~~wife of~~ on the 29 day of August , 1903; that there was born to her on said date a female child; that said child was living March 4, 1905, and is said to have been named Caroline Potts

                            her
                       Sarly x Battiest
Witnesses To Mark: mark
 { Emiziah Bohanan
   Ellen Jones

Subscribed and sworn to before me this 6 day of June , 1905

F. M. Fuller
Notary Public.

My commission expires April 19th 1908

BIRTH AFFIDAVIT.

DEPARTMENT OF THE INTERIOR,
COMMISSION TO THE FIVE CIVILIZED TRIBES.

IN RE Application for Enrollment, as a citizen of the Choctaw Nation, of Caroline Potts , born on the 29 day of August , 1903

Name of Father: Dave Johnson   a citizen of the Choctaw Nation.
Name of Mother: Sarah Potts   a citizen of the Choctaw Nation.

Post-Office: Talihina I.T.

Applications for Enrollment of Choctaw Newborn
Act of 1905 Volume VII

AFFIDAVIT OF MOTHER.

UNITED STATES OF AMERICA,
   INDIAN TERRITORY.
   Central District.

I, Sarah Potts, on oath state that I am 24 years of age and a citizen by Blood, of the Choctaw Nation; that I am ~~the lawful wife of~~ The Father is Dave Johnson, who is a citizen, by Blood of the Choctaw Nation; that a Female child was born to me on 29 day of August, 1903, that said child has been named Caroline Potts, and is now living.

                                  her
                              Sarah x Potts

WITNESSES TO MARK: mark
{ *(Name Illegible)*
  Willard N Everett

Subscribed and sworn to before me this 17 day of May, 1904

                              Sam T Roberts
                                NOTARY PUBLIC.

AFFIDAVIT OF ATTENDING PHYSICIAN OR MID-WIFE.

UNITED STATES OF AMERICA,
   INDIAN TERRITORY.
   Central District.

I, Judy Potts, a midwife, on oath state that I attended on Mrs. Sarah Potts, ~~wife of~~ on the 29 day of August, 1903; that there was born to her on said date a Female child; that said child is now living and is said to have been named Caroline Potts

                                her
                            Judy x Potts

WITNESSES TO MARK: mark
{ *(Name Illegible)*
  Willard N Everett

Subscribed and sworn to before me this 17 day of May, 1904

                              Sam T Roberts
                                NOTARY PUBLIC.

Applications for Enrollment of Choctaw Newborn
Act of 1905 Volume VII

BIRTH AFFIDAVIT.

DEPARTMENT OF THE INTERIOR.
COMMISSION TO THE FIVE CIVILIZED TRIBES.

IN RE APPLICATION FOR ENROLLMENT, as a citizen of the Choctaw Nation, of Caroline Johnson, born on the 29 day of August, 1903

Name of Father: David Johnson   a citizen of the .... Nation.
Name of Mother: Sarah Bohanon nee Potts   a citizen of the Choctaw Nation.

Postoffice   Talihina I.T.

AFFIDAVIT OF MOTHER.

UNITED STATES OF AMERICA, Indian Territory, }
Central   DISTRICT.

I, Sarah Bohanon nee Potts, on oath state that I am 23 years of age and a citizen by blood, of the Choctaw Nation; that I ~~am~~ was the lawful wife of David Johnson, who is a citizen, by blood of the Choctaw Nation; that a female child was born to me on 29 day of August, 1903; that said child has been named Caroline Johnson, and was living March 4, 1905.

                           her
                     Sarah x Bohanon
Witnesses To Mark: mark
{ Chas T. Difendafer
{ OL Johnson

Subscribed and sworn to before me this 10 day of April, 1905

                       OL Johnson
                          Notary Public.

AFFIDAVIT OF ATTENDING PHYSICIAN OR MID-WIFE.

UNITED STATES OF AMERICA, Indian Territory, }
Central   DISTRICT.

I, Judy Potts, a midwife, on oath state that I attended on Mrs. Sarah Bohanon, wife of David Johnson on the 29 day of August, 1903; that there was born to her on said date a female child; that said child was living March 4, 1905, and is said to have been named Caroline Johnson

                       her
                     Judy x Potts
                       mark

Applications for Enrollment of Choctaw Newborn
Act of 1905 Volume VII

Witnesses To Mark:
   { Chas T. Difendafer
   { OL Johnson

    Subscribed and sworn to before me this 10 day of April , 1905

                       OL Johnson
                       Notary Public.

<u>Choc New Born 432</u>
    William Bryant Marion Mitchell
        b. 10-9-02

                              7-5609

            Muskogee, Indian Territory, March 17m=, 1905.

Joseph A. Edwards,
    McGee, Indian Territory.

Dear Sir:

    Receipt is hereby acknowledged of your letter of March 13, 1905, enclosing the affidavits of Ida Mitchell and Dr. J. N. Morris to the birth of William Byrant[sic] Marion Mitchell, infant son of William B. Mitchell and Ida Mitchell, October 9, 1902, and the same have been filed with our records as an application for the enrollment of said child.

                    Respectfully,

                                Chairman.

Applications for Enrollment of Choctaw Newborn
Act of 1905   Volume VII

7-NB-432

Muskogee, Indian Territory, July 8, 1905.

W. B. M. Mitchell,
    Box 201,
        Pauls Valley, Indian Territory.

Dear Sir:

    Receipt is hereby acknowledged of your letter of July 5, 1905, asking if the enrollment of your child William Bryant Marion Mitchell has been approved.

    In reply to your letter you are advised that the name of your child William Bryant Marion Mitchell has been placed upon a schedule of citizens by blood of the Choctaw Nation which has been forwarded to the Secretary of the Interior but this office has not yet been advised of Departmental action thereon.

    You will be advised when the enrollment of your child has been approved by the Secretary of the Interior.

            Respectfully,

                        Commissioner.

BIRTH AFFIDAVIT.

Department of the Interior,
COMMISSION TO THE FIVE CIVILIZED TRIBES.

IN RE APPLICATION FOR ENROLLMENT, as a citizen of the Choctaw Nation, of Wm Bryant Marion Mitchell, born on the 9 day of October, 190 2

Name of Father: W B M Mitchell   a citizen of the United States Nation.
Name of Mother: Ida Mitchell   a citizen of the Choctaw Nation.

        Post-Office: McGee
        Ind. Ter.

AFFIDAVIT OF MOTHER.

UNITED STATES OF AMERICA,
    INDIAN TERRITORY,
    Southern   District.

    I, Ida Mitchell, on oath state that I am 21 years of age and a citizen by Blood, of the Choctaw Nation; that I am the lawful wife of

Applications for Enrollment of Choctaw Newborn
Act of 1905 Volume VII

WBM Mitchell , who is a citizen, ~~by~~ .... of the United States Nation; that a Male child was born to me on 9 day of October , 190 2, that said child has been named Wm Bryant Marion Mitchell , and is now living.

Ida Mitchell

WITNESSES TO MARK:

{

Subscribed and sworn to before me this 20 day of November , 190 2

L P Shi
Notary Public.

AFFIDAVIT OF ATTENDING PHYSICIAN OR MID-WIFE.

UNITED STATES OF AMERICA, }
   INDIAN TERRITORY,
  Southern District.

I, J. N. Norris , a Physician , on oath state that I attended on Mrs. Ida Mitchell , wife of WBM Mitchell on the 9 day of October , 190 2; that there was born to her on said date a male child; that said child is now living and is said to have been named William Bryant Marion Mitchell

J.N. Norris MD

WITNESSES TO MARK:

{

Subscribed and sworn to before me this 20 day of November , 190 2

L P Shi
Notary Public.

BIRTH AFFIDAVIT.

DEPARTMENT OF THE INTERIOR,
COMMISSION TO THE FIVE CIVILIZED TRIBES.

IN RE Application for Enrollment, as a citizen of the Choctaw Nation, of William Bryant Marion Mitchell , born on the 9 day of Oct , 1902

Name of Father: W B M Mitchell   a citizen of the United States Nation.
Name of Mother: Ida Mitchell   a citizen of the Choctaw Nation.

Post-Office: Pauls Valley I.T.

Applications for Enrollment of Choctaw Newborn
Act of 1905 Volume VII

AFFIDAVIT OF MOTHER.

UNITED STATES OF AMERICA, }
    INDIAN TERRITORY.
Southern   District.

I, Ida Mitchell, on oath state that I am 24 years of age and a citizen by Blood, of the Choctaw Nation; that I am the lawful wife of W B M Mitchell, who is a citizen, ~~by~~ .... of the United States ~~Nation~~; that a male child was born to me on 9 day of Oct, 1902, that said child has been named William Bryant Marion Mitchell, and is now living.

                                              Ida Mitchell

WITNESSES TO MARK:
{

    Subscribed and sworn to before me this 13 *day of* March , 1905.

                                              Jos. A Edwards
                                                    NOTARY PUBLIC.

AFFIDAVIT OF ATTENDING PHYSICIAN OR MID-WIFE.

UNITED STATES OF AMERICA, }
    INDIAN TERRITORY.
Southern   District.

I, J. N. Norris, a Physician, on oath state that I attended on Mrs. Ida Mitchell, wife of W B M Mitchell on the 9 day of Oct, 1902; that there was born to her on said date a male child; that said child is now living and is said to have been named William Bryant Marion Mitchell

                                              Dr. J. N. Norris

WITNESSES TO MARK:
{

    Subscribed and sworn to before me this 13 *day of* March , 1905.

                                              Jos. A Edwards
                                                    NOTARY PUBLIC.

Applications for Enrollment of Choctaw Newborn
Act of 1905 Volume VII

Choc New Born 433
    Cyril Gabbert b. 11-19-04

7-5609

Muskogee, Indian Territory, March 23, 1905.

Joseph A. Edwards,
    McGee, Indian Territory.

Dear Sir:

    Receipt is hereby acknowledged of your letter of March 16, 1905, enclosing affidavits of Ella Gabbart[sic] and A. H. Shi to the birth of Cyril Gabbert November 19, 1904; also the marriage license and certificate between T. B. Gabbert and Ella Hyden under date of May 8, 1903, and the same have been filed with our records as an application for the enrollment of said child.

                  Respectfully,

                                      Chairman.

BIRTH AFFIDAVIT.

DEPARTMENT OF THE INTERIOR,
COMMISSION TO THE FIVE CIVILIZED TRIBES.

    IN RE *Application for Enrollment*, as a citizen of the Choctaw Nation, of Cyril Gabbert, born on the 19th day of Nov, 1904

Name of Father: T.B. Gabbert   a citizen of the United States Nation.
Name of Mother: Ella Gabbert   a citizen of the Choctaw Nation.

                  Post-Office: McGee, I.T.

AFFIDAVIT OF MOTHER.

UNITED STATES OF AMERICA,
    INDIAN TERRITORY.
    Southern   District.

    I, Ella Gabbert, on oath state that I am 20 years of age and a citizen by Blood, of the Choctaw Nation; that I am the lawful wife of T B Gabbert, who is a

Applications for Enrollment of Choctaw Newborn
Act of 1905   Volume VII

citizen, by .... of the United States ~~Nation~~; that a Female child was born to me on 19th day of Nov , 1904, that said child has been named Cyril Gabbert , and is now living.

            Ella Gabbert

WITNESSES TO MARK:
{

   Subscribed and sworn to before me this 16 *day of* March , 1905.

            Jos A Edwards
              NOTARY PUBLIC.

AFFIDAVIT OF ATTENDING PHYSICIAN OR MID-WIFE.

UNITED STATES OF AMERICA,
 INDIAN TERRITORY.
 Southern   District.

   I, A. H. Shi , a Physician , on oath state that I attended on Mrs. Ella Gabbert , wife of T B Gabbert on the 19 day of Nov , 1904; that there was born to her on said date a Female child; that said child is now living and is said to have been named Cyril Gabbert

            A.H. Shi M.D.

WITNESSES TO MARK:
{

   Subscribed and sworn to before me this 16 *day of* March , 1905.

            Jos A Edwards
              NOTARY PUBLIC.

Applications for Enrollment of Choctaw Newborn
Act of 1905 Volume VII

DEPARTMENT OF THE INTERIOR,
COMMISSION TO THE FIVE CIVILIZED TRIBES.
F I L E D

MAR 23 1905

Tams Bixby CHAIRMAN.

Certificate of Record of Marriage

United States of America,
    Indian Territory, } sct.
    Southern District.

I, C. M. CAMPBELL, Clerk of the United States Court, in the Territory and District aforesaid DO HEREBY CERTIFY, that the License for and Certificate of Marriage of

MR   T. B. Gabbert   and

M   Ella Hyden

were filed in my office in said Territory and District the 8" day of May A.D., 190 3 and duly recorded in Book G of Marriage Record, Page 251

WITNESS my hand and Seal of said Court, at Ardmore, this 8" day of May A.D. 1903

C. M. Campbell
                              CLERK.

Return this License to the United States Clerk at Ardmore, that it may be recorded, when it will be mailed to the proper address.

Ardmoreite Steam Print.

**Applications for Enrollment of Choctaw Newborn
Act of 1905 Volume VII**

 MARRIAGE LICENSE

UNITED STATES OF AMERICA,
INDIAN TERRITORY,   ss: To Any Person Authorized by Law to Solemnize Marriage, Greeting:
SOUTHERN DISTRICT.

You are hereby commanded to solemnize the Rite and publish the Banns of Matrimony between Mr. T. B. Gabbert of Pauls Valley in the Indian Territory, aged 25 years, and M Ella Hyden of Ardmore in the Indian Territory, aged 18 years, according to law; and do you officially sign and return this License to the parties therein named.

Witness my hand and official Seal, this 8" day of May A. D. 190 3

C.M. Campbell
Clerk of the United States Court.

Certificate of Marriage.

UNITED STATES OF AMERICA,
INDIAN TERRITORY,   ss:
SOUTHERN DISTRICT.   I, J.L. Kelley A Minister of the Gospel

do hereby certify that on the 8th day of May , A. D. 1903 , I did duly according to law, as commanded in the foregoing License, solemnize the Rite and publish the Banns of Matrimony between the parties therein named.

Witness my hand this 8th day of May A. D. 1903

My credentials are recorded in the office of the Clerk of the United States Court, Indian Territory, Southern District, at Ardmore, Book A , Page 161

(NOTE-The person officiating should fill in the spaces for book and page and sign here.)
J. L. Kelley
a Minister of the Gospel

Applications for Enrollment of Choctaw Newborn
Act of 1905 Volume VII

Choc New Born 434
    Samuel Edmond Sullivan
        b. 1-4-03

7-5787

Muskogee, Indian Territory, March 16, 1905.

Edna L. Krebs,
    Cleora, Indian Territory.

Dear Madam:

    Receipt is hereby acknowledged of the affidavits of Edna L. Krebs and Thresa[sic] C. Krebs to the birth of Samuel Edmond Sullivan son of Samuel Sullivan and Edna L. Krebs January 4, 1903, and the same have been filed with our records as an application for the enrollment of said child.

                  Respectfully,

                            Chairman.

$W^m O.B.$

COMMISSIONERS:		
TAMS BIXBY,	**DEPARTMENT OF THE INTERIOR,**	REFER IN REPLY TO THE FOLLOWING:
THOMAS B. NEEDLES,	**COMMISSIONER TO THE FIVE CIVILIZED TRIBES.**	
C.R. BRECKINBRIDGE.		9-N.B. 434.
WM. O. BEALL		
Secretary		

ADDRESS ONLY THE
COMMISSION TO THE FIVE CIVILIZED TRIBES.

Muskogee, Indian Territory, June 5, 1905.

Samuel Sullivan,
    Cleora, Indian Territory.

Dear Sir:

    Receipt is hereby acknowledged of the affidavits of Edna L. Krebs and T. C. Krebs to the birth of Samuel Edmond Sullivan, son of Edna L. Krebs and Samuel Sullivan, January 4, 1903, and the same have been filed with our records in the matter of the enrollment of said child.

                  Respectfully,
                  TBNeedles
                        Commissioner in Charge.

Applications for Enrollment of Choctaw Newborn
Act of 1905   Volume VII

7-NB-434

Muskogee, Indian Territory, July 5, 1905.

Edna L. Krebbs[sic],
   Cleora, Indian Territory.

Dear Madam:

   Receipt is hereby acknowledged of your letter of May 22, 1905, asking relative to the application for the enrollment of your baby Samuel Sullivan.

   In reply to your letter you are advised that the affidavits heretofore forwarded to the birth of your child Samuel Edmond Sullivan have been filed with the records of this office as an application for the enrollment of said child, and you will be notified in event further evidence is necessary to determine his right to enrollment.

   The matter of the allotment of Tushmagaha Dobbs referred to in your letter has been made the subject of another communication.

                      Respectfully,

                                      Commissioner.

Wm O.B.

COMMISSIONERS:
TAMS BIXBY,
THOMAS B. NEEDLES,
C.R. BRECKINBRIDGE.
    WM. O. BEALL
      Secretary

DEPARTMENT OF THE INTERIOR,
COMMISSIONER TO THE FIVE CIVILIZED TRIBES.

REFER IN REPLY TO THE FOLLOWING:

7-NB-434.

ADDRESS ONLY THE
COMMISSION TO THE FIVE CIVILIZED TRIBES.

Muskogee, Indian Territory, May 25, 1905.

Edna L. Krebs,
   Cleora, Indian Territory.

Dear Madam:

   There is enclosed you herewith for execution application for the enrollment of your infant child, Samuel Edmond Sullivan.

   In the application filed in this office on March 15, 1905, the mother gives the date of the applicant's birth as January 4, 1905, while the midwife gives it as January 4, 1903. In the enclosed application the date of birth is left blank, in which you will please insert

Applications for Enrollment of Choctaw Newborn
Act of 1905 Volume VII

the correct date, and, when the affidavits are properly executed, return the application to this office.

In having these affidavits executed care should be exercised to see that all names are written in full, as they appear in the body of the affidavit, and in the event that either of the persons signing the affidavit are unable to write, signatures by mark must be attested by two witnesses. Each affidavit must be executed before a Notary Public and the notarial seal and signature of the officer must be attached to each separate affidavit.

VR 24-4.

Respectfully,
Tams Bixby
Chairman.

9-N.B. 434.

Muskogee, Indian Territory, June 5, 1905.

Samuel Sullivan,
    Cleora, Indian Territory.

Dear Sir:

Receipt is hereby acknowledged of the affidavits of Edna L. Krebs and T. C. Krebs to the birth of Samuel Edmond Sullivan, son of Edna L. Krebs and Samuel Sullivan, January 4, 1903, and the same have been filed with our records in the matter of the enrollment of said child.

Respectfully,

Commissioner in Charge.

7-NB-434.

Sub

Muskogee, Indian Territory, May 25, 1905.

Edna L. Krebs,
    Cleora, Indian Territory.

Dear Madam:

There is enclosed you herewith for execution application for the enrollment of your infant child, Samuel Edmond Sullivan.

In the application filed in this office on March 15, 1905, the mother gives the date of the applicant's birth as January 4, 1905, while the midwife gives it as January 4, 1903.

Applications for Enrollment of Choctaw Newborn
Act of 1905 Volume VII

In the enclosed application the date of birth is left blank, in which you will please insert the correct date, and, when the affidavits are properly executed, return the application to this office.

In having these affidavits executed care should be exercised to see that all names are written in full, as they appear in the body of the affidavit, and in the event that either of the persons signing the affidavit are unable to write, signatures by mark must be attested by two witnesses. Each affidavit must be executed before a Notary Public and the notarial seal and signature of the officer must be attached to each separate affidavit.

Respectfully,

VR 24-4. Chairman.

BIRTH AFFIDAVIT.

DEPARTMENT OF THE INTERIOR.
COMMISSION TO THE FIVE CIVILIZED TRIBES.

IN RE APPLICATION FOR ENROLLMENT, as a citizen of the Chocktaw[sic] Nation, of Samuel Edmond Sullivan, born on the 4th day of Jany., 1903

Name of Father: Samuel Sullivan   a citizen of the White man. Nation.
Name of Mother: Edna L Krebs   a citizen of the Chocktaw Nation.

Postoffice   Cleora, I.T.

AFFIDAVIT OF MOTHER.

UNITED STATES OF AMERICA, Indian Territory, }
Northern   DISTRICT.

I, Edna L. Krebs, on oath state that I am 26 years of age and a citizen by Blood, of the Chocktaw Nation; that I am *not* the lawful wife of Samuel Sullivan, who is a citizen, by White man of the ------------ Nation; that a male child was born to me on 4th day of January, 1905, that said child has been named Samuel Edmond Sullivan, and is now living.

Edna L Krebs

Witnesses To Mark:
  { Jasper S Martin
    F.M. Smith

Applications for Enrollment of Choctaw Newborn
Act of 1905   Volume VII

Subscribed and sworn to before me this   13th day of   March   , 1905.

                                            F.M. Smith

My Com Exp May 21st 1908   Notary Public.

AFFIDAVIT OF ATTENDING PHYSICIAN OR MID-WIFE.

UNITED STATES OF AMERICA, Indian Territory,
    Northern   DISTRICT.

    I, Theressa Kribs[sic]   Mother and , a   Midwife , on oath state that I attended on Mrs. Edna L ~~Sullivan~~ *Krebs* , ~~wife of Samuel Sullivan~~   on the 4th   day of January , 1903; that there was born to her on said date a   Male   child; that said child is now living and is said to have been named Samuel Edmond Sullivan

                                        Theresa C Krebs

Witnesses To Mark:
    { Jasper S Martin
    { F.M. Smith

Subscribed and sworn to before me this   13th day of   March   , 1905.

                                            F.M. Smith

My Com Exp May 21st 1908   Notary Public.

BIRTH AFFIDAVIT.

DEPARTMENT OF THE INTERIOR.
COMMISSION TO THE FIVE CIVILIZED TRIBES.

    IN RE APPLICATION FOR ENROLLMENT, as a citizen of the   Choctaw   Nation, of Samuel Edmond Sullivan   , born on the   4th day of Jany   , 1903

Name of Father: Samuel Sullivan   a citizen of the United States Nation.
Name of Mother: Edna L Krebs   a citizen of the   Choctaw   Nation.

                                  Postoffice   Cleora I.T.

Applications for Enrollment of Choctaw Newborn
Act of 1905   Volume VII

AFFIDAVIT OF MOTHER.

UNITED STATES OF AMERICA, Indian Territory, }
Northern   DISTRICT.

I,   Edna L. Krebs   , on oath state that I am   26   years of age and a citizen by   Blood   , of the   Choctaw   Nation; that I am ~~not~~ the lawful wife of   Samuel Sullivan   , who is a citizen, ~~by~~ ——of the   United States   Nation; that a   Male   child was born to me on   4th day of   Jany   , 1903; that said child has been named   Samuel Edmond Sullivan   , and was living March 4, 1905.

Edna L Krebs

Witnesses To Mark:
{ J.S. Martin
{ F.M. Smith

Subscribed and sworn to before me this   31st day of   May   , 1905

F.M. Smith
My Com Exp May 21st 1908   Notary Public.

AFFIDAVIT OF ATTENDING PHYSICIAN OR MID-WIFE.

UNITED STATES OF AMERICA, Indian Territory, }
Northern   DISTRICT.

I,   T. C. Krebs   , a   midwife   , on oath state that I attended on Mrs.   Edna L Krebs   , wife of .... on the   4th day of   January   , 1903; that there was born to her on said date a   Male   child; that said child was living March 4, 1905, and is said to have been named Samuel Edmond Sullivan

T.C. Krebs

Witnesses To Mark:
{ J.S. Martin
{ F.M. Smith

Subscribed and sworn to before me this   31st day of   May   , 1905

F.M. Smith
My Com Exp May 21st 1908   Notary Public.

Index

ABBOTT
  W E 1
  W E, MD 2
ADAMS
  Henry 137,141
  J A 41
  J A, MD 41
  J Frank 294
AIRINGTON
  Alvin 157,158,159,160,248
  Ella 158
  Ellen 157,158,159,160,248
  Ellon 248
  Noah 157,158,159,160,248
AMDERSON
  Joe 60
AMOS
  Ann 14,15,16,17,18,19,21,22,23
  Annie 20
  Ellen 14,15,16,17,18,19,20,21,22,23
  Sanders 14,15,16,17,18,19,20, 21,22,23
ANDERSON
  Bedford 236,237
  Joe 57,58,59,60,61,64,65
  Josie 57,58,61,62,63,66,67
  Lallis 235,236,237,238
  Lenola 6
  Lyles 236,241
  Rebecca 6
  Robert .. 57,58,59,60,61,62,64,65,66,67
  Robt 63
  Rosa 62,65
  Rosie 57,59,60,61,63,64,66,67
  Rosy 60
  Susie 177
  Tandy 235,236,238,239,240,241,242
  Viola Gladis 236,237,241
  Viola Gladys 242
  Viola Glodis 234,235,236,238, 239,240
  Vola Glodis 235
ANGELL
  W H 4,234
APPLEGATE
  Henry 273
ARCHER

  Arthur O 234
ASHFORD
  James D 61,64,261,262,263,264, 265,266,267,268
  James Harvey 261,262,263,264, 265,266,268
  Lizzie 261,262,263,264,265,266,267
  Thomas 192
AUSTIN
  D J 259,260
  T J 101
BARNES
  T J 87
BATSON
  Dr W V 202
BATTIEST
  Sarly 310
BATTIST
  Sarly 309
BATTY
  Temperence Caroline 138,141
BAYNE
  R A 146
BEAL
  Renn 304,305
BEAMS
  Ada Olive 107,108
  George W 107,108,109
  George W, Jr 109,110
  John J 271,272
  Sallie 108,109
BELVIN
  Annie 10
  Eva 10
  Jonas 10
  Lamos 10
  Lamus 9
  Lena 10
  Raymus 10
  Robert 9
  S J 9
  Sallie A 9
  Sis 10
  Thomas 9,10
  Williamson 9,10
BILBO

Index

C A 300,301
BIXBY
   Commissioner 138,142
   Tams 48,78,117,118,135,136,155,
   180,200,220,221,222,238,243,267,285,
   292,296,319,323
BOBO
   Lacey P 237,241,242
BOHANAN
   Emiziah 309,310
BOHANON
   Sarah 312
BOLLING
   W C 46,47
BOND
   Bensie 229
   Cornelius 229
   Jessie 224
   Mary 224,229
   Sallie 226,231,232,233
   Sally 224
BOND & MELTON 25,291
BONE & MELTON 24
BONER
   W L 215,216,217,218,219,220
BOOTH
   T M, MD 279
   T S 280
   T S, MD 280
BOSTOCK
   George 237
BOWER
   James 11,34,46,47,54,212,250,
   304,305
BOWLES
   R P 306
BOYD
   E Allen 177
BRAND
   E H 273
BREWER
   John Frankling 137,141
   S A 275
   Thos F 147
BRIDGES
   James F 167,169
BROWDER

   J D 41,42
BROWN
   A D 62,65
   Dwight 62,63,65,66
   F M 36,269
   Foster M 269,270,271,272,273
   Hettie A 269,270,271,272,273
   Jim 137,141
   Stephen 268,269,272,273
   Steve 269,270,271
   W E 68,69,70,281,283,285
   W E, MD 70
   Wm C 18
BURGEVIN
   Elizabeth M 172,173
   Elizabeth Mary 171
   Frances E 171
   Francis E 172,173
   Josephine G 171,172,173
BUSH
   Dr F D 168
   F D 166,167,170,201,206
   F D, MD 167,206
   Francis D 51,165,199,200,203,
   204,205
   Francis D, MD 166,204,205
BYINGTON
   Cyrus 212,213
   D J 13

CABEL
   Illegible 177
CALLICOATT
   Virtie 203
CAMPBELL
   C M 195,196,319,320
   Charles R 285,286,287,288,289,
   290,291,292
   Chas R 287,290
   Ella Angelina 285,286,287,289,
   290,291,292
   Ella Angeline 291
   Ella Angilina 286
   Frank Hazel 280,281,282,283,
   284,285
   Frank Hazell 283
   J L 284

Index

James Lee 281,282,283,284,285
Kate 285
Katie 281,282,283,285
Marshall A 285,288,289,291
Susan J 285,286,287,288,289,290, 291,292

CAMPBELUBE
Columbus 12

CAMPELUBE
Columbus 11,12
Ellen 9
Helen 11,12

CANNAWAY
P K 291
Susan J 292

CARLISLE
J H 69,70,282,283

CHAPMAN
T S 71
T S, MD 72

CHATMAN
Alice 137,141

CHILDS
Dr J S 162
J S 162,164
J S, MD 161,162

CHIVERS
Edgar E 198,199
Edgar Eynon 198
Edgar J 198
Margaret 198,199
Maud A 198
Mrs E E 199

CHOATE
Benjamin Paul 35,36,37,38
Christopher C 37
G W 35,36,37,273
Mary E 37
Mary Elizabeth 35,36,38
W F 37,38
William F 35,36,37,38

CHOOTE
Benjamin Paul 35

COHEE
Edmund Macco 138,141

COLBERT
Arella 137,141

Vinn 187,188,190,192

COLEMAN
Belle 84,85,86,88,89,90,91
Belle M 84,87
Billie 86
Clyde R 128,129,130,131,132,133, 134,135,136,137,138,139,140,141,142
Lou Ann 88
Lou Anna 85,86,87,88,89,90,91
R B 2,20
Riley L 130,131,132,133,134, 135,139
Rily L 130
Sarah Caddy 131
Sarah Gaddy 132,133,134
Sarah J 130
Sarah Jane 130,132,133,134,140
W A 84,85,86,87,88,89,90,91

COMPELUBE
Columbus 12,13
Ellen 12,13

CONN
John 209,210
John A 207,208,210,211,213,214
John R 206,210,211,213
John, Jr 211,212
John, Sr 211,212
Leona 206,207,208,209,210,213,214
Minnie J 207,208,210,211,212, 213,214
Minnie Jane 209,210

CONNAWAY
P K 286

CONNOWAY
P K 287,290,291
P K, MD 287,290

COOK
D C 100

COVINGTON
W P 237

CRAWFORD
Katie 162,164

CRESWELL
Mattie 108,109,110

CROUTHAMEL
A H 203,204,206
Ida 203

329

Index

CROWDER
  Mary A 138,141
CULBERTSON
  J W 122
  Katie 113,114,122,124
  W T 113,114,115,116,120,121,124
CURTIS
  W L 246,247
CURTISS
  G W 103
DAMRON
  Amanda 248
  Ethel 248
  W R 248
DAVENPORT
  C J 101,102
DAVIS
  Adeline 295
  Adline 296,297,299
  Bert 295
  Burk 295,296,297,298,299
  Rubie Watson 295
  Ruby Watson 294,295,296,297, 298,299
  Sarah Ann 295,296,297,298,299
DAWSON
  E L 24,25,26,27,29,30,31
  E L, MD 27,29,30,31
  James 116
  L E 122,123
  Lela E 112,114,115,116
DEAN
  W N 293,294
  W N, MD 294
DICKEY
  R P 299,301,302
  R P, MD 301
DIFENDAFER
  Chas T 76,206,312,313
DIXON
  Amber 94,95,96,97,98
  Ruth May 93,94,97,98,99
  Ruthie May 95,96
  W L 99
  Wallace 94,95,96,97,98
DOAK
  Mattie 137,141
DOBBS
  Tushmagaha 322
DOBSON
  Dewey Dewitt 72,73,74
  Dewey DeWitt 74
  Dewey Dewitt 75,76
  Dewry Dewitt 72
  Leonidas 72,73,74,75,76
  Lon 75
  Mary 74,75,76
DONER
  W L 220
DONNELLY
  W C 48,49
EDWARDS
  Jos A 316,318
  Joseph A 313,317
ENGLAND
  Geo 265,266
ESTER
  W N 5
EUBANK
  J A 36,37
  J A, MD 36
EUBANKS
  J A 36,38
EVERETT
  Willard N 311
EWING
  W A 289,291
  W A, MD 289
FANNIN
  E J 48,49,50
FARGO
  Emily 243,246,247
  Emily Jane 244
  Emma J 242,245
FARRILL
  Harriet 273
FLEMING
  John D 141
  John D 137
FLOYD
  Charles W 252,253

Eliza..................................252,253
Jewel................................252,253
FOLSOM
   A E..6,7,300
   Daniel.. 43
   Leora...................166,167,168,169,170
   Leora B...................................165,166
   Nancy.. 43
   Nathan.......................................168,169
   Simpson..46,47
   Unis... 166
   Unis Fay..............165,166,167,168,170
   W W...168,169
   Walter..165,166
   Walter W............166,167,168,169,170
FOSTER
   Betsy.. 183
   Mattie Bell....................................... 279
   Mattie Belle..............................279,280
   Minnie B.. 275
   Minnie F... 274
   Raymond Booth.......................279,280
   William F.. 280
   William T.. 279
FOWLER
   Cline..59,66
FRANKLIN
   Wirt............1,3,13,32,45,46,55,90,108,
   109,110,177,255,261,272,273
FRAZIER
   Cordelia.....................................137,141
FREEMAN
   Jasper M... 8
   Jasper N.............................3,4,5,6,7,8,9
   Maria J.................................3,4,5,6,8,9
   Mariah J... 7
   Pearlie M...............................3,4,5,8,9
   Perley M..6,7
FULLER
   F M... 310
FULSOM
   Eunus Fay.. 169
   Lenora.. 169
   Walter W... 169
FULTON
   Catharine... 53
   Catherine..45,46,47,52,53,54,55,56,57

Catherine, Jr....................................... 45
Florence...............50,52,53,54,55,56,57
J M... 54
Jack........................52,53,54,55,56,57
Jesse.. 47
Jessie..45,46,47
John...48,49,50
John R......................................45,46,47

GABBART
   Ella.. 317
GABBERT
   Cyril..317,318
   Ella..317,318
   T B...........................317,318,319,320
GOLD
   S M...271,272
GORDON
   James M.......................................94,95
GORMAN
   Effie D.....................113,114,121,124
GOTCHER
   Elbert Hubbard..................................2,3
   Susan E..2,3
   Walter E..2,3
GREEN
   W C..56,68
GREGG
   Allen C....................................14,15,17
   B M..14,15,17
GRIFFITH
   C G...242,245,246
   Crado G... 244
   Credo G.....................243,244,245,247
   Emily..243,247
   Emily Jane................................244,245
   Emma J..............................242,245,246
   Ula......................................242,243,245,246
   Ula H...........242,243,244,245,246,247
GRIGGS
   Dora E......................................191,192
   Dora Elizabeth....186,187,188,189,190
   Mary......186,187,188,189,190,191,192
   Willie.. 189
   Willy......186,187,188,189,190,191,192
GRUBBS
   J C... 52

Index

J O 53,55,57
J O, MD 57
GUINN
  John 103
HALLMARK
  Edna 276,277,278
  Edna Irene 273,274,275
  J W 276,277,278
  James 273
  James W 274,275
  Lula 275,276,277,278
  Lula Edna 273,275
  Lulu Edna 274
HAMMOND
  Delia 193,194,195
  E S 193,194,195
HANNAH
  John 244,245
HARLAN
  Aaron 42,43,44
  David Franklin 42,43,44
  Logan 185
  Marietta 42
  Mary Etta 43,44
  Sila 185
HARLEN
  Cilliney. 177,178,180,181,182,185,186
  Logan 178,179,180,181,182,184,186
  Sallie 178
  Sila 179,181,182,184,186
  Silaney 184
  Silany 179
HARLIN
  Cilliney 182,183
  Logan 182,183
  Sallie 182,183
HARLOW
  Sarah A 34,35
HARPER
  Maggie 115,116,122,123
  Maggie E 115
HARRISON
  Robert P 146
HARRY
  Henry 67
HEFLIN

  S A 198,199
HENDRICK
  C B 59
HENDRIX
  R G 95
HICKMAN
  E A 145,151,152
  E L 173,174
  Edwin L 173
  Eugene A 149,150,153,154,155,156
  Houston 145,148,151,152,154
  Houston E 153,154
  Houston Eugene 149
  Katherine K 155,156
  Katherine R 148,150,155
  Lucy 145,149,150,151,152,153,
  154,155,156
HIGHTOWER
  B F 37
HILL
  Dave 24,26,27,28,30,31
  Dave D 28,29
  David 24,25,29,30
  David D 25
  Floy May 51
  Jeff W 51
  Jennie 50,51
  Nellie B 24,25,26,27,28,29,30,31
  Wynema ... 23,24,25,26,27,28,29,30,31
  Wyonia 24
HITCHCOCK
  E A 138,141
HOBBS
  Jessie 48,49,50
HODGES
  D W 61,64
HOMER
  S J 300,301
  Sol J 302
HOPKINS
  Charles H 137,141
  D W 56,57
HORN
  Rosa R 44
HOTUBBEE
  Lyles 237
HOWELL

Index

John C 193
HUDDLESTON
  Frank 254,255,256,257,259,260
  Frank, Jr 255,256,258,260,261
  Frank, Sr 258
  May 254,255,256,260,261
  Nora 254,255,257
HUDSON
  Chas H 184,185,186
  Dr V W 246
  V W 242,243,245,247
  V W, MD 246,247
HULSEY
  Wm J 183
HUMPHREY
  J C 18
  T C 125
HUTCHINSON
  N P 90,91
HYDEN
  Ella 317,319,320

IMPSON
  Melvina 236

JACKSON
  F C 6,7
  J T 158,159
  Lena 158,159
  Sallie 9,10
JAMES
  Bettie 96,97,98
  Betty 96
  Elizabeth 94,95,97
  James D 267
  James Harvey 267
  Lizzie 267
  Martha 262,263,264,265,266,267
JEFFERSON
  Sikey 184,185
JEFFRIES
  E F 75,151,152,153,156
  E T 154
  Lewis Renault 75
JOHNSON
  Alpha 237
  Caroline 312

Dave 309,310,311
David 312
Hamer 176
Harriet 177
O L 76,77,118,119,149,150,
201,206,312,313
JONES
  Albert 137,141
  C E 171,172,173
  C E, MD 172,173
  Dr C E 174
  Ellen 309,310
  Joseph C 34,35
  L G 44
  Mabel M 137,141
  Mulsie 181,186
  Mutsie 179,184
  W W 254,260

KEARNEY
  W M 193,194,197
  W M, MD 193,194
KEESE
  Annie 152
KELLEY
  A S 80,81,82,83,84
  C P 276
  Dr C P 273,276
  J L 320
KENDRICK
  C B 59,66
KENNEDY
  D S 223,224,225,226,227,228,229
  J W 224
KINGKADE
  Andrew 274
KINKADE
  Freddie 18
KREBBS
  Edna L 322
KREBS
  Edna L 321,322,323,324,325,326
  T C 321,323,326
  Theresa C 325
  Thresa C 321
KRIBS
  Theressa 325

Index

LANE
  B H 161
LARECY
  W E 187,191,192
LARRABEE
  C F 138,142,143
LAWRENCE
  Osborne D 264,265
LEDBETTER & BLEDSOE 43
LEFLORE
  John Herbert 137,141
LEWIS
  Amos 138,141
  Bula 137,141
LINDSEY
  Ollie 219,220
LIVELEY
  Rob A 213
LIVELY
  Robert A 207,208,210,211,307
  Robert A, MD 303
  Robt A 174,175,212,213,214,305, 306,307
  Robt A, MD 207,209,210,211,212
LOOMIS
  O H 162,163
LOSENE
  Thos B 6
LOWE
  Eldon 67
LUTTRELL
  J C 194,195

McCANN
  Alice 199,200,201,203,204,205,206
  Austin 199,200,201,202,203, 204,205,206
  Sampson Francis......... 199,201,205,206
  Samson Francis.......... 199,200,202,203, 204,205
McCORD
  E H 81,82
McDANIEL
  B M 144,146
  Cammie 143,147,148
  Lela L 144
  Lelia L 143,145,146,147,148

Lena...144
Marvin................ 143,144,145,147,148
McFARLAND
  J B 88,89,90
  Mattie 137,141
McKEE
  John D 191,192
  Mary A 192
McKEEL
  J F 252,253,254
MACKEY
  B P 127
  Belle 113,116,118,119,120,121, 122,123,124,125,126,127,128
  Ben 120
  Ben P 110,112,113,119,120,121, 123,124,125,126
  Benj P 122,123,125
  Benjamin P 111,112,114,115,116, 117,118,119,127,128
  Beulah A 114,115,116
  Beulah L 126
  Beulah Lois . 110,111,122,123,125,127
  Buelah L 123
  Buelah Lois 120,121,124
  Bula Lois 118,119,128
  Bulah Lois 119,120,126
  David M 114
  Elizabeth.................................121,122
  Elizabeth H 119,128
  James W 110,111,112,113,114,115, 116,117,126,127
  W W 120
MANISS
  Leila A 44
  W J 42,44
  W J, MD 44
MANSFIELD, McMURRAY &
  CORNISH.................. 117,136,139,222
MAPLES
  J B 81
  J B, MD 82
MARTIN
  Eliza 99,100,101,102,103,104, 105,106
  H J 104
  Henry J ... 99,100,101,102,103,105,106

Index

J S 326
Jasper S 324,325
Lewis T 234
Madora Jane 99,100,101,102,103, 104,105,106
Madora May 105,106
W H 4
MATHIES
   Eliza 104
MATHIS
   Eliza 99,100,101,102,103,105
MAYTUBBY
   Peter, Jr 46,55
MEADOWS
   Elmer 137,141
MELTON
   Alger 28,29
   Illegible 30,31
   W J 248
MILL
   W J 138
MILLER
   H C 275
   W J 141
MITCHELL
   Ida 313,314,315,316
   W B M 314,315,316
   William B 313
   William Bryant Marion 313,314,316
   William Byrant Marion 313
   Wm Bryant Marion 315
MOORE
   A J 174
   C B 232
   C D 223,230,231
   E A 173,174
   E O 173
   Nancy 161
   Nancy C 160,162
   R B 270
MORGAN
   Alice F 78,80,81,82,83,84
   Arymond W 83
   Louisa Alice 77,80
   Louisa W 78,80,83,84
   Millie 28
   Raymond W 77,78,79,81,82,84

Raymond Wade 83
Robert A 77,78,79,80,81,82,83,84
Wm 59,66
MORRIS
   Dr J N 313
   Thomas T 33
   Thomas T, MD 32,33
   Thos T, MD 34
MORRISON
   J M 46
MOSES
   Ben 6,7
MULLENS
   Alvin Floid 174,175
   Jasper 174,175
   Tempy 174,175
NABORS
   Alice 216
NAIL
   David O 300,301
   David O, Jr 300,301
   David Oscar 299,301,302
   David Oscar, Jr 299,301,302
   Pearl E 299,300,301,302
   Silas 11,13
NEEDLES
   T B 39,59,73,77,85,104,128,131, 155,179,219,244,267,285,291,296,321
NESBITT
   E F 274,275
NICHOLAS
   W N 184,185
NILES
   M O 263
NOBLES
   Nancy 54
NOLEN
   W T 252,253
NORRIS
   Dr J N 316
   J N 315,316
   J N, MD 315
   T T 34,35
NOVICK
   Lon 183

Index

OAKES
  Thos E 190
OGLESBY
  Minnie 19,20,93
  W J 15,16,19,20,93
OLIVER
  H L 270
OTT
  John 60,67
  John M 67
OWENS
  Estella 248
  John 248,250,251
  Katie 248

PARKER
  Gabe E 67
  R J 265,266
PARROTT
  F C 75,76,149,154
  F C, MD 75
  Farley C 145,152
  Farley C, MD 152
PATTERSON
  Brice 103
  Price 101,102,106
  Price, MD 101
PENNEY
  Annie L 71
  O S 71
  Willie Grace 71,72
PENNY
  Annie L 71
  Willie Grace 71
PERRY
  Clifford 185,186
PERTEET
  Earlie 92,93
  Jno 19,20
  John 92,93
  Lizzie 92,93
  M E 92,93
PHILLIPS
  Charles A 148,207,208,209,211, 307,308
PIATT
  L 204

Mrs L 204
PILGRIM
  James B 97
PINCHEN
  Margret 60,67
PINCHER
  Margret 57
PINCHIN
  Margret 61
PINCHING
  Margret 62,63,64,65,66
  Marguret 62
  Margurete 65
POPE
  Frank 12
  Gilbert 15,16
POTTS
  Caroline 308,309,310,311
  Judy 311,312
  Sarah 308,309,310,311,312
PRUITT
  Henry 138,141
PUSLEY
  Nancy 12,13
  Sallie 11,12,13

QUINCY
  Jefferson 297,298,299

RANDOLPH
  Maude Elizabeth 202
  Nellie P 202
  Thomas M 202
RAPPOLEE
  H E 158,159,160,248,249,250, 251,252
  H E, MD 158,250
  J L 159,160,248,250,251,252
REEDER
  C A 301
  J G 301,302
REID
  T L, Jr 137,141
REIVES
  Cally 138,141
RENICK
  Ella 192,193,194,197

Index

M A 192,193,194,195,196,197
Nora A 192,193,194,197
RICE
   T J 36,38,270
RICHEY
   W H 209,210
RIDDLE
   Sallie... 18
RIDLEY
   Sallie.......................................14,15,23
RIPLEY
   Sallie...16,17,21
RIPLY
   Sallie... 19
RITLEY
   Sallie... 21
ROBERTS
   Sam T 311
ROBINSON
   Aldon Freddie............303,305,306,307
   Aldon Fredie..........................304,305
   C D 250,251
   Jesse....................303,304,305,306
   Jessie...................................303,307
   Sarah..................303,304,305,306,307
ROSE
   J B.. 50
ROSS
   S P 3,113,120,121,122,123, 124,126
   S P, MD 3,114,120,121,123, 124,127
RUNTON
   Carnolie 297,298,299
RUSHING
   G M 217,223
   G M, MD 217
RYAN
   J J.. 103
   T J.. 124

SADLER
   Lark 224
SCHROCK
   Frances 68
   Francis 69,70
   L L 68,70

Lannes L.......................................69,70
Lannes William 68,69,70
SCOTT
   Frank 91
   S F 90
   Sebbie R 10
SEAGO
   Addie A 248,249,250,251,252
   Charles W 248,249,250,251,252
   LaClara A 248
   Laclara A 248
   LaClara A 249
   Laclara A 250
   LaClara A 251,252
SEELEY
   Alfred 183
SEXTON
   Jessie L 1
   Jonas..1
   Richard B 1
   Thos J 304,305
SHARKEY
   Fleny...10
   Impson..9
   Lanca...10
   Lemus..10
   Lupson...10
   Selener...10
   Susan 10
SHARP
   J F 162,164
SHARPE
   J F 163
SHAW
   Robt...263
SHI
   A H 317,318
   A H, MD..318
   L P 315
SHIPMAN
   Ella 195,196
SHONEY
   W A...88,89
SHULER
   James M 143
   Jas L 148
SILER

Index

Otto 56
SILMON
   Lee 15,16,93
SIMMONS
   John 293,294
   Matilda Elizabeth 293,294
   N H 294
   Nathaniel 293
   Nathaniel H 293,294
SITTEL
   Fritz 176,177
   Jennette 176,177
   Malvina 176,177
SLEDGE
   Daniel Oscar 137,141
SMART
   Annie 32,33,34
   James 33,34
   James H 32,33
   Ruth 32,33,34
SMITH
   Anna E 38,39,40,41
   Arlean 39
   Carlton 137,141
   F M 324,325,326
   Francis 39
   Frank 71,72
   Freeman F 38
   Freeman R 39,40,41
   Fulton 39
   J H 172
   J Wesley 172
   L J 151,155
   L J, MD 151
   Larah 90
   Laura 85,86,88,89,90,91
   Lee J 156,157
   May 256,259
   Noland Freeman 38,40,41
   Nowland Freeman 40
SNOW
   Annie Maria 161
   Annie Marie 160,161,162,163,164
   George 160,161,162,163,164
   Nancy C 160,161,162,164
   Sarah E 162,164
SONEY

W B 256
SORRELLS
   Geo W 264,265
STANFORD
   H C 88,89
STATON
   Phebe C 270
   Phoebe C 273
   Phoeby C 271,272
STEPHENS
   Dr L K 130
STEWART
   J A 286,287,288,290
STIGLER
   J S 130,131
SULLIVAN
   Samuel 321,322,323,324,325,326
   Samuel Edmond 321,322,323,324,
   325,326

TAYLOR
   Tobe 35,36
THRELKELD
   W C 254,256,260
   W C, MD 254,260
TIGNOR
   T D 33
TODD
   Cammie 144,146
TOWNS
   Thomas I 152
TURNBULL
   Etta 233,234
   George W 233,234
   Minnie 233,234

WALKER
   Will T 36,37,259,271,272
WARD
   C B 76
   Jane 4,5,6,8,9
WASSAR
   C E 235
   C R 236
WATSON
   America 54
   Edna 223,224,225,226,227,228,

229,230,231,232,233
J J 226,227,228,229
Johnie 14,15
Juilus J 224
Julian J 223
Julius J .. 225,226,227,230,231,232,233
Mary 223,224,225,226,227,228,
229,230,231,232,233

WHITE
Thos J 199
WHITINGTON
J T 196
WILCOX
C E 146
WILHELM
Osborne D 264
P E 60,61,64,67,262,263,264,
265,266
WILKERSON
Coy Smith 215,216
Henry Q 215,216
Mary Ada 215,216
WILKINSON
Ada 216,217,219,220,221,223
Cay Smith 218
Coy Smith ... 214,215,216,217,218,219,
220,221,222,223
H Q 218
Henry L 223
Henry Q 216,217,218,221,222
WILLIAMS
B W 273
Calloway 10
E H 91
Galloway 10
Henry 187,190,191,192
Ida 187,190
J E 95,96,280
WILSON
Lane 10
WINNETT
Nellie 17
WOODARD
Annie 100,105

YORBROUGH
Jas 212,213

YORK
Roza 234
YOUNG
J M 297,298,299
W T 294

www.ingramcontent.com/pod-product-compliance
Lightning Source LLC
Chambersburg PA
CBHW020243030426
42336CB00010B/584